STOPPED ROCKING
and Other Screenplays

By TENNESSEE WILLIAMS

PLAYS

Baby Doll (a screenplay)
Camino Real
Cat on a Hot Tin Roof
Clothes for a Summer Hotel
Dragon Country
The Glass Menagerie
A Lovely Sunday for Creve Coeur
Small Craft Warnings
Stopped Rocking and Other Screenplays
A Streetcar Named Desire
Sweet Bird of Youth
THE THEATRE OF TENNESSEE WILLIAMS, VOLUME I
   Battle of Angels, A Streetcar Named Desire, The Glass Menagerie
THE THEATRE OF TENNESSEE WILLIAMS, VOLUME II
   The Eccentricities of a Nightingale, Summer and Smoke, The Rose Tattoo, Camino Real
THE THEATRE OF TENNESSEE WILLIAMS, VOLUME III
   Cat on a Hot Tin Roof, Orpheus Descending, Suddenly Last Summer
THE THEATRE OF TENNESSEE WILLIAMS, VOLUME IV
   Sweet Bird of Youth, Period of Adjustment, The Night of the Iguana
THE THEATRE OF TENNESSEE WILLIAMS, VOLUME V
   The Milk Train Doesn't Stop Here Anymore, Kingdom of Earth (The Seven Descents of Myrtle), Small Craft Warnings, The Two-Character Play
THE THEATRE OF TENNESSEE WILLIAMS, VOLUME VII
   27 Wagons Full of Cotton and Other Short Plays
THE THEATRE OF TENNESSEE WILLIAMS, VOLUME VII
   In the Bar of a Tokyo Hotel and Other Plays
27 Wagons Full of Cotton and Other Plays
The Two-Character Play
Vieux Carré

POETRY

Androgyne, Mon Amour
In the Winter of Cities

PROSE

Eight Mortal Ladies Possessed
Hard Candy and Other Stories
The Knightly Quest and Other Stories
One Arm and Other Stories
The Roman Spring of Mrs. Stone
Where I Live: Selected Essays

STOPPED ROCKING
and Other Screenplays
TENNESSEE WILLIAMS

With an introduction by Richard Gilman

A NEW DIRECTIONS BOOK

Manufactured in the United States of America

First published clothbound and as New Directions Paperbook 575
in 1984

Published simultaneously in Canada by
George J. McLeod Ltd., Toronto

Library of Congress Cataloging in Publication Data

Williams, Tennessee, 1911–1983
Stopped rocking and other screenplays.
(A New Directions Book)
I. Title.
PS3545.I5365A6   1984   791.43'75'0973   84-6948
ISBN 0-8112-0901-6
ISBN 0-8112-0902-4 (pbk.)

New Directions Books are published for James Laughlin
by New Directions Publishing Corporation,
80 Eighth Avenue, New York 10011

Contents

INTRODUCTION by Richard Gilman   vii

All Gaul Is Divided   1

The Loss of a Teardrop Diamond   95

One Arm   193

Stopped Rocking   293

INTRODUCTION

When Tennessee Williams died in the winter of 1983 he left among his voluminous papers the texts of four screenplays (or, as he referred to several of them, possibly plays for television) none of which had been made into or was even being considered for a film. They had been written at different periods and were of various provenances. Williams was extremely vague about the dates of their composition, but *The Loss of a Teardrop Diamond* and *All Gaul Is Divided* seem to have been written in the fifties, *Stopped Rocking* in the mid-seventies, and *One Arm* most likely in the sixties. *One Arm* is taken directly from his short story of that title, and *All Gaul Is Divided* is an early and longer version of his late play *A Lovely Sunday for Creve Coeur* (Williams wrote that he had forgotten the earlier script when he came to do *Creve Coeur*); the other two scripts seem to have been original works.

That Williams should have written the four screenplays, on his own as it were, without their having been assigned by a director or a studio, shouldn't be at all surprising. He had been, after all, an extraordinarily productive writer in a wide variety of forms, the author of a good deal of poetry, many short stories, several novels, and a long memoir, as well as, of course, the plays that earned him his reputation as the greatest American dramatist of our time.

But even more pertinently he had been much involved with films and film-making from an early point in his career. On a number of occasions he spoke of having been fascinated by movies as a child, and he had introduced into his stage works, even before *The Glass Menagerie*, what are now seen to be cinematic techniques and perspectives, a tendency that would culminate in *Camino Real*.

In 1943, still nearly unknown, he worked for several months as a screenwriter for MGM, where, in a classic instance of an able writer being misunderstood and misused by Hollywood (and misunderstanding the system in his turn), he labored on such projects as a Lana Turner movie, *Marriage Is a Private Affair*, and a script for the child star Margaret O'Brien, and saw his contributions summarily rejected.

The studio also rejected an original screenplay he submitted to them called *The Gentleman Caller*, which, a few years later, was to be the basis, along with a short story, *Portrait of a Girl in Glass*, of *The Glass Menagerie*. Later he wrote another screenplay, which he called *The Pink Bedroom*, with Greta Garbo in mind, but the great star could not be coaxed from her retirement. Then in Italy during the early fifties he had a very minor and obscure writing job on Luchino Visconti's film, *Senso*, and in 1955, at the urging of Elia Kazan, his Broadway director, wrote his one original screenplay to be made into a film, *Baby Doll*, the seeds of which were two of his short plays, *27 Wagons Full of Cotton* and *The Long Stay Cut Short* (also known as *The Unsatisfactory Supper*).

In addition to all this he either wrote or collaborated on the screenplays for a number of adaptations of his own longer plays: *The Glass Menagerie, The Rose Tattoo, Suddenly Last Summer, Orpheus Descending* (filmed under the title *The Fugitive Kind*), and the Joseph Losey film, *Boom*, which Williams adapted from his play *The Milk Train Doesn't Stop Here Anymore*.

Yet despite this varied experience and his evident respect and admiration for films, Williams seems never to have been wholly comfortable as a screenwriter and was far from being a natural one. (If such a being can be said to exist—the best screenwriters are usually directors themselves or writers who execute an imaginative director's wishes.) He did his best work for the movies in close collaboration with and under the tight guidance of strong directors such as Kazan, Losey, and Joseph L. Mankiewicz, but he never seems to have grasped fully the complex esthetic differences between stage and screen or clearly understood just what was technically or artistically possible for a film to accomplish, especially in the evocation of the sort of subtle, evanescent, and highly lyrical qualities with which his best plays are suffused.

Williams recognized his shortcomings in some areas. "In the writing of the film-script," he says in notes found with the typescript of *One Arm*, "I have rarely presumed to indicate to the director the camera-angles and the distance of camera shots," and indeed the four scripts have only the most basic technical or physical directions. But in each of the scripts he asks for effects that are either impossible to achieve or are so essentially literary and abstract that any reasonably intelligent director would be non-plused by them:

> This wide shot should have the appearance of a canvas by a master painter. I think of early Van Gogh and of the early Dutch schools—the emphasis on light and shadow. A poetic *tristesse*, on the surface, a stark desolation of the spirit under . . .

> . . . trees that seem by their transcendent grace and lightness on a fair spring day to be undertaking to annihilate all sense and memory of the sprawling mass of the city.

> This should not look like an ordinary bathroom. . . . Color gives it a curious muted and melancholy radiance. Could it suggest a small apothecary shop near Verona at the time of Romeo's exile from that city?

All this is quintessential Williams in its hunger for emotional chiaroscuro and poetic values, but, as I say, the suggestions would be likely to give a director trying to implement them a rough time. And there are other difficulties the scripts put in the way of pro-spective filming. To begin with there's a relative lack of action, or at least of potential cinematic action, in most of them (the one exception is *One Arm*); they feel like they've been somewhat *willed* from their original existence as dramatic ideas to their pos-sible status as movies. The narrator in *One Arm* is another stum-bling block. His presumable function is to provide an authorial, tale-spinning voice, but his comments are most often either super-erogatory or rhetorically inept: "Summer and fall and winter and spring, yes, time has a habit of passing."

There is also a sense in most of the texts of a superceded era of consciousness and behavior, a datedness in other words. Williams thought that his dealing with earlier times (*All Gaul Is Divided* and *The Loss of a Teardrop Diamond* are set in the twenties and *One Arm* in what appears to be the forties or fifties) was an asset— "A special reality . . . an authenticity of a long past period which only a writer of my age [he was in his middle sixties when he wrote these words] could bring." But the authenticity is mostly on the surface, a matter of references to Pierce Arrows and Stutz Bearcats, trolleys, moonshine, and Elinor Glynn, than of psychic or societal reality.

Well, if these screenplays present such obstacles to turning them into films, what value do they have? What is the point of publishing them now? I'm not one who believes that any scrap of an important writer's work, no matter how trivial or obscure, is a windfall; that's a notion for academia, for the dissertation writers and pedants, in this case for the Tennessee Williams critical or scholarly industry. No, these texts provide their own pleasures and satisfactions, even if none of them seems to me an assured, fully realized creation.

We might begin with the pleasure of recognition, by which I mean the way we're constantly reminded in these scripts of other Williams works, familiar themes and obsessions, other characters, and even familiar lines. For example, Sister Grace's remark in *Stopped Rocking* that "love is perishable as flowers" could have been uttered by any of a dozen Williams characters, and Beulah's line in *All Gaul is Divided*, "There is some people in this world that can't cope with it. . . . They need all the help you can give them," could have been said in reference to a dozen more.

When Jenny, the protagonist of *All Gaul is Divided*, speaks of the "value of kindness" and asks someone, "Don't you believe in kindness—if you don't—what do you believe in?" we think immediately of Blanche Dubois, just as we think of Jenny, in her excrutiating shyness and conviction of being "lost," in connection with Laura Wingfield of *The Glass Menagerie*. Fisher Willow in *The Loss of a Teardrop Diamond* (despite its small scope perhaps the strongest of the four scripts and the most likely candidate for filming) is reminiscent of Heavenly Finley of *Sweet Bird of Youth*, the two sharing a hatred of provincialism and a need, as Fisher says, "to shock and insult, shock and insult." And Oliver

Winemiller, the title figure of *One Arm,* is a locus of many Williams motifs and painful considerations: the ravages of time, the mystery of sexuality, the loss of human innocence and dignity, the bruteness of fact as it assails the spirit.

The screenplay of *One Arm* is greatly interesting, too, for the way it shows Williams "opening out" a text and expanding it, as he did with *27 Wagons Full of Cotton* for the film *Baby Doll,* and for the way he incorporates into it material from other works, including a ferocious landlady from his short story *The Angel in the Alcove* (who also appears in *Vieux Carré*). The differences between the story and the screenplay consist chiefly in the far greater material in the script on Oliver's early life and the consequent relative brevity of the jail sequences, along with the presence, as I've noted, of a narrator through whose voice Williams apparently hoped to compensate for the loss of his own authorial, integumental presence in the story.

In the same way as in *One Arm,* the script for *All Gaul Is Divided* opens up and extends a smaller work, although Williams's claim to have forgotten the existence of the screenplay when he wrote the stage piece would seem to indicate that in this case, and perhaps unconsciously, the process was reversed. Still, we can compare *All Gaul* with *Creve Coeur* and agree with Williams that the filmscript corrects a chief structural flaw of the play, its giving away much of the plot in the early scenes. And there's a degree of fascination in seeing Williams move out from the one-room set of the play to a larger arena for Jenny's life and fate. (Play and script share the misfortune, it ought to be said, of ending on a note, uncharacteristic of Williams, of unconvincing optimism.)

From a biographical standpoint (something that's never crucial to an understanding or appreciation of Williams but offers additional light) *Stopped Rocking* is of special interest. Its central figure, Janet, is confined to a Catholic mental home or sanatorium, just as was Williams's sister Rose at one point in her illness. It isn't too much to speculate that the loving sympathy for Janet the screenplay exhibits, a quality that nearly brings the work off, was informed by Williams's strong feelings toward his sister, his mingled affection, horror, guilt, and pity.

And so here are these scripts, struggling, not fully realized as they may be, but unmistakably Tennessee Williams and therefore an accession to us. It's a commonplace to say that, for the last fifteen or so years of his life, Williams's career was in decline, and we know how much he suffered from what he at times thought was a conspiracy against him on the part of critics and even audiences. It wasn't true and there were moments when he knew it. He had an insatiable need to write and to be esteemed for his writing, and this could blind him to the ebbing of his powers. Yet he wrote in his *Memoirs* that "I cannot help, at times, being totally honest about my work, even now that the years have made this honesty painful." We can assume that this honesty, so magnificent a virtue in his best work, would have been available to him in a contemplation of his lesser.

Richard Gilman
New York City
April, 1984

ALL GAUL IS DIVIDED

PRINCIPAL CHARACTERS
(*in order of appearance*)

MISS JENNY STARLING

FIRST TEACHER

SECOND TEACHER

EDDIE PEACOCK, *a student*

BETTY, *a student*

HENRY, *a student*

MR. PAIGE, *the school superintendent*

A MALE STUDENT

A FEMALE STUDENT

THE SCHOOL NURSE

BEULAH BODENHAFER

ASSISTANT OFFICE MANAGER

HARRY STEED

MISS LUCINDA KEENER

A TEACHER IN THE CAFETERIA

SECRETARY

ANOTHER TEACHER

BUDDY BODENHAFER

THE UPSTAIRS NEIGHBOR, *a stout matron*

AUTHOR'S NOTE

This work has had quite a remarkable history. I would guess that the "teleplay" was written almost twenty years before I wrote the play, *A Lovely Sunday for Creve Coeur*, which appeared last season (1978) at the Hudson Guild Theatre. The most remarkable thing about the teleplay is that I had *totally* forgotten its existence when I wrote *Creve Coeur* in San Francisco about three years ago.

Recently I decided to thoroughly clean out the files of old manuscripts in my New Orleans apartment, files which had long been in storage. Many surprising items surfaced, through this proceeding, of which I suspect that *All Gaul is Divided* is the most fortuitous. The screenplay rectifies the major defect dilemma of the recent play: the giving away of the "plot" in the very first scene. In this initial use of the material, the denouement is saved till the last few minutes of the final scene.

About the style of the work. It belongs to that period in my writing that critics refer to as "the early Williams." It was a time of youthful spontaneity and of true freshness. Better? I no longer am reluctant to admit it. I have not been subjected to any influence but that of Chekhov in my profession. Granting even that influence, I abjure the false modesty of denying that I brought to American theatre a thing that was my own; my kind of theatre was truly mine.

Those things which distinguish this personal quality are not always recognizable until they are exhibited in performance. At least they are not easily appreciated and assessed by the usual contemporary producer. I feel a special reality here, an authenticity of a long past period which only a writer of my age could bring to the period of the play and the teleplay or screenplay.

And I think that the same will be true of *The Loss of a Teardrop Diamond*, another work assumed lost, dug up in those old files. But that one will need a full summer's work to give it the luster, both dark and light, which is my offering to a theatre which has given me life, despite all my transgressions.

Eventually these two works should be published together.

T.W.
June, 1979

ALL GAUL IS DIVIDED

1] INTERIOR. DAY.

A Saint Louis high school classroom, in the late twenties, infected with the sensuous languor of a late and warm spring. It's near the end of the term, the year of bell-bottom trousers and flapper skirts just above the kneecaps.

The teacher, Miss Jenny Starling, over thirty, dresses more youthfully and demurely than the girl students. She has golden curls, unbobbed, but secured to the back of her head with coquettish ribbons or pins. She is like a grown woman playing little girl; when she smiles, you almost expect her to curtsy. Today she has on a pale blue dotted swiss with a sash that ties in back. Her back is to the camera as the film opens, and there is a great deal of suppressed giggling among the pupils behind her as she conjugates the Latin verb "to love" on the blackboard, with perfect Spencerian penmanship and with graceful wrist movements, speaking the forms of the verb in the present subjunctive, in a hushed, reverent voice. A Sousa march, played on a victrola, can be heard faintly but distinctly over the dialogue.

JENNY: I would love?

CLASS IN CHORUS: *Amem.*

JENNY: You, singular, would love?

CLASS: *Ames.*

JENNY: He would love?

CLASS: *Amet.*

JENNY: We would love?

[*They continue with the conjugation. Halfway through, the class door opens a crack, and a female teacher peers in, clasps a hand to her mouth, and lets the door shut again.*]

2] CUT TO: INTERIOR. THE CORRIDOR OF THE HIGH SCHOOL. DAY.

FIRST TEACHER: What does she have on today?

SECOND TEACHER: You won't believe it! She has on blue dotted swiss!

[*They burst into shrill laughter, clutching at each other for support.*]

3] CUT TO: INTERIOR. JENNY'S CLASSROOM. DAY.

JENNY: You, plural, would love?

[*One of the choral voices has a mocking, nasal inflection, very loud, which provokes mounting amusement in the class. Miss Starling suddenly whirls about so violently that her curls come loose from their clasp. She stamps her foot.*]

Stop that, whoever you are! Who was doing that? Was it you, Eddie Peacock?

EDDIE: Doin' what, Miss Starling?

JENNY: Speaking in that falsetto!

EDDIE: Why do you blame ev'rything on me, Miss Starling?

JENNY: Because you're the usual ringleader of any class disturbance! [*Her agitation is unnaturally intense.*] —And I have asked you repeatedly not to sit in the front seat and stretch your legs out like that. If you have to stretch out like that, take a desk at the rear of the classroom. You've failed Latin one term; you're going to fail it a second. Unless your grade on the examination brings you up ten points, you'll be back here next fall to repeat the same term of Latin and I will not accept you in the class if I am still teaching! I won't go through it again, not if they doubled my salary. Not even if they gave me a classroom that wasn't right over the gymnasium so that I wouldn't be constantly distracted by boys jumping up and down to Sousa's marches on that—deafening victrola!

[*Laughter*]

That's enough, stop it! I am not joking with you! This is not any joke! [*She is on the verge of tears.*] —Right here on my desk is my teacher's contract for next year, still unsigned. I'm not yet able to sign it—because of unkindness in pupils still young enough to be kind!

[*Her agitation imposes a respectful hush. A girl in the front row raises a hand.*]

Yes? What is it, Betty?

BETTY: Everyone likes you, Miss Starling. It's just the last week of school . . .

JENNY: Thank you, Betty, but— [*She is now crying.*] —I can't be treated like this!

BOY [*raising his hand*]: Miss Starling?

JENNY: What, Henry?

HENRY: We hope you'll come back next fall, if you don't get married this summer.

[*This deadpan remark may or may not have been meant kindly but it provokes another repressed wave of giggles.*]

JENNY: STOP THAT! —Or I will tear this contract in two right now! I mean it!

[*Silence. Pause. She holds up the contract papers in a shaking hand.*]

4] CUT TO: INTERIOR. CORRIDOR. DAY
The corridor again. Mr. Paige, the school superintendent, hearing Jenny's shrill voice, has stopped outside her classroom. A male student runs upstairs.

MR. PAIGE: Boy? Please go to the school nurse's office and tell her to drop by Miss Starling's right after this period, will you?

5] CUT TO: INTERIOR. CLASSROOM. DAY.

JENNY [*fighting for control of her near panic*]: I do wish it were possible to teach you something more important than high school Latin! —I wish I could be appointed to teach you something that I have learned to be the most important and necessary thing to learn in the world! —Not Latin, not how to conjugate the verb to love, in a dead language, a tongue that's no longer spoken! —But the value of kindness. . . . —Don't you believe in kindness? If you don't—what do you believe in? What can anyone teach you if you don't come to school already believing in kindness! —My father taught me kindness. He used to say to me: "Jenny, be kind, and let who will be clever!" —He died! And on his deathbed, he repeated that to me: "Jenny, be kind, and let who will be clever!"

[*Eddie Peacock slouches and raises a hand.*]

—Eddie Peacock, I have something more to say to this class, this last day before the examination, but I can't say it with you in the room so will you please be excused? Get up, Eddie Peacock, go out! I will see you tomorrow at the examination.

[*There is a pause while he rises, elaborately.*]

EDDIE: —I was just gonna say—

JENNY: NEVER MIND NOW! —You may write me a letter and leave it on my desk during lunch hour explaining your behavior.

[*He goes out.*]

6] CUT TO: INTERIOR. CORRIDOR. DAY.
Eddie Peacock encounters Mr. Paige in the corridor.

MR. PAIGE: What's the matter, Eddie?

EDDIE: Nothin' much. She's just on another rampage, because she thought somebody was makin' fun of her.

MR. PAIGE: You?

EDDIE: She blames it on me, sure, but it's not me, Mr. Paige, it's the gym teacher, Steed, whenever he starts his victrola, she goes to pieces.

7] CUT TO: INTERIOR. CLASSROOM.
The classroom again. Jenny's sobbing is no longer controllable. The classroom falls totally silent except for the music from the gym below.

JENNY: It gets to be too late so early in life, too late to learn to be kind, too late to learn to—*practice consideration*—of *others' feelings!* . . . Excuse me! [*She blows her nose.*] I don't think there's one of you in this class that doesn't know that I'm trying to fight my way back after a—serious—illness. . . . [*She dabs her eyes.*] I don't need to tell you I'm hardly in a condition to—*impose discipline!* —I can't on myself, I can't control myself! —How can I control *you?* If you giggle and mock me, behind my back, if you—make unkind fun of me! What can I do? —I haven't signed my contract for next year. This week is the last week of school. Either you want me back or you don't! I don't know! I can't tell! Maybe you think I'm too funny.

[*The bell rings. The class rises quietly, abashed by Miss Starling's hysterical outburst.*]

WHERE ARE YOU GOING? I DIDN'T DISMISS THE CLASS!

[*A girl comes to her.*]

GIRL: The bell rang, Miss Starling.

JENNY: —Oh, did it? I—didn't *hear* it. . . .

GIRL: Miss Starling? Everyone loves you, you're the most popular teacher in the school.

JENNY: —What?

GIRL: You're the prettiest, too. Honestly, Miss Starling.

8] DISSOLVE TO: INTERIOR. CLASSROOM. DAY.
As the last students go out, the school nurse enters, all in starched white, a hearty, kindly woman.

10

NURSE: How's things, Jenny?

JENNY: —Who told you to come to my room?

NURSE: A little bird told me that you were upset this morning.

JENNY: Well, tell the little bird to mind its own business, please!

[*She slams the drawer shut and turns to the blackboard to erase it.*]

I had to give my class a little talk on how decent human beings should act toward each other because they come from homes where they seem to be taught that sheiks and flappers are the highest achievement of—mankind. . . .

[*The scene begins to dissolve during Jenny's speech.*]

9] DISSOLVE TO: INTERIOR. CORRIDOR. DAY.
Jenny starts into the corridor but retreats as students swarm past. The crowd, the noise, terrify her. She waits till they subside and the corridor is empty. Then she catches her breath, and as if plunging into cold water, she rushes down the corridor to a pay phone near the top of the stairs.

JENNY [*into phone*]: Locust! Wait! Wait! I'm trying to think of the number. Oh. Locust. No! Wait! It's—you'll have to get me the number from Information. It's the Cosmopolitan Branch of the Universal Shoe Company, it's the filing department, it's—Miss Bodenhafer, Miss Beulah Bodenhafer I want to speak to . . .

[*She gasps these instructions again, as the scene dissolves.*]

11

10] DISSOLVE TO: INTERIOR. OFFICE. DAY.
Cut to Beulah at a desk among a hundred identical desks:
she's tried to make hers homelike with bits of bric-a-brac, a
potted cactus plant, etc. She wears a hearing aid which she
conceals with a big artificial poppy. Her name is called from
behind her as she is about to approach a long row of metal
cabinets with a great bunch of papers to file.

VOICE [*crossly*]: Miss Bodenhafer, you're wanted on the
phone.

BEULAH [*visibly surprised—she has a voice of odd sweetness,*
a voice you would more expect to hear in a group of gentle
children than in the office of a wholesale shoe company]: For
me? Oh. Is it my brother, Buddy?

VOICE [*impatiently*]: Naw, it's a woman. How do I know
who it is?

11] CUT TO: INTERIOR OFFICE. DAY.
Beulah is at the phone on a desk at the back of the office.
The occupant of the desk is annoyed by this intrusion. It is
a significant privilege to have a phone on your desk, and it
should not be shared with persons of lesser importance. Beu-
lah crouches as if to sit down but finds nothing to sit on, so
straightens up, murmuring.

BEULAH: Excuse me—to disturb you. . . . [*There's a slight*
German accent in her speech.] Hello? This is Beulah. Is it—?

12] CUT TO: INTERIOR. A PHONE IN THE HIGH
SCHOOL.

JENNY: *Jenny!* I'm *going*, Beulah!

BEULAH'S VOICE: Where are you going, Jenny?

12

JENNY: All to pieces! I've gone! I can't even get home. I can't get home even! I just—broke up!—I guess I'm all through, Beulah . . .

BEULAH'S VOICE: Where are you, Jenny? Where are you calling me from? A phone at the school?

JENNY: Yes, a—phone . . .

BEULAH'S VOICE: Jenny, go to the school nurse. You hear me, Jenny? Go to the school nurse, Jenny, and let her give you something to calm you down. Don't try to go home. You hear me, Jenny?

JENNY: Yes!

BEULAH'S VOICE: You got another class, now? Aren't you free till lunch, now?

JENNY: Yes!

BEULAH'S VOICE: Then stay with the school nurse till lunch. Take my word for it, Jenny. You'll be okay by lunchtime. You hear me? You just rest in the school nurse's room till lunchtime and you'll be all right, Jenny. There's just one more week of school. —We'll have a wonderful vacation together. I got it fixed for me to take my two weeks as soon as you get your vacation, soon as it starts, and Buddy will take his two-week vacation then, too, and drive us down to the Ozarks. You hear me, Jenny?

[*Pause.*]

What was it, Jenny? I mean what upset you, Jenny?

JENNY: Harry Steed's victrola, right under my classroom!

BEULAH'S VOICE: Aw. That gymnasium teacher. You got him too much on your mind.

JENNY: —We met in front of the school when I got here this morning. He was *so* nice to me. Said, "Well, Miss Starling, how many parts is Gaul divided into?"

BEULAH'S VOICE: Aw.

JENNY: I said, "As usual: three!"

[*The voices continue but fade into the sound of the gym victrola where Harry Steed is conducting gym class; male students in gym outfits are leaping up and down, with Indian clubs held above them.*]

13] CUT TO: INTERIOR. BEULAH'S OFFICE. DAY.

BEULAH [*to the Assistant Office Manager*]: I got to use the phone again please excuse me.

ASSISTANT OFFICE MANAGER [*at desk*]: Employees are not supposed to make personal calls on phones here.

BEULAH: I got to. Please excuse me. [*She asks for a number.*]

14] CUT TO: INTERIOR. THE OFFICE OF THE
   SCHOOL SUPERINTENDENT. DAY.

MR. PAIGE: Hello. Hello? Mr. Paige speaking.

15] CUT BACK TO: CLOSE ONE-SHOT OF BEULAH.

BEULAH: Mr. Paige? I'm callin' about my girl friend, Jenny Starling.

MR. PAIGE: Yes, Miss Bodenhafer.

BEULAH: You remember my name!

MR. PAIGE: Yes, and your voice. Is something wrong with Jenny?

BEULAH: Mr. Paige, she scared me. She called me up at the office for the first time. She sounded very panicky, Mr. Paige. You know, like she was when I had to talk to you last winter?

MR. PAIGE: I remember. Did she tell you what's wrong?

BEULAH: She didn't tell me but I think I know. I think it's the new gym teacher. She's been speaking of him so much. She says every day he makes the same crack at her. How many parts is Gaul divided into. She don't know how to answer him, Mr. Paige, you know, he repeats it so often, she don't know how to keep answering him, you know? Mr. Paige! What do you think about it? Is he int'rested in her? Or is he just—you know—fooling? —No man can fool with Jenny. She can't be fooled with. Mr. Paige? I'm trying to work out something between my brother and her.

ASSISTANT OFFICE MANAGER: Not so loud!

BEULAH: Sorry. [*She continues in a loud whisper.*] My brother is with Budweiser. A widower? With one child? Serious? Hard-working? No prize package but serious, hard-working. I just want to know what this fellow Steed is up to. Serious or not serious? With Jenny Starling it's got to be love, Mr. Paige . . .

16] DISSOLVE TO: INTERIOR. JENNY IN THE OFFICE OF THE SCHOOL NURSE.

15

JENNY: Thank you. I feel much better.

[*The bell is ringing in the corridor.*]

NURSE: Don't you think you ought to go home, Miss Starling, for the rest of the day?

JENNY: No, oh, no! I'm really feeling much better. I'll go down for lunch now. Everyone has to keep going, it's just a few days . . .

17] CUT TO: INTERIOR. DAY.
Jenny is descending the stairs to basement: the victrola in the gym in the basement grows louder as she descends.

18] CUT TO: MR. PAIGE A FLIGHT ABOVE HER ON THE STAIRS.

MR. PAIGE: Miss Starling? Oh, Miss Starling?

[*She doesn't hear him but halts on the steps as the gym instructor, Harry Steed, plunges out of the gym in white ducks and a white cotten singlet, transparent with sweat. He makes the costume heroic. . . . Jenny stands frozen on the stairs. Mr. Paige stops short in his pursuit, staring down at Jenny as she stares at Steed.*]

STEED [*shouting to someone behind him*]: Turn that damn thing off!

[*Steed means the victrola, still playing a march tune in the gym.*

[*For some reason Miss Jenny Starling doesn't want Mr. Harry Steed to see her frozen on the stairs, and he doesn't. As soon as he stalks past the staircase without having seen her,*

16

*she continues her descent into the basement where students
are lining up at the cafeteria entrance.*]

19] INTERIOR. CAFETERIA. DAY.
*The high school cafeteria. Windows the size of transoms
are set high in the walls so that beams of dusty gold light
slant down upon crowded tables, tin trays, heavy white
china, etc.*

20] INTERIOR CAFETERIA. DAY.
*Close shot of a table that bears a placard: RESERVED FOR
TEACHERS.*

*Miss Starling arrives at this table with a cottage cheese salad
and a cup of black coffee.*

*Mr. Harry Steed appears opposite her with a tray loaded to
the limit of its capacity, calling out heartily, as he arrives—*

STEED: Well, Miss Starling, how many parts is Gaul divided
into?

JENNY [*breathlessly*]: It's still divided into the same number
of parts, Mr. Steed, "*Gallia est omnia divisa in partes tres!*"

STEED [*unloading his tray with a great clatter*]: All Gaul is
divided in three parts!

JENNY [*almost completely unnerved*]: Yes, in three parts,
Mr. Steed!

STEED: Always in three parts! Monotonous, huh? Ha ha!

[*Jenny laughs, very high.*

[*Steed starts eating with great pleasure and vigor.*]

17

JENNY [*continuing*]: —Yes, it's—rather monotonous, and my chalk scratched today as I was conjugating the verb "to love" on the blackboard: I screamed and the whole class laughed!

[*Steed grins up at her from his food, then swallows with a great muscular swelling of his broad sweat-dampened bare throat.*

[*Jenny drops her fork.*]

STEED: How about the Helvetians? Huh? How about them? How are they doing in the resistance movement against old Julius Caesar today, Miss Starling?

JENNY [*laughing*]: I think it's a foregone conclusion that they will be defeated and he will return in triumph to Rome and write about his triumph for posterity, and I do so wish that he'd never laid down the sword to pick up the pen, no matter how much mightier the pen is supposed to be!

FEMALE VOICE [*interrupting*]: GREETINGS!

21] INTERIOR. DAY.
The camera introduces Miss Lucinda Keener, an "art" teacher with pretensions and some claim to sophistication and social smartness. She has on a dress of the style precipitated by the excavations of King Tutankhamen's tomb in Egypt. Her hair is exotically bobbed and she wears long jade earrings. Her appearance is more striking than appealing.

STEED: Hey, there! —If ole King Tut could see you, he'd turn in his hieroglyphics!

[*Lucinda gives him a playful slap.*

[*Steed promptly ignores her in favor of his food.*]

JENNY [*sadly*]: Why, Lucinda, I thought you always preferred to lunch at the *drugstore* . . .

LUCINDA: It's going to rain any moment, I didn't bring my slicker! Harry? *Harry!*

STEED: Huh?

LUCINDA: I hear you're a *whiz* at *bridge!* 'Sthat right?

STEED: I can hold my own at it.

LUCINDA: Well, I'm in a *desperate* situation! A man just married out of my bridge club. The rule is strictly unmarried, so we're short ONE MAN for next Saturday.

STEED: Don't look at *me.*

LUCINDA: Well, I *AM* looking at you!

STEED: My plans for Saturday night are already made.

LUCINDA: OHHH? What *are* they, Harry?

STEED: Saturday night is the opening of the Municipal Opera. *Blossom Time!* With Vivien Seagall and Allan Jones! —Somebody that's gone to Chicago gave me their pair of box seats . . .

LUCINDA: Box seats? How grand! —I'm not hinting but you DID say a pair! Didn't you say, "A PAIR"?

STEED: You got your bridge club to go to, you can't desert your bridge club and I've already asked Miss Starling! *Haven't* I, Miss Starling?

22] CLOSE ONE-SHOT: JENNY.
A lingering close up of her surprise and rapture.

LUCINDA'S VOICE: Oh! —Why, *Jenny*, aren't you the *lucky* one, Jenny!

JENNY: —*Yes, he!*—just now *asked* me!

STEED: —You haven't accepted yet, though.

JENNY: Oh, the acceptance was a, was a—FOREGONE CONCLUSION! —like the defeat of the HELVETIANS, HA HA HA!

[*She is delighted that she has been able to think of such a prompt and witty remark.*]

23] CLOSE ONE-SHOT: LUCINDA KEENER.
She gives Harry Steed a slyly mocking grimace . . .

24] INTERIOR. DAY.
A shaft of sunlight enters the high transom-like window of the basement cafeteria and falls directly on Jenny Starling's golden curls, her head becomes luminous, transfigured. Her lips begin to quiver, uncontrollably. She lifts a hand to her mouth. Lucinda is watching her wickedly.

LUCINDA: Jenny? Oh, Jenny!

JENNY: What?

LUCINDA: I don't think you ought to drink black coffee at noon, unless you eat something with it. I mean besides a little cottage cheese. It's so bad for your nerves. Honey, you've got a nervous twitch right now, your mouth is twitching. And, honey. I'm going to make an appointment for you with the

20

Maybelle Beauty Shop to get your hair bobbed. You can't keep those little girl's curls forever, Jenny. They're sweet but I think the time has come for you to part with them. Mary Pickford has to keep hers to play child parts in pictures. Like Rebecca of Sunnybrook Farm. But you're not playing child parts in pictures, are you?

STEED: I like Jenny with curls.

LUCINDA: The kids have started calling her Mary Pickford.

STEED: She looks like an angel with curls.

LUCINDA [*to Jenny*]: Where are you going? You haven't finished your salad.

[*Jenny has risen from table.*]

JENNY: I just remembered I have to call my girl friend at her office. Excuse me please.

[*She crosses out of frame.*]

LUCINDA: Harry Steed, you're wicked! Why did you do that to her?

STEED: What'd I do that's wicked?

LUCINDA: Why, she went all to pieces when you made that date with her, and knowing you like I do, I don't think it's fair to poor Jenny. She's one of those girls that think a date with a man is the first step to the altar . . .

[*A teacher starts to take Jenny's place at table.*]

STEED: Hey! That place is taken!

TEACHER: Oh, sorry!

LUCINDA: See? She's coming right back!

[*Jenny returns to the table.*]

What a quick phone call, Jenny!

JENNY: I called my girl friend, Beulah, you know, the one that shares my apartment with me . . .

LUCINDA: Oh! —My date last night drove me out on Art Hill and there was a divine breeze blowing out there last night.

STEED: Was that the attraction?

LUCINDA: I know what you're insinuating, Harry, but public necking is not only common in my opinion, but sort of *unsatisfactory, too.*

STEED [*loudly*]: Any salt on this table?

JENNY: —Art Hill is the highest point of all in all of greater St. Louis, my girl friend Beulah's brother, Buddy—drives us out there sometimes in summer to cool off on—warm summer nights . . .

LUCINDA [*coolly*]: Is that right, dear? How nice! Does Buddy get romantic or does he just enjoy the cool breezes with you?

JENNY: My girl friend Beulah is DETERMINED to start a romance between her brother and me, but her brother, Buddy, not only drinks beer by the quart but can't eat a meal without onions!

LUCINDA: —When we share an apartment, if we do! —No *Beulah*, no *Buddy!* —Promise? Jenny? [*She rises from the table.*] —Now for my cigarette in the girls' lavatory. Will you please excuse me.

JENNY: Yes . . .

STEED: Yeah . . .

[*Lucinda departs, and Steed continues, the speed and energy of his ingestion having abated somewhat.*]

—How did you say the Helvetians made out today?

JENNY [*as if he'd said something witty*]: Oh, the *Helvetians!* —The poor Helvetians were thrown into confusion and panic.

STEED [*reflectively*]: —Into confusion and panic, today, huh . . .

JENNY: Yes! I *do* feel sorry for the Helvetians. Don't *you?*

STEED: —Uh-huh . . .

JENNY: Yes, Caesar's forces made a surprise attack on their rear and threw them into confusion and panic so that half of their force was slain and the other half taken captive.

STEED: That old Julius sure does give the Helvetians a mighty bad time of it! Mm-*MMM!*

JENNY: Yes, every year, every year! —He throws the Helvetians into confusion and panic!

STEED [*eating*]: —How many years has it been?

JENNY: How many years has *what* been, Mr. Steed?

STEED [*still wolfing his food, crouched low over plate*]: Wuh-wuh-wuh-wuh . . .

JENNY: I beg your pardon?

[*Steed laughs, pointing at his stuffed mouth.*

[*Jenny laughs almost hysterically.*

[*A group of senior girls at nearby table burst into laughter, too, and Miss Jenny Starling falls suddenly silent and flushed.*]

STEED [*gulping down a mouthful*]: I said how many years have you been teaching that stuff? Julius Caesar and so forth?

[*He leans back in his chair, his lunch finished.*]

JENNY: Oh, goodness, now, not so long, I mean, well, not for-*ever*!

STEED: Not forever.

JENNY: No, not quite forever. I mean I can still remember a time when I was not teaching first and second year Latin at Ben Blewitt Senior High School. [*Then suddenly, and shrilly, her throat rigid with fury, she shouts.*] GIRLS! GIRLS! YOU GIRLS AT THAT TABLE! STOP THAT GIGGLING AT ONCE OR LEAVE THE LUNCH ROOM! I SHALL TAKE DOWN YOUR NAMES AND REPORT YOUR BEHAVIOR TO MR. PAIGE IF YOU DON'T! [*She is shaking all over, there are tears in her eyes.*] —Excuse me, Mr. Steed. I hate discipline, I mean I hate to have to be severe with students but sometimes their impertinence is just unbearable.

STEED: Gee. You got a fiery temper, you sure did let 'em have it, you practically threw them into panic an' confusion, Miss Starling.

[*Mr. Paige approaches the table.*]

MR. PAIGE: Miss Starling, is something the matter?

JENNY [*barely able to talk, hoarse with agitation*]: Mr. Paige? Mr. Paige? There is a group of girls that occupy that large corner table that come in here every day not to eat lunch but to stare and to whisper and giggle and to make rude remarks which they think are funny, sometimes in such loud voices that I've overheard them plainly.

MR. PAIGE: Remarks about anyone in particular?

JENNY: Most of their humor, Mr. Paige, is directed at *the teachers' table!* They stare straight at you and then whisper something and then all burst into *laughter.* [*She bursts into tears.*]

MR. PAIGE: Pull yourself together, Miss Starling. Oh, Mr. Steed? Oh, Mr. Steed!

STEED: Yeah?

MR. PAIGE: In the interests of propriety, Mr. Steed, I'd like to make the suggestion that you put on an ordinary shirt and jacket when you enter the school cafeteria after this.

STEED: What?

MR. PAIGE: We all know you have a fine chest and powerful arms and shoulders, and we all know that being human your skin is capable of perspiration when you—exert yourself in the

25

gymnasium. But you don't have to make a public display of these virtues at lunch hour, do you? Mr. Steed?

STEED: That's very good, ha ha!

MR. PAIGE: What's "very good," Mr. Steed?

STEED: That little speech you just made, it was full of wit, it was worthy of William Jennings Bryan, the silver-tongued orator, Mr. Paige.

MR. PAIGE: Mr. Steed, I'd like to see you upstairs in my office.

STEED [*aggressively*]: When? Now, or later? Huh? Right now or sometime later? Huh?

[*Mr. Paige stalks away from table. Miss Starling gasps. A bell rings and the room begins to empty with a great clatter of trays and silver.*]

He can see me anytime he wants to, anywhere, and have his— excuse me, Miss Starling.

JENNY: Oh, Mr. Steed! I've gotten you in trouble!

STEED: Believe me, this is no trouble, not for me, anyhow. Anytime I want to go back to pro golf, the doors of the St. Louis country club are wide-open to me, Miss Starling, wide-open. In fact they want me at—Troutdale-in-the-Pines, too . . .

JENNY: —Where is that, Mr. Steed?

STEED: It's in Colorado. President Harding played golf there! —I caddied for him at Troutdale-in-the-Pines in the summer of 1922.

JENNY: —Oh . . .

STEED: I took this job at a financial sacrifice to me because I thought it might be a stepping stone to a job as athletic coach at a state U or something . . .

JENNY: I'm sure it will be, Mr. Steed.

STEED: What's he want me to wear in his damn cafeteria? White tie an' tails? And change back into my gym clo'se in five minutes to—? Gimme your check, Miss Starling, you're my guest.

[*They cross to cashier.*]

JENNY: Oh, now, you mustn't!

[*He ignores this protest.*]

STEED: Got any mints? No? Give me some chewing gum, then . . .

[*He has paid the check and waits for her by swinging doors on basement corridor.*]

JENNY: Well, thank you so much, Mr. Steed.

STEED: —What're *you* doin' here? In this *dump*? A girl with your looks, still young? Why don't you marry out of this stupid, boring business? The monotony of it, the mo-not-o-ny of it, the damn mo-NOT-o-ny of it!

[*He kicks the door of a half-open locker in the basement corridor. Two female teachers pass and pause a little beyond, or behind.*]

—Huh? How come a girl like you hasn't got herself married out of this dump an' quit dead languages like Latin an' raised some live kids! Huh? I'm asking you a perfectly serious question! Miss Starling. What's your first name?

[*Jenny whispers her first name in confusion and panic.*]

Jenny! —I want to have a talk with you. About this whole situation. Where'll you be at three-thirty, after the— ?

[*A secretary rushes up.*]

SECRETARY: Mr. Steed, Mr. Paige is waiting for you in his office, he says to tell you that your next class has been dismissed, so—

[*A long pregnant pause. Steed grunts and nods and hitches his belt and his shoulders and starts upstairs under the destroyer escort of Mr. Paige's secretary.*]

25] INTERIOR. MR. PAIGE'S OFFICE. DAY.
Mr. Paige sits benignly at desk, with a cigar as Steed enters, with a display of independence.

STEED: She says you wanta talk to me.

MR. PAIGE: I thought I made that plain in the cafeteria.

STEED: I said when and you didn't answer the question. Well?

MR. PAIGE: Sit down, Harry, and get that chip off your shoulder.

STEED [*sitting on the corner of the desk*]: I got no chip on my shoulder, Royal. You don't object to me using your first name, do you?

MR. PAIGE: No, why should I? Teachers are not employed by principals, they're employed by the Board of Education.

STEED: What's that got to do with it? You can fire me if you want to and I can quit if I want to. Don't forget *that*!

MR. PAIGE: You've still got that chip on your shoulder. Get it off so we can talk.

STEED: I'm talking. Then you can talk.

MR. PAIGE: Thanks, Harry!

STEED: You're welcome, Royal. Okay! I'm not quitting unless I got to quit because, well, I've got a serious attitude toward this job. Not that I intend to stay here the rest of my life, by no means, no! I want to leave here with a good record behind me. But there's certain things I won't take, Royal. I won't let myself be bawled out publicly. You bawled me out in front of another teacher! I won't take that off you, Royal. Look. You're principal, here, but you're a very young guy to be principal of a city high school, and I treat any man, even a man much older, as equal to me. I never treat any man as inferior to me but I treat any man, even a man I work for, if I got to work for him, as *equal* to me! Do you get what I mean about that, Royal!

MR. PAIGE: Yes, it's not hard to get. Will you cool down a little? That little incident outside the cafeteria has no importance at all.

STEED: To you, maybe *no*, to me, *yes*! You bawled me out in front of another teacher, and it was—humiliating!

MR. PAIGE: I didn't bawl you out, I simply made a suggestion about the way you ought to be dressed, I mean ought *not* to be dressed, after a lively workout in the gym when you enter a cafeteria in the high school of which a fair number of patrons are silly-age girls! If you had taken a shower before you entered—

STEED: I took a shower! —This morning. I got a half hour for lunch. How can I have lunch and take a shower? Both? In half'n hour!

MR. PAIGE: Harry, I want to talk to you about something else.

STEED: Well, go ahead. What else?

MR. PAIGE: Miss Jenny Starling. She's our *problem* teacher. You'd better not fool with her, Harry. She'll take it seriously, Harry. And she's one of those people that need to be loved so badly that if they're just paid a little—sentimental attention, they—well, they—imagine it's *love*! Of course if it *IS* love, that would solve their problem. *ALL* their problems. But if it turns out to be just a passing interest, their mistake about it could put them back in a sanitarium, Harry . . .

STEED: —Is it all right if I take her to the Muny Opera Saturday to see *Blossom Time*?

MR. PAIGE: —Yeah, but just be careful!

26] DISSOLVE TO: INTERIOR. CORRIDOR. DAY.
Two teachers, Lucinda Keener and another.

LUCINDA: —The school nurse gave her something to calm her nerves . . .

OTHER: Has she gone home?

LUCINDA: Oh, no, she's meeting her classes. I dropped by her classroom and she was in it with her two-thirty class.

OTHER: You know her history, don't you?

LUCINDA: I've heard she was out of her mind.

OTHER: In the asylum.

LUCINDA: Gracious . . .

OTHER: Yes! But Mr. Paige took her back because they said she'd recovered. Well, she hasn't recovered.

LUCINDA: No, she hasn't recovered.

OTHER: Of course she hasn't recovered, they don't recover completely from something like that.

LUCINDA: Harry Steed should be shot! —Flirting with that poor girl, to amuse himself!

[*The bell rings, there is a shrill outcry.*]

OTHER: Bridge tonight?

LUCINDA: Yes. At eight-thirty . . .

[*She turns back a few paces and enters a classroom as students swarm out.*]

27] INTERIOR. JENNY'S CLASSROOM. DAY.
Lucinda Keener waits by door till the room is emptied. Jenny is weeping with her face to the blackboard.

LUCINDA: Jenny! Jenny! Stop that . . .

JENNY: Who is that? *OH! You!* —Lucy . . . [*She gasps.*] Where is my monitor? My monitor's left without erasing the blackboard! Oh! My monitor's left without sponging off the blackboard!

LUCINDA: Jenny, Jenny, stop that right this minute! What *is* the matter with you?

JENNY: I! —Feel! —*Awful* . . .

LUCINDA: —Where is your sponge? I'll clean the blackboard for you.

JENNY: No, I—I WON'T BE TREATED LIKE THIS! [*She rushes into the corridor, and returns almost instantly with a male pupil.*] NOW! GET OUT YOUR SPONGE AND SPONGE THAT BLACKBOARD OFF!—and DON'T *EVER!*—FORGET TO, AGAIN!

[*They watch in silence as the sulky boy sponges off the Latin conjugations from the sunlit blackboard. Miss Jenny sniffs once or twice.*

[*The boy goes out soon as he is finished.*]

LUCINDA: Jenny?

JENNY: —How did I get lost, Lucinda? What happened to me? Why did I lose myself? Why? Why did I get so LOST!? Do you understand, can you tell me, what's happened to me? I spent nearly two years in a—NO! [*She tries to laugh.*] Have I got everything? Oh, I'm still in my smock! Have you got—? Oh! —Lucinda? Would you please walk home with me?

LUCINDA: How far is it, Jenny?

JENNY: Just a few blocks east of here on West Pine.

LUCINDA: I live in the opposite direction, but I do think we should have a serious talk, Jenny, not only about sharing an apartment, but I feel I should also give you a bit of advice about the dashing young gym instructor who is escorting you to *Blossom Time* at the Muny . . .

28] DISSOLVE TO: EXTERIOR. A PARK ACROSS THE
STREET FROM THE HIGH SCHOOL.
Jenny and Lucinda leave the school and cross the street. Lucinda directs Jenny to a bench in the small park that faces the high school. Lucinda is obviously reluctant to go out of her way and finally succeeds in getting Jenny to sit down.

LUCINDA: Let's just sit here and talk, Jenny. Now about Harry Steed. [*Lucinda settles herself with the air of someone imparting great wisdom.*] Harry Steed has had a remarkable social career in St. Louis. Did you know that, Jenny? He has created a legend about himself, Harry Steed. He's been quite clever about it. The invented background—was very wisely put at a safe distance, Honolulu! [*She laughs lightly.*] As far as that! People were given to understand that Harry Steed was born in Honolulu, the son of a Lt. Colonel in the American military forces stationed there.

JENNY: Wasn't Harry Steed born in Honolulu, Lucinda?

LUCINDA: Oddly enough, that part of the legend is true. But the rank of his father was elevated above the truth of the matter which is that Harry Steed's father was a non-commissioned officer in the military force there. He was just exactly this—he was a cavalry sergeant!—and also a drunk who finally wound up in a veteran's home there—as hopeless!

JENNY: —How did you get hold of this—information—about Harry Steed?

LUCINDA: Honey, I go out with a captain at Jefferson Barracks; I had him do a little sleuth work for me. About Mr. Harry *Steed*!

JENNY: *Why*? Were you *interested*?—Lucinda . . .

LUCINDA: The woman hasn't lived on this earth that has taken a good look, or even just a glance at Harry Steed, especially in his white ducks and cotton lisle undershirt after conducting a strenuous boys' gym class at Blewett High!—who wouldn't and isn't intensely interested in Harry Steed!—*at first*!—till she's found out more of the truth as opposed to the glamorous legend. Well—he carried on a little flirtation with me. Like he's now doing with you.

JENNY [*sadly*]: Oh.

LUCINDA: And Harry Steed is a society adventurer of the first water, Jenny!

JENNY: Oh?

LUCINDA: Just let me give you a little history of his social career in St. Louis. I think I'd better because you're all worked up, practically hysterical, over the fact that he's asked you to go to the opening of the Muny Opera with him! —Saturday night.

JENNY: Lucinda, I'm convinced that Harry Steed is sincerely interested in me. I'm scared to death that I'll—*spoil* it.

LUCINDA [*drawing on her cigarette*]: That's why I think you ought to know his background. Will you listen?

JENNY: Yes.

LUCINDA: Harry Steed won a free-for-all golf tournament when he first came to St. Louis, three years ago, when he was still under thirty, and as a result of that, he became the golf pro at the St. Louis Country Club which I don't have to tell you is the best club in St. Louis. This was of course before he graduated downwards to being the boys' gym instructor at Blewett, Jenny. Well! —He'd gotten in with a wealthy society crowd at the St. Louis Country Club and also at the Glen Echo which is the second most socially important country club in St. Louis.

[*Jenny is looking into space.*]

Now, then. At the St. Louis Country Club where he was the golf pro, he made himself very attractive to that beer baron's widow, you know the one that I mean, you've seen her name in society pages I'm sure, although she is common as pig tracks and has no more business in the most exclusive country club in St. Louis than I have at this high school! . . . Well! He became her pet! —Daphne Hammerschlogger, that's her name! Can you believe it? —She's worth twenty million and looks it, especially around the middle! She is pushing—no, she's *past* fifty! *But*! —She's blondined her hair and starved herself skinny and takes part in Charleston contests at the St. Louis Country Club. Naturally, he would have preferred to stay the golf pro at the St. Louis Country Club. But he got in a little scandal with one of his female students, they stayed too long in the woods looking for a lost golf ball. Hours, I've heard. Never found it. He was politely dismissed from that lofty position and then he came here. But don't imagine he plans to stay here long because he doesn't. This is just a fill-in. The scandal at the Country Club was his first foot up in smart society in St. Louis. It divided the club in two camps. Some for and some against him. Now he plays golf there every weekend and drives a flashy Stutz that the beer baron's widow gave him. That's his present background. He went to the Veiled Prophet Ball. Not only went to it but escorted one of the maids of honor. Now seriously.

35

Do you think his so-called attentions to you are to be trusted, Jenny?

JENNY: Lucinda, thank you. I had no idea that he was involved in that crowd.

LUCINDA: I thought you should know since you're going to *Blossom Time* with him.

JENNY: Yes. I guess I should. But I still think, I still hope, that maybe his interest in me is genuine.

LUCINDA: Jenny, you're so naive that it breaks my heart for you. —Now let's switch the subject. How about it, now, Jenny, are you or are you not going to share my new apartment the first of next month? I have to know. We have to make the deposit, right away, Jenny. Now it's obvious to me that you are going to be going out with Harry Steed, at least for a while, and if you play your cards right, you can make some good contacts through him, as long as you just don't take him seriously as a beau. Well. You'll need an attractive place and it won't do for you to receive him in the place you stay now with that fat middle-aged typist who is your present companion. You can't let him call for you there. You need a place where you can entertain the smart new crowd you'll be meeting through Harry Steed.

JENNY: I know, but Lucinda . . .

LUCINDA: What?

JENNY: It's—*really* quite a—*decision*!

LUCINDA: To move from a sordid background to a smart one?

JENNY: No, to—hurt poor Beulah . . .

36

29] DISSOLVE TO: INTERIOR. THE APARTMENT
JENNY SHARES WITH BEULAH.

*A large window, twice or three times the size that the win-
dow really would be, frames one of those delicate young city
trees that seem by their transcendent grace and lightness on a
fair spring day to be undertaking to annihilate all sense and
memory of the sprawling mass of the city. The walls are
lilac-colored; the light is misty except the beams that fall on
Jenny placing a dish on the drop-leaf table in front of the
giant window and the young tree.*

*The camera follows Jenny back to the kitchenette of the
apartment she shares with Beulah Bodenhafer. Beulah is at
the sink and Jenny picks up a dishtowel lying on the counter;
they are washing and drying dishes, Beulah with competence,
Jenny very vaguely.*

JENNY: He sat down at my table today in the school cafeteria.

BEULAH: Who did, honey?

JENNY: Mr. Steed, Harry Steed, the boys' athletic coach. *You*
know! I've told you about him. I've mentioned him to you
often. Don't you listen?

BEULAH: Oh, *him*! —Sure. What happened?

JENNY: —Well—when he came to the table, he said to me,
"How many parts is Gaul divided into today, Miss Starling?"

BEULAH: Ain't that what he said last time you had a talk with
him?

JENNY: That's how he starts every time, it's his little joke, and I never can think of anything bright or funny to answer, I just—sort of—laugh and—

BEULAH: I wouldn't know how to answer that joke, not if it was thrown at me time after time.

JENNY: I said, "The usual number." I said, "All Gaul is always divided into three parts."

BEULAH: That's a good enough answer—did the talk go on after that?

JENNY: I was afraid it wouldn't. He started eating. He eats enormous lunches; he always has more on his tray than you'd think it could hold, sometimes dishes are piled on top of each other! [*She laughs.*] —But stays as thin as a boy, and I have to starve myself to keep from getting too plump!

BEULAH: You worry too much about weight. Look at me. Do I worry?

JENNY: No. That's the trouble . . .

[*Beulah chuckles good-humoredly. She is a good-humored person.*]

Well, he ate and ate, and then—

BEULAH: Then what, Jenny?

JENNY: I—lingered at the table, although I had practically finished my salad when he got there, I—just had a few bites left but I chewed each bite a long time, and, finally—I thought he never would! —He looked up at me again and gave me the sweetest smile I've ever seen in my life. He has such perfect teeth, he has such a wonderful set of teeth in his mouth it's hard to believe that they're real. Honestly, that's so, Beulah, it's hard to believe they're real teeth.

BEULAH: —Buddy's got teeth like that . . .

JENNY: —Every time that I mention a man to you, you mention your brother to me!

BEULAH: —Well, my brother's the only man I'm interested in or is interested in me. Don't you like Buddy? I ask you that because I know he likes *you*. He thinks you're an *absolute knockout*!

JENNY: Huh!

BEULAH: Why did you say "Huh"? You don't like Buddy?

JENNY: Buddy's just fine, fine. But I wish you'd stop trying to push me at him or push him at me like you seem to be doing because I'll tell you frankly, it won't work, ever! It could never possibly work . . .

BEULAH: I'm sorry to hear it because I think that him and you are both lonesome and two lonesome people, both attractive and the right age for each other, can give each other a lot of comfort in life. If Buddy wasn't my brother, I sure would set my cap for him because I could do a lot worse, any girl that I know could do a lot worse than Buddy. And I'm not pushing him at you, I'm just telling you that he has taken a serious interest in you, and Buddy's got him a good job at Budweiser that might develop into a better one, you never can tell. I'm very hopeful about it . . .

JENNY: Beulah, you're hopeful about everything.

BEULAH: No. Not everything, Jenny—I wouldn't say I was hopeful about myself. I think I'll be typing and filing down there at the Universal Shoe Company till the place shuts down or I'm retired for old age. But I am hopeful about my brother, Buddy, and I don't understand why you can't see the good points in him.

JENNY: I've got nothing *against* him.

BEULAH: I wish you could find something *for* him. He's just waiting for the "go" sign. You know, next Sunday, they start running the open air streetcars out to Creve Coeur Lake, and I thought I'd make us a nice picnic lunch and we could all go out there on the open air streetcar and have a picnic by the lake. It's a lovely ride out. You go through such lovely country. You remember? The time you first met Buddy when I arranged that picnic out there for us? I thought that he made a good impression on you, you seemed to get along real good together, and you sat in the backseat of the streetcar coming home and I purposely sat up ahead with Little Pretty but I opened my compact and seen in the mirror he had his arm around you and once he kissed you! You must have liked Buddy, then.

JENNY: Yes, but I wasn't enchanted with Little Pretty. After all, Buddy is a widower with a very unmanageable little girl on his hands, and he's getting fat, too.

BEULAH: He's not fat yet. But Buddy's been drinking too much beer with the boys and it's been putting weight on him too fast lately. I told him so. He agreed to stop it. It's just beer fat and as soon as he quits drinking beer every night with the gang of boys from the plant that extra weight will drop off him just like magic. You watch! It will! —Like magic . . . —But the point of this talk is that I know Buddy and I know you, and I feel in my heart, very deep, that you are meant for each other and I am going to keep on doing all that I have in my power to bring you together—eventually, because—I'm so attached to you both . . . and admire you both so—highly!

JENNY: —Beulah? Last spring I was still just recovering from my nervous breakdown and I was very insecure and very lonely. But, now, Beulah, it's different. I am back on my feet, nervously speaking, I mean. And, Beulah? I think I'm in love and I think that I may be able to make him love me. I mean Mr. Harry Steed. Beulah? He's invited me to the theater with him Saturday. He has tickets to *Blossom Time* at the Muny Opera. I'm going with him. He's the handsomest man I've ever laid my two eyes on, and if, if, *if!* —I can manage to be somewhat brighter? —I think I can build up his present interest in me to a point where—*well* . . . something *might happen* . . .

BEULAH: Okay, honey. But just don't set your heart on it, because you're easily hurt by disappointments in people, the same as I am.

JENNY: —Beulah, we're very different. We are opposite types. You are easygoing. You accept things as they are and make the best of them, which is very, very, very admirable in you and one of the many fine things that I respect in your nature, but Beulah. I *dream* of—I *dream* of—finding my true heart's desire! It all depends on how things go on this date.

BEULAH: Good luck with it, honey. I mean it. And Buddy would wish you the same. . . .

[*Fade out.*]

30] INTERIOR. APARTMENT. EARLY EVENING, SATURDAY.

Jenny emerges from the bedroom, dressed for Blossom Time. *She has on a dress like a little girl's birthday party dress:*

starched white organdy with a pale blue silk sash. The golden curls have never appeared so golden or so luxuriant. Beulah is understandably startled.

Beulah whistles in amazement.

JENNY: It isn't too much, is it, Beulah?

BEULAH: —Too much what, honey?

JENNY: Too *much* . . .

BEULAH: All I can say is you look like a dream, you look like a real dream in it. Oh, I—hope it don't rain!

JENNY: Does it look like rain?

[*She crosses to window with a great rustle of skirts. The light outside has a curious green luster. The young tree framed by the window gleams as if made of glass.*]

Why, it's been raining, Beulah!

BEULAH: Oh, no, no, there was just a little—light shower, just a—sprinkle! I think it's all cleared off now.

JENNY: —If it rains, I'll die!

BEULAH: If it rains, it rains! You get rain checks if it rains; that way you go out with him twice. Huh, Jenny?

JENNY: I hope going out with him twice doesn't depend on the weather! Where can I sit down without getting messed?

BEULAH: What's wrong with the sofa?

JENNY: I wish I hadn't put so much starch in these ruffles; they make such a noise when I move.

BEULAH: They make a wonderful rustle.

JENNY: I'd better sit on that piano stool till I hear his car pulling up.

[*She lifts the back of her skirt so that she won't sit on it. It falls all around the piano stool like a snowy white bell. Her eyes are wide and brilliant, her voice trembling.*]

—What time is it?

BEULAH: It's a quarter past seven.

JENNY: He said he'd be here at seven! [*There is a note of anguish in her voice.*]

BEULAH: Oh, now, honey, you know how the traffic is crossing Olive and—Delmar . . .

JENNY: Feel my hand! Is it icy?

BEULAH: Jenny, for God's sake, Jenny! Don't work yourself up like this!

[*The window glimmers.*]

JENNY: *Lightning!*

BEULAH: It's clearing up—slowly. What kind of wrap are you wearing?

JENNY: I'm not wearing a wrap. I'm just going to carry my shawl in case his car top is down—to protect my hair a little.

43

BEULAH: Which shawl?

JENNY: My rose-colored shawl that Aunt Flo bought in Sorrento.

BEULAH: Why don't you wear the Spanish one with the roses embroidered on it and the long silk fringe?

JENNY: Because it would be too much! That's why . . .

BEULAH: "Romance, Romance, may come in the spring or fall!"

[*Pause: another faint glimmer of lightning.*]

[*She sings the second line.*] "Romance, Romance, be eager to heed its call!"

JENNY: Beulah! Don't! Please!

BEULAH: Honey, be honest with me! You want me in or out of this room when he gets here?

JENNY: Well, to be honest—I'd like to receive him alone.

BEULAH: Okay. I'll be out.

JENNY [*sharply*]: Don't misunderstand me! —It's just that he doesn't know I'm sharing my apartment with anyone—else . . .

BEULAH: You don't have to explain a thing to me, ever, Jenny; you ought to know that by this time. —Shall I go out, now? So I won't have to break my neck getting out when he gets here?

44

JENNY: What time is it now?

BEULAH: It's twenty-two past seven.

[*Jenny springs up.*]

—Him?

JENNY: I think so! Hurry!

BEULAH [*going out*]: I can't help wishin' you had this date with Buddy!

[*The bell rings. Jenny gasps, then draws herself up heroically as she crosses to admit Harry Steed with a high gasp of laughter.*]

STEED [*blinking at her in doorway*]: —Gee! —Jenny . . .

JENNY: All Gaul! Is divided!

[*Steed laughs a bit uncomfortably and looks at his watch.*]

I was actually ready when you arrived! Shall we go now, right now, or—?

STEED: —I think we ought to go now. It's been raining a little. I guess you know about *that*. —Got everything?

JENNY: Everything but—excuse me a moment! [*She rushes out for her shawl and comes back with it.*] "Rain, rain, go away! Come again some other day!" —Ha, ha! I mean evening . . . [*She sweeps out into the hall of the apartment.*]

[*He looks after her with an air of troubled perplexity.*]

45

STEED: —You look wonderful, Jenny . . . [*But the tone of this comment is ambiguous.*]

[*They go out. It glimmers again outside; his car is heard driving off. Beulah comes back in with a scared look. She calls Buddy's number on phone.*]

BEULAH: Buddy? Beulah! Jenny just went out to the Muny Opera opening with that high school gym teacher. Buddy, I'm awful worried about her. She dressed up too much, Buddy, you know what I mean? She had on a sort of a little girl's party dress and it was a little too much. She even had a—a big blue silk sash on it with a big bow in the back, and—her eyes looked very strange, Buddy, and her voice was so—high? Excited? —Suppose it rains at the Muny! You know how everybody rushes for the shelters when it rains there, Buddy. Jenny can't stand a crowd! —Buddy, I'm worried sick! I told her, I couldn't help saying it to her, Buddy, that I wish it was you she was going out with tonight. This man is too good-looking and Jenny is too excited! —Buddy? Do me a favor? Come over and sit with me till she gets back from the Muny. —Can't you? — Oh. —Well, Buddy, I want to have a talk with you tomorrow night. I'll come to your place. —I'm terribly worried, Buddy!

[*Fade out.*]

31] EXTERIOR. NIGHT.

Jenny and Harry Steed are in his car, a Stutz "bearcat" roadster, blood-red, wire-wheeled, the smartest little car of the day.

STEED: We still got half an hour before the show. You want to park on Art Hill and feel that wonderful breeze Lucinda was talking about?

JENNY: —Oh, I'd love to, I'd love to!

32] CUT TO: EXTERIOR. ART HILL IN ST. LOUIS. NIGHT.

STEED: I don't feel much breeze. Do you?

JENNY: No. But the view is heaven.

STEED: Not many cars here tonight.

JENNY: No, it's nearly deserted.

[*Harry puts his arm about her. Jenny is wildly expectant of his next move if any.*]

STEED [*tightening his arm about her*]: How many parts is Gaul divided into? Tonight?

JENNY: It's not divided, tonight, it's—*unified! Completely!* [*He turns her face to him and holds her close.*]

STEED: —May I?

JENNY: Yes! Yes, please!

[*He pulls her face tight to his. When he finally releases her, Jenny exclaims.*]

OH!

[*Harry laughs gently. Jenny sighs and leans on his shoulder.*]

STEED: —I've been wanting to do that for a long time. Jenny—I got to make a decision!

JENNY: What decision?

STEED: I can't talk about it yet.

JENNY: Talk about it to me! I'd never tell!

STEED: —See that lightning?

JENNY: It's a long way off.

STEED: I bet it rains before the opera's over.

JENNY: —What decision were you talking about? —You said you had to make a decision. What is it? You can trust me! —I've got to make one, too.

STEED: —What's yours?

JENNY: You saw the place I live in when you picked me up there tonight. I was ashamed for you to. It's so terribly tacky. You didn't meet my girl friend, the friend that shares it with me. It's her place, not mine, I moved in with her after my— breakdown, I had a slight nervous breakdown. —Maybe you've heard about it? —I'm sure it's known at the school. Well. Beulah is my girl friend. The kindest person that I have ever known. But I—had to ask her not to come in when you—I didn't want you to meet her.

STEED: Why?

JENNY: Well, she's like the apartment.

STEED: Then I think I'd like her, Jenny.

JENNY: Oh, yes, but—I'm gradually trying to weed out some of those knickknacks she's got all about. It isn't easy. She comes in and says, "Where's Happy hopped to?" Know what Happy is? A huge green china frog which she thinks is ornamental!

—Isn't that hilarious? [*pause.*] —Didn't you speak of having to make a decision?

STEED: Yeah. But I shouldn't bother you with it.

JENNY: Close as we are now? You think I'm not concerned? You think I'm only concerned with the number of parts that Gaul was divided into twenty centuries ago?

STEED: —You're strange and sweet and—may I?

JENNY [*offering him her lips*]: Ordinarily I—

[*They kiss, lingeringly.*]

—I hold a very strict line with a man and would never consider these intimacies on a first date, but—Harry? Tell me about the decision you want to make? Is it a personal or a professional decision, does it concern your—emotions or—?

[*Distant orchestra.*]

STEED: I hear the overture! —We're going to be late.

JENNY: Why don't we forget the Muny? I've seen *Blossom Time* before.

STEED: Jenny?

JENNY: Let's stay here. I'll sing you the sweetest song, my favorite song in the opera.

[*In a voice quivering with emotion she sings "Kiss Me Again."*]

49

STEED: Beautiful, honey, but it's supposed to be a duet. We better get moving.

[*There is a close shot of her face, disappointed, as the car starts off.*]

33] DISSOLVE TO: A BOX AT THE "MUNY OPERA" IN FOREST PARK.

The closing number of Blossom Time *is in progress. A summer storm is approaching. Lightning flashes behind the huge trees that tower above the open stage. The flimsy scenery has begun to flap alarmingly in the wind. Anxious murmurs are heard at each lightning flash; a few spectators have begun to hasten up the concrete aisles of the amphitheater . . .*

There is a close up of Jenny and Harry Steed. She is "simply enchanted!" Steed is bored and restless. Now and then Steed glances at her exalted profile. His glances contain three elements, a certain tenderness, a good deal of amusement, and some irritation . . .

STEED [*after a particularly brilliant flash of lightning*]: Jenny? Jenny?

JENNY: Enchanting, simply enchanting! Allan Jones is *so* handsome. Don't you think he's the handsomest tenor they've ever had at the Muny?

STEED: Jenny? It's going to rain any minute.

JENNY: —Not yet. It's almost over . . .

STEED: How are you in a riot? When the storm breaks, everybody is going to rush for the shelters.

[*On either side of the concrete bowl is a gravelled aisle with a solid roof and trellised sides which serves as a shelter when a performance is interrupted by rain.*]

JENNY: *Shh! This part is so lovely* . . .

[*More and more people are shuffling up the rather steep concrete aisle beside the iron-railed box.*]

STEED: Jenny, it's okay with me, but you don't look like a girl that ought to be caught in a stampede if it rains. Imagine what it would do to your golden curls!

JENNY: AHHH! AHHH! SO ENCHANTING . . .

[*She leans back, enraptured, her head tilting toward his shoulder, eyes fluttering, hand to throat.*

[*Abruptly the storm breaks. The anxious murmurs turn to excited outcries. Lights flicker on stage as performers rush into wings.*

[*Scenery collapses; shrieks; panic; pandemonium.*]

STEED: *My God, it's a cyclone!*

[*He seizes Jenny and pulls her into an aisle. A stampede of fleeing spectators sweeps them apart. He calls her. He is answered at a distance by her wild screams* . . .]

34] CUT TO: A SHELTER.
He is carrying Jenny, whose screams have fallen to strangled sobs.

STEED: Let me through! I got to get this woman to a hospital! Hey, let me through . . .

51

35] CUT TO: INTERIOR. JENNY'S APARTMENT.
    NIGHT.
They enter Jenny's apartment, admitted by Beulah.

*Jenny is drenched and dazed; the Mary Pickford curls are
ravished by storm, the organdy is a wreck . . .*

BEULAH: OH! Fo' heaven's sake! *I known it!*

STEED: I think you better take over. She had a bad time at
the Muny when the storm broke.

BEULAH: Jenny? Jenny! It's all right, honey, you're home.

[*Jenny begins to sob. Beulah shepherds her to her bedroom,
calling back.*]

Sit down, Mr. Steed. I got some hot cocoa for you . . .

[*He sneezes, then looks about the odd little apartment. Rosie
the bulldog approaches him, waddling and sniffing. He gives
a slight, incredulous laugh. After a moment, Beulah comes
back out.*]

—Mr. Steed, I'm Beulah Bodenhafer, Jenny's roommate. You sit
down.

STEED: I'm too wet to, Beulah. I'd spoil the chair. [*He sneezes
again.*]

BEULAH: Oh, my goodness, I hope you're not catchin' a cold.
Why don't you take off those wet clothes in the bathroom and
put on a robe? I got a nice quilted bathrobe you can put on.
Of course it will be a little bit short for you, but it'll be warm.
The radio says that we caught the tail of a cyclone, just the tail
of it, though. The head of it struck in East St. Louie, they say.

52

. . . Now you go in the bathroom and I'll hand you the robe through the door!

STEED: Thanks, Miss Bodenhafer, but I'm goin' home, now.

BEULAH: Aw, naw! Jenny would be heartbroken!

[*The phone rings.*]

Aw, that's Buddy, my brother. Enquiring how it is here. I told him Jenny was goin' out to the Muny. . . . [*She crosses to the phone in the hall.*] Hey! Buddy? Jenny just got back from the Muny, Buddy. She got caught in the stampede but she wasn't hurt, just scared. She seems to be kind of dazed, Buddy. She come in the door like she didn't know where she was.

36] CUT TO: INTERIOR. PARLOR.
Beulah's voice continues as Steed crosses to the front door. Behind the bedroom door Jenny's voice calls, "Beulah!"

Steed goes out quietly.

BEULAH: Just a minute, Buddy. Jenny's calling. [*She sets down the receiver and rushes to the bedroom.*]

37] CUT TO: INTERIOR. JENNY'S BEDROOM.
Jenny sits panting on the bed, coming out of her shock.

JENNY: Beulah! Where's Harry Steed?

BEULAH: He's in the front room, honey.

JENNY: *Dry my hair! Help me! Where's my robe?*

BEULAH: Right here, Jenny.

JENNY: *SHH! Not so loud!*

BEULAH: It's all right, honey. I think he understands.

JENNY: Understands WHAT! Will you please give me my robe?

BEULAH: Sure, honey. I got it for you. Here. But you're not dry yet.

JENNY: How is my hair? Is it hopeless?

BEULAH: Naw, it looks lovely, honey.

JENNY: I don't dare look in the mirror. See if Mr. Steed is all right, Beulah.

BEULAH: Honey, don't you think I better excuse you? You know you ought to go right to bed now, Jenny.

JENNY: NO! [*She rushes to the door.*] Harry? Mr. Steed? Harry?

[*There is no answer. She enters the parlor. There are wet tracks on the carpet, the front door is ajar, but there is no Harry Steed. She begins to sob wildly.*]

BEULAH: What's the matter, honey?

JENNY: HE'S GONE, HE'S GONE, I'VE LOST HIM! I'VE LOST HIM, HE'S GONE, HE'S GONE!

[*She screams and rushes into the hall of the apartment building. Beulah rushes after her. There is the sound of a struggle in hall. After a moment she drags Jenny back in. They cross the camera, into the bedroom again. After a moment Beulah*

54

rushes back out and turns around distractedly. Buddy's voice is heard calling on the phone. Beulah rushes to phone.]

BEULAH: Buddy, Buddy, come over quick! Bring a doctor! She's had a terrible—shock—a real—*attack*!

38] DISSOLVE TO: INTERIOR. THE APARTMENT ENTRANCE. SUNDAY EVENING. CLOSE TWO-SHOT: BUDDY AND JENNY.
Buddy looms awkwardly, beaming at Jenny.

JENNY: Why, hello, Buddy. What an unexpected—

BUDDY [*heartily*]: Hi, Jenny.

JENNY: Where's your sister?

BUDDY: Aw, Beulah's doin' the dishes.

JENNY: I'd better help her with them. I don't know why Beulah always wants to cook in. It's too much for her after a day's work at the office to prepare and serve and clean up after a meal at home. We have such a nice little restaurant right around the corner from us now, the Martha Washington Kitchen. Such a sweet little place with Colonial style decorations, little hurricane lamps with pink chimneys on each table and very reasonable prices. They serve a chicken-pot-pie every night, that's their specialty, for seventy-five cents, including a vegetable and a salad and a dessert and—coffee . . .

[*Her mind and her voice seem to wander. Beulah enters from the kitchenette, but stands stock still, listening intently with a bright smile. She is matchmaking, she hopes!*]

Beulah?

BEULAH: What, honey?

JENNY: Can I help you in there?

BEULAH: No, no, no! Everything's finished. You stay in front with Buddy!

BUDDY: Jenny?

JENNY: What, Buddy?

BUDDY: You sure do resemble Mary Pickford with those beautiful curls.

JENNY: I've always worn curls since I was a tiny girl. I'm not trying to look like Mary Pickford.

BUDDY: Oh, I didn't think that. I just thought you did look like her. Ha ha! I meant to give you a compliment, ha, ha . . .

[*The shot broadens to include the living room and kitchenette. Beulah echoes his nervous laugh in the kitchenette.*]

JENNY [*somewhat coolly*]: Thank you. —Beulah? Come on in if you are through in the kitchen.

BEULAH: In a minute. I got to put things away. Don't worry about me, Jenny.

JENNY: I'm not worried about you. —How are things at Budweiser?

[*The question is directed to Buddy as she takes off her hat and gloves before the mantel mirror.*]

BUDDY [*rising and coming up behind her*]: Fine! Fine! How are things at the high school?

JENNY: Things at the high school are sufferable at best, just sufferable, at best . . .

BUDDY: Maybe you ought to get out of that high school, Jenny?

JENNY: Into what, Buddy?

BUDDY: You're not getting any younger; why don't you get married, Jenny?

[*Jenny rises abruptly—she shuts the kitchen door.*]

JENNY [*returning*]: —Buddy, I know you didn't intend that remark to be unkind but it was! I shall get married, Buddy, but not because I'm "not getting any younger" and have to accept the first opportunity of marriage that's offered to me. I have romantic ideas about marriage. I think it has to be based on mutual attraction and on complete suitability of the two persons, since it's something that ought to last for a lifetime like my parents' marriage. *Don't do that!*

[*He has put his arms about her waist and planted a kiss on the back of her neck, lifting her curls to expose it.*]

—I said don't do that! So DON'T! —Excuse me. I'm going to rest because I—have a headache.

[*She rushes into the bedroom.*]

BEULAH [*coming into the living room*]: WHAT DID YOU DO?

57

BUDDY: What makes you think that Jenny and me could ever get together?

BEULAH: If you'd do what I tell you! Just be nice with her, Buddy! What did you do? Try to kiss her?

BUDDY: What's wrong with that?

BEULAH: Nothing except you done it too quick, Buddy. You'd better go home, now, Buddy. It's spoiled for tonight. I knew by her voice that she's in a nervous condition.

BUDDY: Yeah, as always. Why are you so anxious to push me at her?

BEULAH: I understand Jenny's problems, and you are lonesome as she is.

BUDDY: I don't have much trouble with other girls.

BEULAH: I'm trying to get you the right one.

BUDDY: What's right about her? For *me*? A prissy cold-blooded schoolteacher that's over thirty?

BEULAH: You ruined everything by saying "You're not getting younger." Don't you think she knows it?

BUDDY: She's too touchy for me. I don't know what to say to her.

BEULAH: Y' don't have to say the wrong thing every time, Buddy. As for her being past thirty, she's just thirty-two. You are thirty-nine, face it! And a widower with a child. —Jenny's a lady! —And a very pretty and well-educated young lady that, if you would just approach her in the right way, not like a bear,

58

like a bull, would make you the wonderfullest wife and mother of children that you could ever hope for!

BUDDY: —She feels superior to me. Superior to you, too.

BEULAH: NOT SO LOUD. —She can hear you.

BUDDY: —G'night. I'm going, Sis. Thanks for supper.

BEULAH: Oh. Wait. Here's something for Little Pretty. [*She hands him a package.*]

BUDDY: What's this?

BEULAH: A jumping rope and a set of jacks and a pretty new blue hair ribbon.

BUDDY [*putting on his jacket*]: Thank you, Sis, she'll love 'em.

BEULAH [*as he goes out*]: Don't forget next Sunday.

BUDDY: What about next Sunday?

BEULAH: The picnic at Creve Coeur Lake! The open-air streetcars are starting next Sunday.

[*He is out. Beulah rushes to window.*]

—Buddy! —Don't forget that, will you?

BUDDY'S VOICE: NAW!

BEULAH: Without Little Pretty! Huh, Buddy? Make some other plans for her!

BUDDY'S VOICE [*further off*]: Okay!

39] DISSOLVE TO: INTERIOR. SCHOOL. THE FOL-
LOWING MONDAY MORNING.

LUCINDA: Jenny Starling, *not* blue dotted swiss, again.

JENNY: What's wrong with it, Lucinda?

LUCINDA: Nothing except it's only for little girls, Jenny.

JENNY: Does it look silly on me? I hesitated about it quite a
while.

LUCINDA: Not quite long enough, and it reeks of camphor.
Come in my room a minute. I've got something to tell you of
the *utmost* importance!

[*They enter Lucinda's classroom.*]

Now! First tell me about Saturday night! Were you caught in
the rainstorm at the Muny?

[*Jenny bursts into tears.*]

Jenny! What's the matter? Sit down. I'll lock the door so we
won't be disturbed. I knew there was something wrong when I
saw Steed. I said, "Well, how was *Blossom Time*, Harry? Was
it absolute heaven?"

JENNY: What did he say about it?

LUCINDA: He can be funny, you know. He does have a sense
of humor.

JENNY: What did he say? What was funny?

LUCINDA: It wasn't so much what he said but the face he made.

JENNY [*stricken*]: What face?

LUCINDA: Oh, I can't imitate it!

JENNY: —Would you say that he was—making *fun* of me?

LUCINDA: He makes fun of everything, honey, nothing is sacred to him. Was it a real disaster? Did your curls get wet?

[*The bell rings in the corridor.*]

JENNY: There goes the bell . . .

LUCINDA: Jenny, I've found the place for us! Guess where? Westminster Place!

JENNY: That's not in the school district.

LUCINDA: You can't find a smart apartment in the school district, Jenny.

JENNY [*crossing to the door*]: How much is it?

LUCINDA: You can't build your life on the rock of economy, honey. You know that, don't you? You've got to be *bold* and *plunge*! Now assuming that Harry Steed is serious. In his attentions? Are you satisfied to receive him where you stay now? Don't you want a modern, smart place in a fashionable location to entertain him for bridge suppers and so forth?

JENNY: If what you say about the face he made—perhaps I've seen the last of him, outside of school . . .

61

LUCINDA: —I was just teasing you, dear. You want to know what I hear? Wedding bells! This summer! If you play your cards right. What's your address?

JENNY: West Pine. Five two oh four, West Pine . . .

LUCINDA: —I'll be there on Saturday. A deposit has to be made on the apartment to hold it!

JENNY: —When?

LUCINDA: Close to six. —You won't regret it, Jenny. Sometimes a single decision, if it's the right decision, can determine the whole course of your life in this world, Jenny.

40] DISSOLVE TO: INTERIOR. CORRIDOR. DAY.
The sound of a march tune is heard on the victrola in the gym.

It suddenly stops and Harry Steed lopes out of the gym ahead of his gym class. Jenny is in the basement corridor, before her locker.

STEED: Hey, Jenny! How many parts is Gaul divided into?

JENNY: Harry! —You startled me, Harry!

STEED [*gaily as he goes*]: All Gaul is divided into three parts, huh?

JENNY: *Harry?!*

[*He doesn't appear to hear her.*]

—All Gaul is—divided into—three parts . . .

41] DISSOLVE TO: INTERIOR. JENNY'S APARTMENT.
LATE AFTERNOON, SATURDAY.
*Jenny has been trying on summer dresses. The bed is piled
with them. The doorbell rings. She admits Lucinda.*

LUCINDA: Well! I was prepared for something but not quite
this! What a fantastic clutter of little objects, why, it's like a
little souvenir shop in some tacky resort town such as Niagara
Falls or Chatauqua or Atlantic City, New Jersey! [*Her voice is
shrill with disdain.*] Where did all this stuff come from?

JENNY [*embarrassed*]: Her mother died lately and—

LUCINDA: Oh. And she inherited all of these little knickknacks?
How sweet! Ha ha!

JENNY: Beulah's very devoted to her family . . .

LUCINDA: Are all the family heirlooms in the parlor?

JENNY: They're scattered about the apartment.

LUCINDA: What is that noise?

[*There is a loud asthmatic snuffing sound.*]

JENNY: Beulah's bulldog, Rosie.

LUCINDA: Oh, no! Where is this creature?

JENNY: In the bedroom.

LUCINDA: Does she suffer from asthma?

JENNY: All bulldogs do, more or less. They're very short
nosed, you know.

63

LUCINDA: What an extraordinary noise she makes breathing! Does she always do that?

JENNY: It's always louder when she smells a stranger.

LUCINDA: I hope my perfume is agreeable to her. Does she like Chanel?

JENNY: She's very funny. Would you like to see her?

LUCINDA: Oh, yes, do let me see her but just for a moment, I just want to peek through the door . . .

[Jenny opens the bedroom door and an old bitch bull waddles out.]

No! Not possible, really!

[Jenny laughs uneasily.]

Please don't let her jump on me!

JENNY: She's too old to jump.

LUCINDA: Good! She has one virtue. Jenny, may I use your phone?

JENNY: Rosie, go back, Rosie.

LUCINDA: Jenny, where is your phone?

JENNY [*vaguely*]: —Phone?

LUCINDA: Yes. It's short for telephone, dear! That ghastly apparatus that Mr. Alexander Bell brought into our lives to wreak havoc.

JENNY: Oh! —It's in the back hall.

LUCINDA: Will you please lead the way? I'll try to follow! [*She knocks over something on the table by door.*] Oh, I've *broken* something! Some hideous little what-is-it, oh, hooray, there's one less! Will she be brokenhearted?

JENNY: Oh, that can be mended, I guess . . .

LUCINDA: You don't mean to say she'll put it *together* again! My heavens, what utter darkness. Is there a light of some kind?

JENNY: Yes. Wait there a second, just a— [*She switches on the light.*] There!

LUCINDA: Jenny, no wonder you're a victim of chronic depression. I've been here less than ten minutes and feel so sad I could weep. I'm going to call the sweetest young married couple! They live in Webster Groves, have the sweetest little home there, just half a block from the Webster Groves Country Club. Of course that isn't one of the *very* exclusive country clubs, but they have an attractive young married crowd and their Saturday night dances are fun! I went to one last month. I was the only unmarried girl on the floor and the husbands gave me a rush! —I swung from partner to partner till I collapsed from exhaustion! It's a rather sophisticated young married crowd, getting started. You know? Flirt with each other's husbands and no one gets stuffy about it. Let's see, now. Here's Carters, a long string of them. Mr. J. Brandon Carter, they call him Brandy. Isn't that a cute name? It's Webster 6-0400. . . . If they're having a dance tonight and invite me to it would you like to go, too?

JENNY: Why, I—

LUCINDA [*to operator*]: Webster 6-0400, please. I have a hunch they're having a dance there tonight . . .

[*There is the sound of a door opening in the kitchen beyond.*]

Who's that?

JENNY: Beulah.

LUCINDA: Oh! Could you keep her out of here till I've finished this call?

[*The door opens on Beulah.*]

JENNY: Beulah? Lucinda's making a phone call. Would you mind waiting back there till she's through?

BEULAH: Aw. Naw. Excuse me. [*She backs out. There is some noise.*]

LUCINDA: Jenny, please close that door!

JENNY [*at the door*]: What on earth is that racket?

BEULAH: Just putting some things for the picnic tomorrow in the icebox . . .

[*Jenny closes the door firmly.*]

LUCINDA [*into the phone*]: Brandy! How are you, darling? It's so good to hear your voice! I'm going to give you a little telephone kiss. [*She makes a kissing sound.*] Did you catch it? All right, now you give me one, give me a telephone kiss and make it a *big* one. Ahhhhh! I'm all goose pimples! —*Really! Ha, ha!* [*There is a slight pause.*] You know, I don't think I called you to tell you what a wonderful time I had at the country club dance a week ago Saturday. It was simply *peachy*! And you?! You *sheik*! I didn't know you had such wild blood in you; Valentino will have to look to his laurels! Was Agnes cross? A little? Who with, with you or with me? Both of us? Oh. I thought she was more broadminded. I'll have to talk to that girl. She can't pick out a good-looking husband like you and expect to keep him all to herself all the time on all occasions, ha, ha, ha . . . Brandy? I'm not hinting, of course, but tonight is Saturday night and I never had such a good time in St. Louis County as I had at that last country club dance. Is there going to be one tonight? *Ohhhh*? There *issss*? —I'm *waiting*! Oh, don't be coy, you know what I'm waiting for, an invitation, of course! I have a marvelous new formal that I could wear, I'm a knockout in it . . .

[*The icebox door slams in the kitchen.*]

Aw, you're adorable. Look, Brandy. I had a date for tonight, of course, but something happened suddenly, a death in his family, no, no, not a death but a sudden stroke that's serious, though. Now I just wondered if you could get someone for me. Not as handsome as you, that would be asking too much, but someone attractive and unattached. Some of those *wives* had *blood* in their eyes last time! —I don't want to be murdered on a dance floor! —Oh, come on. Put on your thinking cap! UH! I have an idea. Just a moment. Jenny? I just can't talk when someone is standing over me like that. Would you mind going in the— [*She indicates the kitchen where Beulah is making a remarkable lot of racket.*]

JENNY: Oh, I'm sorry. Surely . . . [*She crosses out.*]

LUCINDA: Close the door, please, Jenny, she's making *such* a racket in there! [*Then, when the door is closed, she continues in a hushed voice.*] Brandy? Don't you know Harry Steed, that

67

was the golf pro at the Glen Echo last year? I knew you did.
Well, he is now the boys' athletic director and gym teacher at
the school where I teach. Brandy? Would you do me a great
big beautiful favor tonight? Would you ask him for me? And
don't say it's for me! Say it's for someone wonderful but don't
say WHO! —Give him my address and tell him to pick me up
but don't say who I am. It'll be such FUN! —You know? We'll
both laugh our heads off when he steps in the door, and there I
am in my lovely new evening gown! —With something suitable playing on the victrola. . . . Will you? Just *try*? It's one
chance out of a hundred he is *free* this evening, but will you
just give it a try? You sweet thing, you. I'm going to give you
another telephone kiss, the nice thing about a telephone kiss is
it leaves no lipstick traces. Bye, bye, honey. Call me back in
one hour, my number is in the phone book.

[*There is a slight pause. Beulah enters the living room. Jenny
follows.*]

JENNY: Oh, Lucinda, this is Beulah, Beulah Bodenhafer, Miss
Lucinda Keener.

BEULAH: Didn't catch the name. Would you mind repeating
the name?

LUCINDA [*regarding her coolly*]: Keener.

BEULAH: —I got one of the new electric hearing aids. I'm
still self-conscious about it. I cover it up with this big paper
poppy.

LUCINDA: Oh, is that why you—! [*She utters a sharp little
giggle.*]

[*Jenny is intensely mortified by this encounter.*]

JENNY: Shall we? —Will you excuse us, Beulah? Lucinda and I have to discuss something privately.

LUCINDA: Oh, Jenny, we can't talk now, I have to RUN. They asked me to the Saturday dance at their club. They have a gorgeous date for me if I can trust the description they gave me: *lyrical*—mature but not potbellied. Such a rare combination!

[*She has crossed into the front room, followed by Jenny who is about to close the door which is blocked firmly by Beulah.*]

JENNY: Aren't you lucky.

LUCINDA: How's your Charleston, Jenny?

JENNY: Oh, I

LUCINDA: I don't mean this Saturday, I mean next Saturday, they're having a Charleston contest at the club. I'm going to get you in with this little crowd.

JENNY: —Perhaps I—

[*She is thinking of Harry Steed as a Charleston partner.*]

BEULAH: She practices the Charleston all the time, like a fiend!

LUCINDA: Oh? Is that right, Jenny?

JENNY: Doing it alone is one thing, but doing it with a partner is another.

LUCINDA: A couple of martini cocktails will solve that problem.

BEULAH: Jenny don't drink, never drinks, it don't have a good effect on her.

JENNY: BEULAH, WILL YOU PLEASE!

BEULAH: —What, Jenny?

JENNY: —Allow us to have the front room to *ourselves* for a minute?

BEULAH: Excuse me. I got to start supper. [*She turns about and starts back to hall. She stops at door.*] Miss Keener, that's a smart little suit you got on. A girl down at the office where I work has got one like it.

LUCINDA: I hope not exactly like it.

BEULAH: Well, it has the same cut, the same nipped in waist and lapels and pleats in the skirt. It's very slenderizing. I can't wear nothing like that. Where did you get it, Miss Keener?

LUCINDA: I get my clothes at Scruggs.

BEULAH: I bet it cost you twice what she paid for it at Famous and Barr . . .

LUCINDA: —Why?

BEULAH: Your material's better. But the effect is the same. Can I ask you how much you paid for that suit?

LUCINDA: I'm sorry but I don't like talking about the cost of my clothes. Good-bye, Miss—? Oh! —Bodenhafer . . .

BEULAH: Yeah, that's right, Bodenhafer. Your name slipped my mind, too. [*She crosses out with a shrug.*]

LUCINDA: Now I understand why you're practically on the verge of a nervous breakdown. How can you possibly occupy an apartment with that creature?

JENNY: I'm so indebted to her.

LUCINDA: Financially?

JENNY: Not just that. Lucinda, she's so devoted!

LUCINDA: She's attached herself to you because there's nobody else would put up with her.

JENNY: Oh, she's very popular at her office. On her last birthday they gave her an office party; she came home loaded with presents.

LUCINDA: Those are her kind of people. Are they *your* kind of people? Jenny, you've got to get out, this move is imperative, Jenny! Come to the front door with me. I'm sure that woman is eavesdropping on us. [*She leads Jenny into the outside hall.*] —What a hideous entrance! Is there anything tackier than imitation marble stairs, and that chandelier reminds me of mushroom soup . . . with dead flies in it. [*They descend the steps to the street.*] Jenny, make a decision! Make it right now!

JENNY: But I haven't even seen the Westminster Place apartment.

LUCINDA: I've described it to you in every detail. It's smart, modern—in a fashionable location! Look. Give me the money for the deposit now and tomorrow you can inspect it, you can look at it Sunday, and if for some reason it doesn't happen to suit you, the deposit will be refunded with no difficulty. All right? Agreed?

[*Jenny looks bewildered.*]

Now let's assume that Harry Steed, for instance, is seriously interested in you. Could you receive Harry Steed in that apartment, and introduce him to Miss Beulah the Slob? Jenny, you're one of those vague people that have to have decisions made for them. All right. I'll make it for you. You just go back in and bring me out the deposit for the apartment. You will see it tomorrow. You'll be enchanted with it, but if you're not, you'll get the deposit right back! Now isn't this the right program?

JENNY [*drawing a deep, sighing breath*]: —I'm putting all my eggs in one basket—Harry Steed! And how do I know that Harry's still interested in me? Since that awful evening when we were caught in the storm at the Muny Opera—it's been a week since he's even asked me how many parts Gaul is divided into!

LUCINDA: Steed is waiting for you to make the next move, Jenny. He's spoiled, socially.

JENNY: If only I could somehow—!

LUCINDA: Jenny? —*Jenny!*

[*Jenny's thoughts have drifted into space.*]

—The next invitation has got to come from you, the next step's yours because Harry Steed won't make it. Follow the program. Give me the money for the deposit right now, inspect the place tomorrow, Sunday morning, and have him over one night for a little bridge supper or something. With my own little crowd, without the slob, Beulah. Go right in there and get me the deposit, and soon as I leave, have a quiet talk with Beulah, explain to Miss Bodenhafer that you can't stay on her level for the rest of your life if you want to have one worth living!

[*Pause.*]

JENNY: —Beulah's been so kind to me . . .

LUCINDA: Now you're trying my patience! I'm not going to wait any longer. Stay with that slob forever if that's the kind of future you're prepared to accept!

JENNY: Wait. —I'll get the, the—money . . . [*She sucks in her breath again, then turns back to the apartment entrance. She halts with door pushed open.*] —Lucinda, I don't understand the money arrangement we'll make. I pay the rent? Then how can—

LUCINDA: I explained it to you. You pay the rent, I pay the household expenses.

JENNY: And how much is it, again? The rent?

LUCINDA: Ridiculously little for what you get. Please, honey, do *hurry*! I'll have to run my legs off if I'm going to keep my appointment with that real estate man.

JENNY: Oh, dear. I locked myself out.

LUCINDA: Then ring the doorbell for Beulah the Slob. I'll wait outside on the walk, I don't care to see her again. [*She clatters down the stairs on her high heeled pumps and goes out the door to the sidewalk and fading gold sunlight . . .*]

[*Jenny rings. Beulah lets her in.*]

JENNY: Locked myself out.

BEULAH: —Who was she?

JENNY: That was Lucinda Keener.

BEULAH: From school?

JENNY [*impatient*]: Yes, Beulah, from school, from school. May I please get by?

[*Beulah is occupying the bedroom doorway.*]

BEULAH: Sure, sure, go by . . .

[*Jenny starts rooting in a dresser for something.*]

— I don't like the looks of her.

JENNY: Naturally not, since she's a friend of mine. And I don't care for the looks of those slobs that *you* work with.

BEULAH: The girls at my office are honest hard-working girls, if that's slobs. I wouldn't describe them as slobs . . .

JENNY: I'm sorry, but I would.

BEULAH: —Maybe you think I'm one, too. Huh? Jenny, you—! —Something's been wrong with you lately. If you tell me what you're looking for, maybe I could help you find it, Jenny.

JENNY: I am looking for my—! [*She clasps her forehead as if the word won't come.*]

BEULAH: Huh?

JENNY: Pocketbook, the—

BEULAH: The patent leather?

JENNY: Yes, the—

BEULAH: I put it away safer for you.

JENNY: Where?

BEULAH: On the top closet shelf.

JENNY: Will you please get it for me? And I'd appreciate it if you'd let me take care of my own things myself after this.

BEULAH: I just thought I'd better lock it up in the closet while the wallpaper men was here, Jenny, one of them looked kind of shifty.

JENNY: Hurry! Lucinda's waiting outside.

BEULAH [*producing the purse from the closet*]: Aw. She wants money, huh? She looked like a sponger to me. I bet she spends all her money on her clothes and then has to borrow. We had one of them at the office before the war, and—

[*Jenny rushes out, giving the dog a slight kick as it stands in doorway.*]

42] CUT TO: EXTERIOR. THE SIDEWALK.
Lucinda is waiting crossly.

LUCINDA: Now I'm so late I'll have to go in a taxi.

JENNY: She'd hidden my extra pocketbook in the closet. Let's see now. [*She counts out the bills.*] That's just it, I believe.

LUCINDA: I'll have to ask you for taxi fare, too, I'm afraid.

JENNY: How—how much would that—?

LUCINDA: This will cover it. [*She snatches another bill.*] Now you've really made up your mind? It's settled, is it?

JENNY [*panting*]: Yes! Completely, Lucinda! I can't afford it but I've got to somehow! I must have a place to entertain my friends without—

LUCINDA: Without embarrassment, yes. Jenny, you're looking haggard. Go in and rest a while, darling. [*She moves off crisply, her heels clacking out of the sound track.*]

[*Jenny is exhausted. On the way into the apartment building she passes an upstairs neighbor with a bag full of empty bottles. The woman greets her cheerfully. Jenny barely returns the greeting. She stops a moment to catch her breath, then rings the doorbell. We hear Beulah's voice on the phone, muted, talking to her brother.*]

43] **INTERIOR. APARTMENT HOUSE.**

BEULAH [*offstage, through the door*]: The open-air streetcars start running out to Creve Coeur tomorrow, Buddy, and like I said, I thought it would be nice if we took out a picnic, y'know, like we did last summer . . .

[*Jenny rings impatiently three short times.*]

Excuse me, Buddy. Jenny's locked herself out. [*She shouts.*] COMING! [*Then she opens the door and Jenny enters, still panting, and distracted.*]

[*Jenny crosses rudely past Beulah to the shallow bay window facing the street and looks out tensely. Beulah stands uncertainly behind her, forgetting the phone.*]

Honey? Jenny? I'm sorry I made remarks about y'r friend.

[*Jenny shrugs.*]

Anybody you like is okay with me.

[*Buddy's voice, calling, becomes audible over the abandoned phone.*]

Aw! Ha, ha! —I forgot I was talkin' t' Buddy. [*She rushes back to the phone.*] So Buddy? Is that agreeable with you, the plan for tomorrow? Well, good.

JENNY [*shrilly, turning from the window*]: COUNT ME OUT, IF YOU HAVE COUNTED ME IN!

[*There is a slight interval of silence.*]

BEULAH: —Nothing, Buddy. I, I'll—call yuh back later. Give Little Pretty my love! [*She hangs up and returns anxiously to the front room.*]

JENNY [*furiously*]: I love the way you assume, just assume, that I have nothing better to do on my Sundays than go out with you and Buddy, your fat brother!

BEULAH: —Buddy ain't fat, just solid.

JENNY: Solid! Hah . . . that's a nice way to put it!

BEULAH: You don't know his good points yet.

JENNY: I don't think I'm likely to, Beulah. I have other interests than the good points of Buddy. —I might be seeing Mr. Steed again.

BEULAH: —Then why're you in a bad humor?

JENNY: I am not in a bad humor, I'm just—exasperated!

BEULAH: What over, Jenny?

JENNY: You have no life of your own and—you have no life of your OWN! Everybody must have her own life but you don't! You're constantly trying to hang onto mine for some reason! Well. You can't, it won't do. We have too little in common.

[*Pause.*]

BEULAH: —Oh, Jenny, Jenny . . .

JENNY: Self-pity?

BEULAH: Jenny, you got to go back and have a talk with your doctor. You're very upset over something and since you won't tell me, you better go and tell him. I think I know what it is. It's Harry Steed at the school. I want you to know I sincerely hope that it will work out okay. But I dread to think of how you'll be if it don't.

JENNY: I can take care of my own affairs!

BEULAH: —No. You need help, Jenny. Some people do and you are one of those people. . . . Some people need somebody to help them, Jenny. I don't mean that as an insult. You are a wonderful person but a person that needs to have somebody to lean on a little. I want you to let me help you because I'm devoted to you as a friend and companion. We been good companions since—I met you at the City Sanitarium when me and Buddy was visiting our mother. After Mother died I kept coming back to visit you and we got to be good friends. You made wonderful progress. I don't claim I was responsible for the progress but I made a great effort to overlook your, your, your—

moods and—so forth. —But, now, Jenny, this Harry Steed business has set you off again. I don't think it's serious, awf'ly, but it's got to be coped with and I can't do it alone. Tomorrow Jenny you got to go see your doctor and talk about it with *him.* So he can advise you. Advice from me would be worthless because you've turned against me. When people're under this kind of strain, they turn against their good friends before they do against others. I noticed that fact at the hospital when I was visiting there, Jenny. The last time you got so disturbed, the doctor said, get married, you need to be loved. That was when I introduced you to Buddy. All right. You didn't take to him. You didn't appreciate the very fine qualities in him. But now, Jenny, maybe you'll see him different. He's took off a whole lot of weight. You'll see he's not fat but just solid. But first I want you to go have a talk with the doctor. I'm going to call him right now and tell him it's an emergency and he's got to talk to you early on Sunday morning, here or at his office, because you look to me like you're about to be a very sick girl again, Jenny. [*Pause.*] —On the way home I stopped by Werner's and bought some new sheet music. Let's sing a little together, huh, Jenny?

[*She sits at the upright piano and opens the sheet music. She plays "Carolina Moon" and sings with it in a rich and pleasant contralto. Jenny remains motionless for a while. Then she sighs and picks up an empty wastepaper basket and goes around collecting and depositing in basket the many, many knickknacks on the tables and shelves.*]

BEULAH [*stopping short*]: What're you *doin'*, Jenny? *What are you—*!

JENNY: *I can't spend another evening in a room full of little objects without going mad!*

[*Fade out.*]

44] INTERIOR. APARTMENT. SUNDAY.

Beulah is in the kitchenette preparing a picnic lunch. There is a knock at the fire escape door. She admits a stout matron who has descended the fire escape from the apartment above with a section of the Sunday paper.

WOMAN: Did you see *this*? [*She points out a photograph with a caption in the society section of the paper.*]

[*After reading the caption, Beulah draws a sharp, pained breath.*]

BEULAH: Oh, this is terrible, terrible. This will be a terrible shock to Jenny. She better not see it!

WOMAN: How are you going to keep her from seeing it?

BEULAH: —Well, she'll hear about it sooner or later but—I don't want her to see it right away. She had her heart set on him.

WOMAN: —Hunh . . .

BEULAH: What a stinker! —He took her to see *Blossom Time* at the Muny Opera last Saturday. She come home in a *daze*!

WOMAN: Well . . .

BEULAH: I'm gonna hide this from her.

WOMAN: The other teachers will be phoning the news to her right away.

BEULAH: Oh! —Yeah! —I better not let the phone ring . . . [*She draws another pained breath as she rushes to the phone and stuffs a crushed matchbook under the cradle so it won't ring.*]

WOMAN: I knew from what you told me that she was headed for a disappointment, Beulah. A man younger than her and so good-looking? Naw! I knew this would happen . . .

BEULAH: What a stinker to lead her on and never mention that he was about to have his engagement announced to a society girl in a classy suburb!

WOMAN: Your doorbell's ringing, Beulah, I got to go up . . .

[*She exits onto the fire escape as the bell rings impatiently. Beulah goes to answer. She admits Lucinda, very smartly dressed.*]

BEULAH: Aw. Hello. Afraid I've forgot your name.

LUCINDA: My name is Lucinda Keener. You were Miss Bodenhafer at our last encounter.

BEULAH: Yes, and I still am.

[*Slight pause.*]

LUCINDA: —May I come in? I am calling for Jenny.

BEULAH: Sure. Come in. Excuse me. I just had a shock. Have you seen the thing about Mr. Steed's engagement in the morning paper?

LUCINDA: Ha, ha! —Yes, of course. —Has Jenny seen it?

BEULAH: No. She hasn't come out, yet . . .

LUCINDA: May I sit down and wait for her to emerge for the day?

BEULAH: Yeah. Sit down. Want coffee?

LUCINDA: Thank you. Yes.

BEULAH: Well, pour you'self some coffee. I got to get rid of this paper before she comes out.

LUCINDA: Do you mean you're planning to hide it from her?

BEULAH: Yeah, I think I'll wrap up the devilled eggs in it. [*She goes out to the kitchen.*]

[*Lucinda helps herself to coffee at a drop-leaf table in the living room.*

[*A canary warbles sweetly in its cage.*

[*Lucinda looks at it with disdain. There is radio music from a room adjoining and the sound of Jenny counting aloud, breathlessly, doing exercises.*

[*White curtains drift in languidly from the gold spring Sunday outdoors . . .*

[*Beulah's voice is heard on phone.*]

BEULAH [*offstage, in a hushed tone*]: Buddy? Buddy! You got to get over here for the picnic to Creve Coeur Lake with me and Jenny today, don't say no, it's important! And don't take Little Pretty, leave her with the people next door because she makes Jenny nervous. Something awful has happened to poor Jenny that I'll explain to you in private. I'm not alone now in the apartment, Buddy. Will you go? And be very sweet to

Jenny. And do what I told you to do, and wear your pinstripe, Buddy, wear your pin-striped suit with a clean white shirt and a—and a—Buddy? Wear that light blue silk tie that Mama give you her last Christmas. Huh? Huh, Buddy? —And bring some beer and meet us at the Creve Coeur streetcar station, the open-air cars are starting to run out today, and it will be so lovely at Creve Coeur Lake—I'll talk to yuh later . . .

[*She restores the crushed matchbook to keep the phone from ringing and returns to the living room to engage in conversation with the caller.*]

—Excuse me for leaving you alone with your coffee.

LUCINDA: That's quite all right. There's no better company in the morning than a cup of hot coffee.

BEULAH: I always make two pots, one for me, one for Jenny, because hers has got to be weaker. You know how nervous she is.

LUCINDA: Miss Bodenhafer—can she hear us in there?

BEULAH: With the victrola on? No. She's taking her exercises. She didn't hear the doorbell. Why? You want to say something private?

LUCINDA: —Did she have a nervous breakdown, or was it mental?

BEULAH: —Miss Keener, there is some people in this world that can't cope with it, and Jenny's one of them people. They need all the help you can give them, and sometimes they need even more . . .

LUCINDA: That doesn't answer my question.

BEULAH: You got to stand between them and, and, and—
Life! —Y'know what I mean? — You got to act like a screen, a
shield, or something! —I just now called my brother. He's nuts
about Jenny! —He's willing to pop the question at any time,
and I just now let him know that now is the right time to pop
it. We're going to Creve Coeur Lake on the open-air streetcar.
It starts running today. I'll leave them alone together. He'll pop
the question. Now of course I know that Jenny will not accept right away. Not knowing about the gym instructor's engagement. She'll probably turn Buddy down or put him off
with some answer like, "Thank you so much. I'll have to think
it over." —You know what I mean, Miss Keener?

LUCINDA: Yes, Miss Bodenhafer, but I am mystified by your
interest in arranging a marriage between your brother and
Jenny Starling. What is your brother's position? Does he have
a pretty good position?

BEULAH: Buddy's with Budweiser.

LUCINDA: Oh, he works in a brewery?

BEULAH: Yes, he works with Budweiser. He's not gonna be
vice-president in ten years but he's still going to be working
for 'em, that you can count on, and having something to count
on is having something.

LUCINDA: —Miss Bodenhafer—

BEULAH: Why don't you call me Beulah. What's your first
name?

LUCINDA: —Beulah, I think that—*animal*—wants to go out.

[*Rosie, the bulldog, is standing patiently by the front door.*]

BEULAH: Yeah, she does. You know I was so upset I didn't notice her at the door? —Excuse me again. You want to come out with us?

LUCINDA: No, thank you. I think I'll wait.

[*Beulah takes Rosie out. Lucinda crosses to bedroom door.*]

Jenny? May I enter?

JENNY: OH, LUCINDA! WHEN DID YOU ARRIVE?

LUCINDA: Ages ago! —What on earth are you doing?

JENNY: My setting-up exercises. I'm nearly through.

LUCINDA: I've been having the most *enchanting* conversation with your devoted companion! I can't wait to tell you about it. Oh! —Here's the society page of the *Globe-Democrat!* —I see you have your coffee . . .

[*Beulah enters and picks up the society page which Lucinda had placed on bedside table.*]

BEULAH: Aw, it's full of June brides! Mind if I look at it first? [*She turns the radio up very loud.*] Miss Keener? Let's go have some more coffee. Jenny hates being watched at her exercises . . . [*She grips Lucinda by wrist and propels her out of the bedroom and kicks the door shut.*]

45] CUT TO: INTERIOR. THE PARLOR.

LUCINDA: Will you kindly let go of my arm?

BEULAH: You're a bad person. Get out. Get out of this apartment right this minute and don't ever come here again.

LUCINDA [*calling out*]: Jenny!

BEULAH [*snatching up a flower pot that holds a cactus plant and threatening Lucinda with it*]: OUT! OUT! OUT!

JENNY [*offstage, from the bedroom*]: What did you say, Beulah?

BEULAH: Don't answer! Just go! Quick! Or would you like to be crowned with a cactus plant? In a pot?

JENNY [*offstage*]: Beulah, what did you say?

BEULAH [*shouting*]: Nothing, honey. Finish your exercises.

LUCINDA: —I believe that you *would*!

BEULAH: You *bet* I would! And I'd LOVE it! —ROSIE? ROSIE?

[*The bulldog waddles back in.*]

—Okay, now, you go!

LUCINDA: —Jenny and I are going to share an apartment. You will not be welcome. [*She marches out.*]

[*A church hymn starts next door as Jenny turns off victrola.*

[*After a few moments, Jenny comes out of the bedroom.*]

JENNY: —Where is Miss Keener?

BEULAH: Oh. She said to tell you that she had to visit a—cousin of hers—with the flu . . .

JENNY: —How strange! She didn't tell ME!

BEULAH: —Naw, well, she told me to tell you. Honey, get dressed. I got the picnic lunch packed. Buddy is on his way to the Creve Coeur streetcar station, without Little Pretty. I knew you'd be glad to hear "without Little Pretty."

JENNY: —Beulah, I'm not going out to Creve Coeur with you and Buddy, even without Little Pretty. You know what I think? I think you said something offensive to Lucinda.

BEULAH: Me? Oh, no! —I gave her two cups of coffee.

JENNY: —Why did she run away? Without a word?

BEULAH: —Jenny, I gave you the word. She's gone to see a sick cousin at a hospital and will call you—tomorrow . . .

JENNY: But we had an appointment to—

BEULAH: —Did you have an appointment to look at apartments?

JENNY: —Oh. She told you, did she?

BEULAH: Why didn't *you* tell me, Jenny? Why'd you leave *her* to do it?

JENNY: Because I'm a coward, Beulah.

BEULAH: We've got such a sweet little place here. Don't you think we got a sweet little apartment?

JENNY: *Yes, yes, yes, but I can't stay in it forever!*

BEULAH: Now, Jenny, don't get worked up.

87

JENNY: Beulah, it's painful to break up a thing you're used to but that's how people go forward, that's the way that progress is made in life.

BEULAH: —Aw. Progress in life . . .

JENNY: That's how we make it, it's painful but necessary. Try to see it my way. I MUST have a place where I can receive my new friends.

BEULAH: Like her? Lucinda Keener?

JENNY: No! Like—Mr. Steed, Harry Steed!

BEULAH [*sadly*]: Aw. Like him.

JENNY: He's made it clear that he's seriously interested in me: all this spring! He's only going to be here a week or two more. Then he's going to direct sports and entertainment at a very exclusive hotel in Colorado! —I'm in love with him, Beulah!

BEULAH: —Yeah, I know you are, Jenny . . .

JENNY: But I can't leave it all up to him. I've got to *indicate*—my *feelings*!

BEULAH: —How are you going to indicate them, Jenny? To Harry Steed?

JENNY: By MOVING AT ONCE! —To a place where I can ask him over for a bridge supper. And so forth . . .

BEULAH: Wait a minute. My tin ear's out of whack. I got a loud buzz on it . . . [*She adjusts the hearing aid concealed by the paper poppy.*]

JENNY: Oh, Beulah, Beulah! You're making it *so* hard for me!

BEULAH: Now, then. The buzz ain't so loud. What was you sayin' about that phys ed instructor?

JENNY: Nothing! —NOTHING!

BEULAH: Aw. Excuse me, Jenny. I wish that you would compare him to my brother.

JENNY: Are you sure you want me to compare him to Buddy? All right. I will. If you are sure you can take it. Without being hurt, because I don't want to hurt you. Well. To begin with. Buddy is employed in a brewery and he looks it.

BEULAH: —I'm not hurt. But Buddy is takin' off weight . . .

JENNY: He also ACTS it, Beulah. His manners are something that leave something to be desired! I'm not a snob. But I can't reconcile myself to keeping house the rest of my life in the South Side, in the brewery district, for a man who has never read a book or been to a symphony concert in his life.

BEULAH: —Jenny, he's got season tickets to the Muny. He got 'em because I said to. I hoped he would take you to ev'ry new show at the Muny, not one, but ev'ry new show . . .

JENNY: Beulah, Beulah! Can't you get it through your head that I love Harry Steed so much that I nearly—

BEULAH: Yes. I know, I know, Jenny! —But Buddy—

JENNY: —Buddy WHAT?

BEULAH: Buddy is ready and willing to accept you on faith.

89

JENNY: HOW *NOBLE* of BUDDY! —What do you mean "on faith"?

BEULAH: —He knows you been through a breakdown but that don't phase him. He still has faith in your future.

JENNY: Well, isn't that wonderful of him, isn't that just— NOBLE!

BEULAH: He's crazy about you, Jenny. He thinks you're the prettiest, sweetest little thing that ever came down the turnpike.

JENNY: —What strange things you say! —I never came down a turnpike in my life.

BEULAH: That's just a saying.

JENNY: BEULAH, I AM FED UP WITH THIS CONVERSATION! Accept my word for something! —*I! DON'T! WANT! BUDDY!*

BEULAH: He could make you want him. And want to have kids with him.

JENNY: You don't seem to see that I am in love with Mr. Harry Steed, Beulah. —Where's the society section of the *Globe-Democrat*? Everything's here but the society section, and that's the one part of the paper that I am interested in. —You took it out of the bedroom. Where did you put it?

BEULAH [*evasively*]: —I don't remember. I better go put the picnic lunch in the boxes . . . [*She shuffles out to the kitchen.*]

[*Jenny looks after her with emotion: pity and resentment of feeling pity.*

[*She draws a deep breath, then follows Beulah into the kitchen.*]

46] INTERIOR. THE KITCHEN.

JENNY: Beulah, it's not just the place, but you've spoiled me, Beulah. —You've been—well, excessively kind! You know it's a kind of tyranny? A tyranny of—kindness! You've made me—dependent on you for too many little things like—seeing the laundry goes out, seeing the bills are paid and sometimes paying the bills, and cooking and keeping house for us in spite of the fact that sometimes you have to pay more than your share of the rent instead of—fifty-fifty like we agreed on at first . . .

BEULAH: —Jenny? I had to, Jenny?

JENNY: —It's robbed me of my independence, Beulah!

BEULAH: I never meant to but I had to, Jenny! What else could I do? *You* being *you* . . .

JENNY: —What do you mean by that, Beulah?

BEULAH: Somebody had to keep you going, Jenny, or otherwise it would of been many times you would of gone to pieces and had to quit teaching school because—Jenny? —You are very high-strung and you are sometimes—peculiar . . .

JENNY: Beulah, I am very fond of you. How could I be otherwise? You've been a mother to me.

BEULAH: No, honey, just a big sister.

JENNY: But, Beulah, it can't continue, it's too much of a rut and I really do have to have a decent place, I mean a smarter place, to entertain in. Don't you *see* that?

91

BEULAH: —All right. I won't argue with you . . . [*She continues packing the picnic lunch.*]

JENNY: Beulah? Where is the Sunday paper?

[*Beulah continues as if she didn't hear her.*]

Beulah! The *Globe-Democrat*! Will you please give it to me?

BEULAH: — Here. [*She hands her the paper.*]

[*Jenny crosses to front room with it. After a moment or two Jenny goes back into the kitchen.*]

—Where's the society section? I want to see the pictures of the June brides and that section seems to be missing . . .

BEULAH: Oh! The society section? What do you want with that, Jenny?

JENNY: I just told you, I wanted to see the photographs of the June brides!

BEULAH: I'm afraid it's too late to. I wrapped up the deviled eggs in it.

JENNY: Unwrap the deviled eggs and give me that part of the paper; you know it's the part that I'm most interested in!

BEULAH: —Unwrap it you'self, I got a headache this morning, Jenny, and I—

JENNY: Where are the deviled eggs?

BEULAH: They're in the icebox, honey.

92

JENNY: Beulah, I am not intending to go to Creve Coeur on a picnic.

BEULAH: All right, Jenny.

[*Jenny unwraps the deviled eggs. The society page announcement catches her eyes. Her body stiffens. She gasps and the gasp is followed by a sick moan. She remains still for a minute, then wanders in a dazed way out of the little kitchen.*

[*Beulah looks after her with sincere sorrow. Then she gently closes the Frigidaire door and begins to ready herself for the picnic. She puts on a flowered straw hat, and sadly collects the items for the picnic, and packs them in two or three shoe boxes. On her way out, she replaces the phone on its hook, and she closes the door as quietly as possible.*]

47] INTERIOR. LIVING ROOM.
We see Jenny again. She is sitting stiff as a poker in a big overstuffed chair under a fringed floor lamp, the radio playing beside her.

After a little while she gets up and crosses to the phone and calls a number.

JENNY: Is this the Creve Coeur streetcar station, please? I have an important message for somebody there, for Miss Beulah Bodenhafer, who will be there in a minute. You will know her by her hat. It's a straw hat with, with, with—silk roses on it, and she also has a paper poppy over one ear to conceal her—hearing aid—she's a bit deaf. —Will you please tell her that Miss Jenny Starling is coming to join her and her brother for the Creve Coeur streetcar. . . . Thank you—I'll try to get there in time . . .

[*Fade out.*]

THE END

THE LOSS OF A TEARDROP DIAMOND

PRINCIPAL CHARACTERS

(*in order of appearance*)

FISHER WILLOW

JIMMY DOBYNE

OLD MAN DOBYNE

THE SECRETARY

MISS CORNELIA FISHER

SUSIE, *a maid*

WILLIAM, *the butler*

A NURSE AT THE ASYLUM

MRS. DOBYNE

MR. CRAIG VAN HOOVEN

CAROLINE, *a debutante*

CAROLINE'S RELATIVE

MIKE

JULIE FENSTERMAKER

VINNIE McCORKLE

ESMERALDA BACHELDER

MATHILDE BACHELDER

MR. FENSTERMAKER

A NURSE

MISS ADDIE

MRS. FENSTERMAKER

A BOY AT THE HALLOWEEN PARTY

HANK

AUTHOR'S NOTE

To prepare this script for submission, messy as all the rewrites have made it, I will probably have to engage a typist to work under my supervision so he or she can consult with me continually about it. Then, too, it should be studied, when typed, by a good script-editor for tightening, etc.

I feel that *The Loss of a Teardrop Diamond* (on film) will require a great deal of visual magic, the kind that added so much to such recent films as *Coal Miner's Daughter*, *The Deer Hunter*, and *Apocalypse Now*.

I do not collaborate with anyone in my writing, but I am eager for the advice and suggestions of sensitive directors and producers.

T.W.
May, 1980

THE LOSS OF A TEARDROP DIAMOND

1] EXTERIOR. DAY.

Close shot of Fisher Willow, daughter of a Delta plantation owner and a debutante of the season in Memphis. She has driven straight home from a late party in Memphis and is still dressed for the evening. She has on a leopard-skin coat inspired by Elinor Glynn.

2] EXTERIOR. DAY.

Shot of Fisher's Pierce Arrow and the porch of the plantation commissary. Jimmy Dobyne emerges from the store with evident reluctance as blackbirds call harshly and a watery sunlight dazzles his sleepy eyes. He's a tall, lean youth in his early twenties. Blinking, squinting in the sun, he looks like the hero of a romantic ballad. He greets Fisher Willow from the door, approaching no closer.

JIMMY: You up mighty early, Miss Willow.

FISHER: Haven't been to bed yet.

[Jimmy offers no comment on this. Old Man Dobyne starts to come out but Jimmy keeps the screen door closed firmly against his father's fumbling effort.]

DOBYNE: Le' me out.

JIMMY *[under his breath, without moving his lips]*: Stay in there, you stinker.

FISHER: Huh?

JIMMY: I noticed you car's headed *in*.

FISHER: Yes. I'm still in a pahty dress. See? [*She opens the leopard-skin coat to reveal a crystal-beaded coral satin sheath.*]

[*Old Man Dobyne mutters loudly, irritably, still pushing from the inside. Jimmy jerks the door open suddenly and kicks the old man's shin, quickly, smartly, and shuts the door again, all without appearing to move and with the same lazily genial look on his face. From inside the old man's outraged voice can be heard. As Fisher laughs, Jimmy stops smiling.*]

FISHER: Come on out, Mr. Dobyne! Don't let him bully you that way.

JIMMY: HEY, DAD! Come on out here, Dad! Fisher Willow wants to see you, Dad.

[*He swings the door wide open for the old man who comes out with the chuckling, grinning trajectory of colored field-hands.*]

Exhibit you'self to her, Dad. That's right. Go right on down there, Dad—careful! Careful!

[*He springs forward to steady the old man on the steps.*]

—Miss Willow, you know my father, Mr. James Dobyne, don't you? He's in charge of your father's commissary. He's had the job nearly two weeks, and that's a record for him, yeah, yeah, that's a world record for him, longest time he's held down a job since the Spanish-American War when Admiral Hobson recommended him to Congress for the citation for "Exceptional Valor Above and Beyond the Call of Duty." Admiral Hobson was a distant cousin of ours and so was the Governor of Mississippi . . . then. Well, here he is, bright an' early on—Monday. . . .

[*In the above speech there is the kind of sad rage that we feel for someone loved deeply whom we can't help.*]

DOBYNE [*with a crooked old pirate's grin*]: Ha, ha, ha! Miss Willow, this is my boy. Yes, Ma'am, this is my boy, James Dobyne the Fifth.

FISHER: I know your son, Mr. Dobyne.

JIMMY: That's right, Dad. Blow your stinkin' bad hooch breath in her face so she can give a complete description of your condition at eight o'clock this mawnin' to Mr. Alex Willow, her father. That'll fix ev'rything up real good, just perfect!

FISHER: Mr. Dobyne, I think your condition is *fine*. I wish my condition this morning was half as good. Jimmy? Get in the car! Drive up to the house with me; I want you to do somethin' fo' me. Will you let him go, Mr. Dobyne? I'll bring him back in one hour.

DOBYNE: Sure, sure, Fisher. They all want credit this mawnin' an' I'm not givin' 'em none 'til they're paid up through last summer. Now what I wanted to tell you is I think that I found out why—[*He spits.*]—small planters in this country don't like your daddy. It's 'cause last spring he blown up the south end of his levee so the rest wouldn't break, an' consequently the planters south of his place were under water, under ten foot of water, from where he dynamited as far south as Friar's Point an' further! Consequently your father's not popular with them. In fact they hold him person'ly responsible for the damages they suffered, destruction of houses, loss of livestock, an' drownin' of two white man, and one ole cripple white lady, and five or six nigras! Now what I—

FISHER: Mr. Dobyne, my father knows about that, but he didn't dynamite that levee without a telephone warnin' to ev'ry place south of here!

3] INTERIOR. CAR.
Fisher starts the car motor. Jimmy remains by the door, furious, despairing. Blackbirds caw; their wings flap. . . . It starts raining again.

JIMMY: You gonna git wet out there.

FISHER [*commandingly*]: Come on, get in the car!

JIMMY: I can't go car-ridin' now.

FISHER: Just up to the house? Will you PLEASE? I've got to ask you something!

4] EXTERIOR. PORCH.
He sighs, flips away his cigarette, and descends to the car. He starts around it to the opposite door.

FISHER: No, *you* take the wheel, I'm so ex-*HAUST*-ed! —It was almost daybreak when I lef' Memphis . . .

[*He shrugs and starts back to her side of the car. She slides over, calling out gaily.*]

—Hold up that porch Mr. Dobyne; don't let it fall down on you!

[*Old Man Dobyne has retreated to the porch and is hanging onto a post supporting its tin roof.*]

5] INTERIOR. CAR.

JIMMY: —Well, I reckon that's that . . .

FISHER: What's what?

JIMMY: My old man's talked himself out of another job, huh?

[*Fisher laughs lightly.*]

JIMMY: Isn't that what he just did?

FISHER: Light a cigarette for me, will you, please?

JIMMY: —Shoot . . .

FISHER: No. Daddy won't fire your father; he never *hired* your father. It's *your* job, not *his!* We all know that you manage the commissary for your "old man," Jimmy. —Let's stop here, I can't smoke in the house.

[*The car draws up under the poplars flanking the drive. It is still raining lightly. Blackbirds caw back and forth between the near and far trees.*]

—It's funny how people just think about their own problems. It never entered my mind to speak of your father's condition.

JIMMY: My old man was on the wagon 'til this weekend, but, you see, on Sundays we always go out to Lion's View.

FISHER: *Where? Oh!* —The asylum . . .

JIMMY: —Yeah. The state—sanitarium where they put—my mother. . . . Going out there always knocks him off the wagon!

103

FISHER: —Excuse me for sounding like the Goddess of Wisdom, but people aren't *knocked* off the wagon, they always *jump* off it, Jimmy. Oh, they always find something to excuse the jump, but it's still a *jump*, not a *fall*—they're never *pushed* off, they *jump* off . . .

JIMMY [*with some reserve in his voice*]: —You're very understanding about the problem.

FISHER: I hope you'll understand *mine*. I need you, Jimmy.

JIMMY: —How?

FISHER: —I—feel *embarrassed*—to *tell* you.

JIMMY: —What?

FISHER: —It's very humiliating to admit such a thing . . .

JIMMY: What thing?

FISHER: My only dependable date to debutante parties in Memphis is a forty-five-year-old bachelor who's my Aunt Fisher's lawyer. You see, I—returned from Europe to discover that I'd acquired certain social disadvantages despite my aunt's prestige, my fancy trappings.

JIMMY: What disadvantages in particular, Fisher.

FISHER: The most particular disadvantage is the one your father mentioned. Apparently *my* father's selfish action last spring, with its tragic consequences to a number of helpless persons south of here, is very well-known in Memphis. —I wonder if their moral objections are as strong as mine. I barely speak to my father anymore. —But they find it convenient to hold it against me, you see. Oh, I'm sure they also resent other things about me probably even more. My foreign education, my tendency to make sharp remarks about things that strike me as stupidly provincial—I'm considered sarcastic—I—*want to escape!*—But Aunt Fisher's determined that I have this debut. And I have to go through with it to please her, so she won't leave five million to the Episcopal Church when she dies but to me.

JIMMY: Don't you have enough money already?

FISHER: A person of my kind never has enough money.

JIMMY: You don't mean you're greedy, do you?

FISHER: No, I just know that I'll have to buy most everything that I want. . . . Why don't you look at me. I'm looking at you, Jimmy.

JIMMY: I guess I'm still—embarrassed. And don't know what you want.

FISHER: —You.

JIMMY: Me?

FISHER: Yes.

JIMMY: Why?

FISHER: —To take me out in Memphis, to escort me to these agonizing parties.

JIMMY: How could I? —In these clothes?

FISHER: Clothes are just the cover of the book and books can be re-covered as handsomely as their contents. —Now drive on up to the house, please.

JIMMY: How could I take you to these "agonizing" parties in Memphis and run the commissary and watch out for Dad?

FISHER: I'd just need you nights. Two or three nights a week? The rest of the time Aunt Fisher's lawyer will do. He's not so bad. A gentleman, of course, presentable enough, but—something happens between forty-five and fifty. I mean when he's fifty I'd be half his age. More like a daughter than a wife and I don't want a father, another father—unpleasant associations are attached to that, if you understand.

JIMMY: Surely, Fisher, he's not your only prospect.

FISHER: Auntie Fisher would never permit me to be seriously involved with someone outside her circle of acquaintances, either direct or by reputation, Jimmy. I could have married a titled Italian in Venice, dashing, romantic. When I intimated my infatuation with him, Aunt Fisher cabled me, "Come home at once." —I started not to, but practical considerations seem to run in my blood as well as—sensual . . .

[*Pause. Poplars bend and sigh in the wind; blackbirds caw; the dappled light on their faces sways and fades and brightens again. A hound dog barks in the distance.*]

I hope you've listened to me and understood me.

JIMMY: Oh, yes, I had a scholarship to Ole Miss.

FISHER: I know. —Now drive us up to the house.

6] EXTERIOR. DAY.
The camera follows the car as it drives up to the house.

FISHER [*continuing*]: They *hate* me! —You wouldn't, would you?

106

JIMMY: They hate you? It's strong as that?

FISHER: *Most* of 'em, *yais!* Why *not*? They know they bore me—almost beyond endurance—I can't conceal it! So naturally they are not quite crazy about me. Oh, I've got a reputation of some kind anyhow, which is something to accomplish. I mean I'm good for some LAUGHS! —But, Lawd! —I don't know why! I don't seem able to stop it! —I just have to shock and insult, insult an' shock, fo' some reason! —What am I fighting? I don't know what I'm fighting! —It's senseless. —I'm not on the guest list for th' most important comin'-out party this season, in spite of Aunt Fisher's position! —They left me off it. —She's frantic! —Jimmy? Jimmy?

JIMMY: —What?

FISHER: —Isn't it lovely, this cool, wet air on your face! —We're going to have a great big country breakfast in the kitchen, cawn-meal cakes an' molasses and bacon an' coffee, and then you're goin' upstairs t' be measured for a tuxedo, tails, and—a regular jelly-bean—wardrobe!

JIMMY: What'n Sam Hill would I do with a tuxedo? Did you say "tails"? Me? —Why!

FISHER: —Because I need a properly dressed young escort! Handsome, young, distinguished! —Otherwise I'll have to disgrace Aunt Fisher by goin' out only with fawty an' fawty-five-year-old bachelors all season! —Because fo' some reason the Memphis boys can't stand me . . .

JIMMY: —Huh!

FISHER: —Huh?

JIMMY: I don't understand. What reason?

FISHER: —Jimmy, I've got a tongue that I CAN'T *control!* —I just *will* say what I *think.* I can't conceal what I FEEL! —And people don't *like* it! —Fawty-five-year-old bachelors think I'm clever! EVERYONE thinks I'm clever! —But only fawty-five-year-ole bachelors seem to be able to stand my company, long. An' bachelors of that age don't REALLY like girls. They just pretend to, for social reasons, that's all . . . —because they're snobs and liars and cowards, an' so forth! —I have ABSOLUTELY! *NO* INTEREST OR *DESIRE!!* —TO BE A SOCIAL SUCCESS IN PROVINCIAL SOUTHERN SOCIETY! —HOWEVER! —I've got to please Aunt Fisher; I've got to avoid an absolute social fiasco! —So Jimmy, you've got a new job. You're going to be my steady escort. Here's the house.

JIMMY: Yeah, I recognize it.

[*He walks around the car to let her out.*]

FISHER: Thanks. Come in.

7] CUT TO: AN UPSTAIRS ROOM.

FISHER [*continuing*]: Open the shutters, Jimmy.

[*He obeys, warily. The camera stays on him.*]

JIMMY: Who's going to measure me?

FISHER'S VOICE: I shall, with your assistance. Take off that sloppy old sweater. —Hold your arms out for the tape.

[*He does, warily. She enters the picture frame.*]

Of course, you're going to need shirts, evening shirts, and— Jimmy, don't hold your arms over your head like this was a hold up. Hold them straight out to your sides like a *cross*. —But don't suffer on it so much!

[*He lowers his arms to his sides. The measurements continue.*]

JIMMY: Fisher? There's one thing I want you to know about my old man. He's a sincere, honest person. A stinker, yeah, an old stinker, but a sincere, honest person and what he told you about the local attitude toward your father was meant—*good!*

FISHER: —Jimmy, will you please help me measure your legs. Hold the end of the tape at the inside top of your thigh while I

JIMMY: —Oh . . . yeah . . .

[*Absently, he obeys her directions. Fisher mumbles a figure.*]

—Were you listening to me? About my old man?

FISHER: Yes, you said that he was a stinker.

JIMMY: I said that he was a stinker but a sincere, honest man and what he said was—

8] CUT TO: THE PORCH OF THE COMMISSARY.
Jimmy's dad is still clinging to the thin wooden post on the porch, his face glazed and tranquil. Sounds are heard: a car driving up, a door slamming, a car driving off. Jimmy mounts the steps to the porch. He turns to give a parting salute to the car heard driving off. Blackbirds caw.

FISHER'S VOICE: Bye!

JIMMY: *Yeah!* [*He turns to his father.*] —Know what she done? Measured me for clothes to take her to Memphis parties! . . .

DOBYNE: Well! —She's set her cap for you, Jimmy.

[*He releases the porch pillar and stumbles down the three wooden steps and squints into the beginning sunlight.*]

JIMMY'S VOICE: I ain't set mine for her.

[*Dobyne stumbles forward and falls. Jimmy rushes to him and helps him up.*]

JIMMY: —Dad? Will you go back to bed?

9] INTERIOR. DAY.
A men's tailor shop in Memphis, where the next few scenes take place.

FISHER [*to tailor*]: A week from Saturday isn't soon enough. You see, my brother lost *ev'rything* in the fire, literally doesn't have a suit to his name, just a few borrowed things that don't fit him . . .

TAILOR'S VOICE: Why didn't your brother come in to be measured here, Miss Willow?

FISHER: Because he was slightly injured—leaping out a second-story window! —I don't suppose there'll even be time for fittings, but even if the fit isn't perfect, he's the sort or man that *any*thing looks good on, so just do the best you can with the measurements I gave you and I'll pick the suits up no later than a week from Thursday, charge me extra if that's necessary. Well, I—have to *run* now . . .

10] CUT TO: MANSION. EXTERIOR. DAY.
Fisher is seen driving up to her aunt's palatial residence in Memphis. A chartered bus of "garden pilgrims" is being received in the porte cochere by uniformed servants and a secretary. Miss Cornelia Fisher suddenly appears in window and cries out.

CORNELIA: *Pilgrims with dogs not admitted, no dogs can enter the gardens!*

SECRETARY: I'm very sorry, Madam, but Miss Fisher can't allow dogs to enter her gardens because last fall a dog was very—destructive . . .

11] DISSOLVE TO: ENTRANCE HALL OF MANSION.
    INTERIOR. DAY.
Fisher has entered. It is dim and elegant and austere. The maid follows her in.

FISHER [*throwing off her coat*]: Susie, will you please take this beast upstairs, and then will you please bring me up a steaming hot glass of milk and a hot water bottle an' tell Auntie Fisher I'm going to sleep for hours and to get Miss Grace to cancel any engagements on my list fo' today? Say I'm *dead*—or something else to amuse them.

MAID: You still got your pahty dress on!

CORNELIA'S VOICE: Fisher, was that Fisher?

[*Fisher closes her eyes desperately for a moment. Then flings the leopard-skin coat to the maid and advances into the room from which her Aunt had called.*]

FISHER: Yes, Auntie, that was she.

12] CUT TO: A LONG ONE SHOT OF
MISS CORNELIA FISHER.

Cornelia Fisher is a kind of female dragon of the human species, seated at an opulently gleaming table, behind her a "Tudor" casement of leaded panes, lightly tinted green. It is an occasion for the richly visual effects of the film to be established. The wealthy old spinster has a certain resemblance to her niece, Fisher.

13] CUT TO: TWO SHOTS OF FISHER
AND HER AUNT.

Fisher dutifully approaches the old woman and gives her a peck on the cheek.

FISHER: Morning, Auntie.

CORNELIA: I think you mean afternoon.

FISHER: I wouldn't be surprised. William wants to serve you.

[*A Butler has entered the scene with a soup tureen.*]

CORNELIA: Bouillon, just bouillon?

WILLIAM: Yes, Miss Fisher, bouillon.

CORNELIA: What's that floating in it?

WILLIAM: Bits of toast.

CORNELIA: I guess you mean croutons. Fisher, sit down.

FISHER: Oh, please, I—only want some hot milk upstairs, I'm bone tired.

CORNELIA: Miss Fisher will have some bouillon, too, buttered toast and—

FISHER: Nothing more. It would make me vomit.

CORNELIA: I see. —Bring my niece a bowl of hot bouillon, William.

[*He shuffles away.*]

FISHER: Auntie, why don't you pension that old man off?

CORNELIA: William would have no life outside of my service, but that is not the subject I want to discuss. What kept you out all night?

FISHER: Drove home to the Willows.

CORNELIA: Drove to your father's place?

FISHER: Yes.

CORNELIA: WHY!

FISHER: Experienced an insult I couldn't accept last night.

CORNELIA: I phoned the Cartwrights at nearly daybreak, Fisher, to ask why you were still out.

[*William reenters the scene with Fisher's bouillon.*]

FISHER: Didn't the Cartwrights tell you what happened? My escort went upstairs and never came back down, at least not the front way. Perhaps he made his escape by the back stairs.

CORNELIA: Or perhaps you didn't wait long enough?

113

FISHER: Nearly half an hour in the hall. Should I have waited longer.

CORNELIA: After a few minutes you should have sent up for him.

FISHER: Auntie, we both have pride. Do you want me to give up mine?

CORNELIA: Fisher! Fisher Willow! You're ruining yourself in Memphis.

FISHER: And? I wonder why!

CORNELIA: I've heard you antagonize people!

FISHER: —How?

CORNELIA: That's what I'm asking you! How? How do you do it?

FISHER [*rising from the table*]: —They don't seem real. Nothing, nobody seems real.

14] DISSOLVE TO: FISHER'S BEDROOM. DAY.
Fisher enters and turns, as if dazed, to a mirror. She looks into it without expression.

FISHER: "As silent as a mirror is believed . . . realities plunge in silence by . . ."

15] DISSOLVE TO: JIMMY DOBYNE AT LION'S VIEW.
INTERIOR. DAY.
Jimmy Dobyne is calling on his mother at Lion's View, a state asylum for the insane. A nurse brings the woman into the sun-room and guides her to a wicker chair.

114

JIMMY: Mama? Mama? It's me, it's Jimmy, Mama! How have you been Mama?

16] CLOSE-UP OF MRS. DOBYNE.
The prematurely aged woman is working her jaws, spittle dribbling from the corners of her mouth. Her eyes are first glazed, then fixed and furious. She suddenly snatches out her dental plates and hurls them at her son. He closes his eyes— tight. Then he begins to sob helplessly.

NURSE: —Mr. Dobyne? Your mother's disturbed today. You'd better see her next week.

MRS. DOBYNE: POISON TEETH IN MY MOUTH, POISON TEETH IN MY MOUTH, GIVE THEM BACK TO THEM, GIVE THEM—

[*Jimmy has fled from the sun-room.*]

—Who was that? Was that—?

NURSE: Let's go back to the cottage, Mrs. Dobyne.

MRS. DOBYNE: —My teeth! I—!

NURSE: —You broke your teeth, Mrs. Dobyne, you've been a very bad lady. Now let's go back to the—

17] DISSOLVE TO: INTERIOR. EVENING.
The scene is Fisher's bedroom at her aunt's house in Memphis.

MAID [*entering*]: Miss Fisher?

FISHER: Yes?

MAID: A young man has arrived in a truck and says he's expected by you.

FISHER: Did you say a truck?

[*She rushes to window and glances out.*]

—How is he dressed?

MAID: Looks like work clothes to me.

FISHER: Don't let Aunt Cornelia see him. Rush him straight up the back stairs.

MAID: Where to?

FISHER: Here.

MAID: Oh, but Miss Fisher, your Aunt would have a fit if you brought him to your bedroom.

FISHER: Oh, when she knows who he is, she'll take a more tolerant view. How do I look?

MAID: Can't you see yourself in that full-length mirror?

FISHER: What you see in mirrors is not what other people see necessarily, Susie. In the mirror I see a well-dressed witch; that's always what I see in that goddam mirror. Is he upstairs?

JIMMY's VOICE: Fisher?

FISHER [*flying to the door*]: Jimmy, in here, Jimmy. I'd nearly despaired of your arrival. The party's been on for an hour. Look. All your dress clothes are laid out on the bed, please get into them lickety-split. —Jimmy, you look—dazed! Is something wrong?

JIMMY: I—visited Mother. She—didn't know who I was. She's in the violent ward; it's called the Drum.

FISHER: Jimmy, she'll soon be out.

JIMMY: Mama was—committed.

FISHER: There are better places; arrangements can be made; it's just a question of time. Get out of those wet things. Susie, bring Jimmy a brandy. Or would you like champagne? You've had a shock. Make it champagne laced with brandy.

JIMMY: I—avoid drinking much because—it runs in the family, Fisher. Gee. I'm undressing right in front of you like you weren't a—girl . . .

FISHER: Propriety is a waste of time. We don't have time to waste.

JIMMY: Where can I—?

FISHER: Your underwear's wet, too. You needn't wear any. Get right into the tuxedo.

CORNELIA FISHER'S VOICE [*from below*]: Fisher? Fisher?

FISHER: Christ, what a name! I suppose I can bear it for a million dollars.

JIMMY: This thing looks complicated.

FISHER: Susie will help you. Or would you accept help from me?

117

JIMMY: —Susie? —Please.

FISHER: I see. Well, Susie, make sure he comes down to be presented to Aunt Cornelia impeccably dressed in the contents of that box. [*She crosses to door.*] This is going to be the first debut party of the season at which I will shine with—pride.

18] SHOT OF FISHER AT THE TOP OF THE STAIRS.
Her nostrils flare as she draws a deep breath.

FISHER: Oh, God, let it be, let it happen.

CORNELIA FISHER'S VOICE: Fisher! Mr. Van Hooven's waiting!

FISHER [*now descending the stairs*]: Who? Oh, my goodness, did I forget to tell him that my escort tonight is James Dobyne—the Fifth?

CORNELIA'S VOICE: What? What?

FISHER [*mocking*]: "What, what?"

19] CUT TO: CORNELIA FISHER'S DRAWING ROOM.
Cornelia Fisher is with Mr. Van Hooven, a middle-aged bachelor with a glazed look. He stumbles up as Fisher enters.

FISHER: Oh, Van, don't get up. I've news that ought to please you. You're relieved of duty tonight. I have another escort, so you and Aunt Cornelia can spend the evening together, discussing old times.

CORNELIA: I don't understand this at all.

FISHER: The explanation is about to enter.

[*Jimmy enters.*]

Mr. James Dobyne, Aunt Cornelia Fisher and her attorney, Mr. Craig Van Hooven. Well.

CORNELIA: Dobyne? Dobyne?

FISHER: Oh, Aunt Cornelia, surely you remember Governor Dobyne?

CORNELIA: This young man is—

FISHER: His grandson. Goodnight, Auntie, we're terribly late. [*She kisses her formally.*] Have fun together—play cards or discuss litigations or—consummate the long romance between you. Is the Pierce Arrow out?

20] CUT TO: THE ENTRANCE.

FISHER [*continuing*]: Oh. I knew I'd forgotten something. Excuse me a moment. Aunt Cornelia, may I wear the teardrop diamond earrings tonight. It's such a special occasion, please, Auntie.

CORNELIA: Those earrings are worth ten thousand dollars, Fisher. The clasps are getting loose and you're so careless with things.

FISHER: Ten thousand dollars, fancy that. Do I inherit them, Auntie?

CORNELIA: Certainly not if you lose them.

FISHER: I'll have my ears pierced for them.

[*The old lady rises slowly and crosses into her study.*]

21] CLOSE-UP OF FISHER BEFORE AN OVAL MIRROR.

FISHER: Jimmy, fasten them for me, my fingers are shaky tonight, too much black coffee.

[*He complies with grave care.*]

I'll wear my hair back of my ears. There! Lucky I've had it shingled.

CORNELIA'S VOICE: Van, please make sure that those earrings are insured. My mother wore them when she was presented to Queen Victoria in England and at the coronation of the Czar.

22] DISSOLVE TO: THE FRONT WALK.

FISHER: Run, run, it's still raining.

JIMMY: Who's in the driver's seat?

FISHER: The chauffeur, silly.

JIMMY: Jesus.

FISHER: Yes, God's Son, nailed to a cross, redeemed the sins of the world!

[*She hops into the backseat of the car, the door opened by the uniformed chauffeur.*]

CORNELIA [*calling from the door*]: Fisher, do you have the key this time?

FISHER: Yes, Auntie, and have a room made up for Mr. Dobyne; he'll have to stay overnight.

JIMMY: Jesus . . .

FISHER: You mentioned him before. —Now let me put in your shirt-studs.

JIMMY: I've never been to one of these things. I don't know how to behave.

FISHER: Trust your instincts, Jimmy. I doubt that the worst possible behavior would obscure your dashing appearance . . .

[*She is adjusting his shirt-studs.*]

JIMMY: —Mama didn't even know me today . . .

23] CUT TO: THE BALLROOM OF THE HOTEL PEA-BODY IN DOWNTOWN MEMPHIS. CLOSE TWO-SHOT OF FISHER AND JIMMY.

FISHER: The receiving line's breaking up!

JIMMY: What do I do?

FISHER: Wait till the lady extends her hand, then just take it and smile.

[*She approaches a slightly wilting debutante.*]

Why, Caroline, you've got that all-nigger band that played so divinely at Jessie Strutt's! I bet when I walk in they'll strike up my favorite number.

CAROLINE [*coldly*]: Which is what?

FISHER: One moment, let me appear! [*She rushes into the ball-room, calling out—*] Fats, Fats, my song!

[*From the ballroom comes rich laughter. The band strikes up "See the Boat Go Round the Bend."*]

CAROLINE [*to a sour-faced relative*]: She tips that band leader fifty dollars at every dance he plays faw.

RELATIVE: I wonder what she tipped the Governor's grandson?

CAROLINE: Shall I enquire?

RELATIVE: I dare you.

CAROLINE: Accepted! Mr. Dobyne? I'm released for the waltz.

JIMMY: Sorry, Miss, uh—

CAROLINE: Caroline!

JIMMY: But I'm not employed by you.

FISHER [*rushing back to him*]: Jimmy!

JIMMY: Excuse me.

CAROLINE: Did you hear what he said, "I'm not employed by you?" —Isn't it killing?

RELATIVE: Susie Bracken says Fisher Willow is not on the list for her Halloween Ball.

CAROLINE: Would she dare?

RELATIVE: When a girl's already engaged, her first year out, her audacity knows no bounds.

24] CUT TO: FISHER, ALONE. A CLOSE ONE-SHOT.

FISHER: Has anyone seen my escort?

VOICE: Mr. Van Hooven?

FISHER: No, no, Mr. James Dobyne the Fifth.

VOICE: Have you looked in the gentlemen's lavatory, Fisher?

FISHER: Vulgarity won't get you everywhere, Dotty.

VOICE: It will get me to Susie Bracken's Halloween Ball.

FISHER: Possibly that far, but not much further. Oh, there's Jimmy. Jimmy, Jimmy, where were you?

VOICE: Sounds panicky!

VOICE: No wonder! —Where's he been hiding his candle?

VOICE: Apparently in her employment . . .

25] CLOSE TWO-SHOT OF FISHER AND JIMMY.

FISHER [*shrilly*]: Where on earth were you, what were you doing?

JIMMY: I promised Dad I'd call him about Mama's condition.

FISHER: *Did* you?

JIMMY: It was a promise. I said I'd found her fine.

FISHER: Your instincts are infallible and you're the sinecure of all female eyes at the party. Let's—

JIMMY: Huh?

123

FISHER: Cool off on the roof.

JIMMY: Whatever you say.

26] MEDIUM SHOT.
They cross through couples chattering between dances.

VOICE: Fisher?

FISHER [*impatiently*]: Yes?

VOICE: What lovely earrings!

FISHER: Thank you. My teardrop diamonds.

VOICE: Your ears are weeping diamonds?

VOICE: Where'd you get them?

FISHER [*sharply*]: Naturally from Woolworth's.

VOICES Oh. I thought Kresge's!

FISHER: May we get through, please, will you let us get through. This room is suffocating!

27] CUT TO: THE ROOFTOP OF THE PEABODY
   HOTEL. CLOSE TWO-SHOT OF FISHER
   AND JIMMY.
Fisher's arm is linked through Jimmy's.

FISHER: How cool, the river wind.

JIMMY: Mmmm.

FISHER: Music is so much nicer from a distance.

JIMMY: Mmmm.

FISHER: There's the *Delta Blossom*, coming in, band still play-ing. Why, it's the number I always request. [*Fisher sings tensely.*] "See the boat go round the bend, goodbye, my lover, goodbye. All loaded down with boys and men—" [*She discovers herself abandoned.*] Jimmy? Jimmy?

VOICE: Has your escawt escaped you, Fisher?

FISHER: Mr. Dobyne is calling our chauffeur!

[*She rushes, almost like a competitive runner, through the roof-gathering. She catches sight of Jimmy.*]

JIMMY!

[*A girl ascending the stairs hisses "Muderer's daughter!" at Fisher. She stumbles on the stairs. There is laughter as she tumbles.*]

JIMMY: SHUDDUP! —Are you hurt, Fisher?

FISHER: Not at all now. Where were you going?

JIMMY: If I said to pee would it be embarrassing to you?

FISHER: Oh, Lawd, Jimmy! I'm not sure if embarrassment is still an emotion I could feel. —I wasn't embarrassed when in-fawmed that I'd been omitted from the guest-list for Susie Bracken's Halloween Ball. I wasn't even embarrassed by the hilarity provoked when I fell down the stairs. —But do let's go home at once. —You can pee outside, between cars . . .

125

28] CUT TO: THE BACKSEAT OF THE LIMOUSINE.

JIMMY: Did I behave okay?

FISHER: You were bawn to that, under all circumstances. —Somebody told me you struck a man in the lavatory.

JIMMY: He grabbed hold of my—

FISHER: What?

JIMMY: Nothing.

FISHER: Mentionable? Oh, Jimmy! [*She leans her head on his shoulder. He doesn't respond.*] I hope you'll soon learn that nothing's unmentionable between us—not even your— Is it shyness, or indifference, Jimmy?

[*There is a long pause.*]

JIMMY: Fisher, I think it's pride.

FISHER: That makes a bond between us. —Something to begin with . . .

29] CUT TO: THE NEXT MORNING. LONG SHOT OF THE BREAKFAST TABLE.
Cornelia Fisher is seated austerely at the head of the table. Fisher enters in something between a silk negligee and a morning gown.

FISHER: Good morning, Auntie. Hasn't Mr. Dobyne come down?

CORNELIA: William says he couldn't stay overnight; he had to drive back to—where did he have to drive back to?

FISHER: —Oh . . .

CORNELIA: That doesn't exactly answer my question, Fisher.

FISHER: What was your question, Auntie?

CORNELIA: Do you know where he drove back to?

FISHER: Why, to his father's plantation.

[*She sits at the opposite end of the table with a look of desolation. The butler removes the cover from a plate of bacon, eggs, grits. She pushes it away.*]

Is this my mail?

CORNELIA: Go through it after breakfast.

FISHER: I have to go through it right now.

CORNELIA: William, put Miss Fisher's plate on the warmer.

FISHER: First, pour me a cup of black coffee. [*He does. She drains the cup.*] Another, please.

CORNELIA: Fisher, you shouldn't begin a day with two cups of black coffee.

FISHER: What should I begin it with, Auntie?

CORNELIA: If my hands shook like yours, I'd switch to hot chocolate.

FISHER: I must have missed it. This is the latest that it could have arrived if it was ever going to.

CORNELIA: What are you referring to, Fisher?

FISHER: My invitation to Susie Bracken's party.

CORNELIA: Let me go through the mail for you.

FISHER: You wouldn't find it, either. She ignored me completely last night—so I'm not surprised.

CORNELIA: I am.

FISHER: It's not the end of the world.

CORNELIA: Nor the beginning.

FISHER: Who knows. I have an excellent alternative. An invitation to a Halloween party at Julie Fenstermaker's place.

CORNELIA: Where is her place?

FISHER: North of father's, of course, and so less affected by the—incidents surrounding last spring's floods.

CORNELIA: Susie's mother Emily is indebted to me for the survival of her gift shop. I made her a loan that tided it over the period when it was— [*She rises grandly and crosses to a phone.*] —threatened with bankruptcy.

FISHER: Aunt Cornelia, it's odd that I should have to tell you how little people are influenced by help in a time of crisis when the crisis is past. Oh, please don't do what I think you're about to do. Even had Susie Bracken invited me to her pointless coming-out party—

CORNELIA: Pointless? How pointless?

128

FISHER: She's engaged. Debut parties are only for the purpose of announcing to the world that a socially eligible young lady is on the market for a proposal from a socially eligible male, and Susie having been removed from the market almost before the start of the season—

CORNELIA [*at phone*]: Emily, dear, you answer your own phone, how brave you are! No fear of creditors or their outraged lawyers now? Well, things must be going *much* better at the gift shop. I've just heard a rumor that your sweet little Susie's the first debutante of the season to be spoken for, and so I presume her coming-out party will also be an announcement party. I'm thrilled and so is Fisher. —Why, my niece, of course. You know my niece, don't you, Emily? Tell me, Emily, who is the lucky young man? An out-of-towner from—why, certainly, Emily, I'm sure that calls must be pouring in from all sides.

[*She hangs up.*]

Said that she had an urgent call from her other phone. —She has no other phone. —I shall have Van demand immediate repayment of the loan plus interest on it and I shall—

FISHER: May I use the phone, now, Auntie?

[*Cornelia, rigid with fury, appears not to hear her. She crosses to a number of buzzers, and presses one.*]

CORNELIA: [*into the speaker by the row of buzzers*]: Ash!

FISHER: No longer Ashley? Reduced to Ash?

CORNELIA: My dear, you still sound a bit groggy. I suspect you disregarded my warning about that sleeping medication. Ash! Must I cut off the supply at the drugstore? Do you really prefer to be only half-conscious for at least half the day?

129

FISHER [*to herself*]: Probably—understandably . . .

[*She crosses to the phone and calls the Fenstermaker planta-tion, north of her father's. The scene begins to dissolve.*]

CORNELIA [into speaker]: Please have your coffee and do this at once. Call my lawyer, call Van, and tell him to demand im-mediate repayment with interest on my loan to Emily Bracken, long overdue. Did you understand me, Ash?

[*Complete dissolve.*]

30] EXTERIOR. PORCH OF COMMISSARY. DUSK.
Jimmy and his father are seated side by side, Jimmy in his tuxedo and his father, drunk, in workclothes.

DOBYNE [*softly*]: Son?

JIMMY: Huh, Dad?

DOBYNE: If your mother don't recognize you anymore, wouldn't it be better not to visit her anymore? Your mother has pride, y'know, and I think maybe it would be a relief to her if you—stopped going out there. —Like I did. She don't want to be seen by her son in her—present awful condition.

JIMMY: Somebody's got to check on her "present awful con-dition" to see that it doesn't get worse.

DOBYNE: How could it get any worse?

JIMMY: There are very few conditions in life that can't get worse if nothing's done to even try to—check them. —Dad? You know what I could do?

DOBYNE: Check it? —How?

JIMMY: Well, I—could serve Fisher Willow as more than an escort to parties. She's hinted repeatedly, Dad, that she would like—intimacy with me.

DOBYNE: Just—

JIMMY: The intimacy would have to end up with marriage. Maybe not first, but—soon. —Here comes the Pierce Arrow, Dad.

DOBYNE: I'll step inside, I'll—step inside till she—

JIMMY: Take your bottle, Dad . . .

31] EXTERIOR. DUSK. A COUNTRY ROAD.
Fisher and Jimmy are driving in the convertible on their way to Julie Fenstermaker's party.

FISHER: We're getting close to the river, the air is fresher.

JIMMY: Would you move your knee just a little so I can shift gears? We're coming to the junction with Highway 7—there's a stop light on it, don't know why, practically no traffic.

FISHER: Excuse me. I didn't realize I was crowding you, Jimmy. You know—excuse me for making such a frank confession—you're the only American boy that I instinctively draw close to, that's the truth.

JIMMY: Thanks.

[*He halts the car at the junction.*]

FISHER: There's just practically no traffic, Jimmy, there's no traffic at all, so why are you—

JIMMY: I'm used to obeying signals.

FISHER: I love rebelling against them.

[*An open-top car approaches the junction.*]

VOICE: HEY, THERE!

FISHER [*frantically*]: BLOW THE HORN, BLOW THE HORN, JIMMY! THEY'RE GOING TO SHOUT SOMETHING AT ME!

[*She leans over him and presses the horn down with her fist to drown out the shout.*]

JIMMY [*after the car has passed*]: —Gee!

FISHER: —What did they yell? Did you hear them?

JIMMY: Gosh . . .

FISHER: What was it? You can tell me?

JIMMY: —All I heard was the horn. Why'd you stop up your ears?

FISHER: I heard them hollering something and I preferred not to know what.

JIMMY: Yeah, but you stopped up your ears before they hollered, Fisher.

FISHER: I knew they were going to holler.

JIMMY: How'd you know they'd holler?

FISHER: Because they do, nearly always. They recognize my Pierce Arrow, and if they've been drinking, they almost always shout out something obscene or insulting to me. —You know why . . . I'm a murderer's daughter! Oh, here's the road that goes up to the levee. Let's go up on the levee. You've passed the road. —Back up the car and go up it; I want to breathe river air.

JIMMY: We're already late to the party.

FISHER: I don't care! Back up the car and drive it up on the levee!

[*There is a shrill note of command in her voice. He obeys, his face set.*]

32] DISSOLVE TO: EXTERIOR. NIGHT.
The car is parked on top of the levee. Jimmy lights a cigarette.

FISHER: Why didn't you offer me one?

JIMMY: Aw. I keep forgetting you smoke.

FISHER: Give me yours a moment, I just want a puff.

[*She takes the cigarette from his mouth. He is obviously uncomfortable. She moves closer to him. He slides away.*]

Am I crowding you?

JIMMY: No, but—

FISHER: What?

JIMMY: I hear the party music.

FISHER: These country parties, it's just old victrola music.

133

[*During a moment of silence, he drops the cigarette pack in his lap. She picks it up, restoring the contact of their bodies.*]

—Camels?

JIMMY: Yeah.

FISHER: Good. I'm going to test your powers of observation. Describe to me the scene on the package, tell me what all's in the picture on the Camel package.

JIMMY: —A camel. A man on the camel. A palm tree. A pyramid in the background and—that's all I remember.

FISHER: —Most people forget the figure behind the camel, the man on foot behind the camel rider.

JIMMY: Aw. I hadn't noticed him either.

FISHER: So lovely, so peaceful here. I almost never feel really peaceful, you know. —When I accepted Julie's invitation to this Halloween party I was killing two birds with one stone.

JIMMY: Which two birds you mean?

FISHER: Julie was really my only good friend at All Saints College before I went to the Sorbonne in Paris.

JIMMY: [*with a touch of the sardonic*]: Gee.

FISHER: The other bird, well, I've missed you, Jimmy, my only attractive escort to Memphis parties.

JIMMY: I doubt your dad thinks I oughta be running up there every whipstitch to go to a—debut ball.

FISHER: Doesn't mind a bit. I've called and gotten his approval each time.

JIMMY: And I worry about my own father, when I'm away he's most likely to hit the bottle.

FISHER: Your dad never makes any trouble.

JIMMY: No, just kills himself maybe. [*He starts the motor of the car.*]

FISHER: Don't go yet, there's no hurry. Why're you so anxious to leave this enchanting place?

JIMMY: —I'm—not anxious.

[*She leans her head diffidently against his shoulder.*]

JIMMY: You're shivering, Fisher, you must be chilly.

FISHER: People don't always shiver because they're chilly, and how could I be chilly in my leopard-skin coat? Really, you *are* silly, Jimmy. Is that why I like you, aside from the fact you're the best-looking boy I've met or anyone's met this side of—the Atlantic.

[*She has drawn up her legs on the car seat to face him, a hand on his shoulder, but he remains staring straight ahead at the mist rising off the river.*]

JIMMY: Thank you for those compliments, Fisher Willow.

FISHER: But—sometimes I feel that if you were passing my car on the road you'd shout insults at me, too.

JIMMY: What gives you that crazy idea, Fisher Willow?

135

FISHER: The way you say my full name, Fisher Willow, instead of just "Fishie."

JIMMY: "Fishie"! —When you say something is fishy, it means not quite all right.

FISHER: Yes, well, friends tell the truth.

[*A hoot-owl has been heard several times.*]

Listen, Minerva's bird calling.

JIMMY: What's calling?

FISHER: The hoot-owl's the bird of the Goddess of Wisdom, Minerva.

JIMMY: Oh, Greek mythology—pretty ignorant of that.

[*He starts the car abruptly as she leans her head against him again.*]

FISHER: *Mon Dieu!* —Such—something! —Reaction to what?

33] DISSOLVE TO: CLOSE TWO-SHOT OF
FISHER AND JIMMY.
Their faces are barely visible through the heavy mist rising and rolling off the levee. A car approaching from the other direction cuts through the mist. Fisher's teardrop diamonds catch the light a moment before she, automatically, covers her ears with her hands. Jimmy's grin flashes as he shouts a greeting to the driver of the Model T Ford.

JIMMY: Fisher, you did it again.

FISHER: Did what? Again?

JIMMY: Covered your ears like you thought you'd be hollered at.

FISHER: I wasn't conscious of it. Who did *you* holler at?

JIMMY: Old friend, Mike.

FISHER: Leaving so early?

JIMMY: Probably just to get a bottle of moonshine.

[*There is the sound of the hoot-owl.*]

FISHER: Is that the same owl? Has it flown after us here?

JIMMY [*impatiently*]: I don't hear any owl.

[*He shifts gears, slowing the car down. Fisher abruptly leaps out. The camera view widens to take in the drive.*]

JIMMY: *Hey!*

[*He slams on brakes and leaps from the car on driver's side and follows Fisher up the gravelled drive.*]

Why'd you do that?

FISHER: *What?*

JIMMY: Jump out before the car stopped. You could've got hurt.

FISHER: *What?* [*Her voice is almost as sharp as a rifle shot.*] *Hurt? Me? Never!* —But thanks for your solicitude. —Delicate as my bones are, they never break. —How far is the house?

137

JIMMY: In walking distance, but—

FISHER: I have time to arrange my hair.

[*With rapid, jerky movements, she snatches a comb from her beaded bag and fusses needlessly with her shingled hair. Suddenly she gasps.*]

Oh, Lawd, d'you know what's happened?

[*He responds with a baffled stare.*]

One of my teardrop diamonds has fallen off! I mustn't move. I think it fell off right here, where I'm standing. Isn't it lucky I was still on the drive. The Fenstermakers never cut their grass. Light a match.

[*He does, crouching with it.*]

See it?

[*She crouches too.*]

No. It isn't here. Look in the car seat, it must have come loose in the car. I'll stand here. Where I stopped. It may be under the gravel that you kicked around. Those earrings are treasures, they're worth five thousand each.

[*Julie Fenstermaker, Vinnie McCorkle and a few other guests approach along the gravelled drive.*]

JULIE [*calling out*]: Who's there? —*Mike?* —Back already?

FISHER: It's me, it's us, I mean.

JULIE: Fishie! —I'd really hoped she'd be busy in Memphis.

VINNIE: —Why?

JULIE: I expect you'll discover why. I happen to like her but you'll notice later that—

VINNIE: Huh?

JULIE: —Nothing. They seem to be looking for something . . .

FISHER'S VOICE [*sharply*]: It might be a good idea to turn the car lights on, don't you think, Jimmy?

[*Julie now rushes up to Fisher. They embrace. Vinnie goes past them toward the car as the lights are turned on. She suddenly bends to pick up something.*]

JULIE: Have you lost something, Fisher?

FISHER: Nothing less than a five-thousand-dollar teardrop diamond, honey.

JULIE: My Lawd, *where?*

FISHER: Somewhere between the car and where I'm standing.

JIMMY [*calling*]: See it on the drive, Fisher?

FISHER: No. Do *you* see it in the car?

JIMMY: Looking, still looking.

FISHER: Go get a flashlight from the house, all you're doing with matches is burning your fingers.

JULIE: Is that Jimmy Dobyne in the car?

139

FISHER: Yes, but that's scarcely my concern at the moment.

JIMMY: It's nowhere in the front of the car.

FISHER: It's GOT to be in the front of the car! I had it on when I got in the car and I didn't get out of the car anywhere on the way here, did I?

JIMMY: You're out of the car, now, Fisher.

FISHER: Well, look around where I'm standin'.

JIMMY: I'll go ask for a flashlight.

FISHER: All right. I'll stand right here so we'll know where to look in the drive.

JIMMY: Fisher, you walked halfway to the house before you discovered you'd lost it.

FISHER [*crossly*]: I DID NOT! I didn't walk more than a couple of feet from the car, before I discovered I'd lost it?

JIMMY: Look. You got out before I could open the car door for you and you walked clean around the car. I couldn't see you even. You'd disappeared in the fog when I heard you holler you'd lost your—

FISHER [*angrily*]: I GUESS I KNOW HOW FAR FROM THE CAR I WALKED! Will you please borrow a flashlight from the house? Is that too much to ask of you?

JULIE: Don't get hysterical, Fisher. I'll bring you a flashlight!

34] LONG CAMERA SHOT OF JIMMY.
Jimmy stops in the drive to greet Vinnie.

FISHER: Who is that common-looking little tramp talking to my escort?

JULIE: My cousin, Vinnie. —Excuse me, I'll get the flashlight.

[*Fisher starts toward the car.*]

JIMMY [*following her, Vinnie with him*]: Fisher, I thought you were going to stay where you thought you dropped it.

FISHER: I'm retracing my steps to the car. I'm sure to see it if it fell in the drive.

[*She is not looking at the drive but staring rather fiercely at Vinnie.*]

VINNIE [*to Jimmy*]: —Never expected to see you again in my life!

JIMMY: God. I'm glad you're here, Vin. [*He lowers his voice.*] It's gonna be a rough night if we don't locate that earring.

35] EXTERIOR. NIGHT. CLOSE THREE-SHOT.

FISHER: I don't want to interrupt your reunion. Old friends, are you, Jimmy?

VINNIE: I'm Julie's cousin, Vinnie McCorkle.

FISHER: How do you do? Julie's gone for a flashlight. Obviously—

JIMMY: What?

FISHER: The earring dropped off before I got out of the car.

JIMMY: Just where'd you do that? Why, you were out before I'd stopped it like a—jumping flea!

FISHER: A charming simile. —So you are Julie's cousin?

VINNIE: Didn't I say so?

FISHER: I suppose—

VINNIE: What?

FISHER: Sometimes there's no resemblance between relations.

JIMMY: I'm going to back the car up since you jumped out before it had stopped.

FISHER: I did not.

JIMMY: You did.

FISHER: I wouldn't dare, my ankles are thin as—

VINNIE: Toothpicks?

FISHER: Don't move the car. I'm going to help Julie locate the flashlight.

[*She stalks up the drive, out of the shot.*]

36] TWO-SHOT: JIMMY AND VINNIE.

VINNIE: What did she say that lost earring is worth?

JIMMY: Five thousand.

VINNIE: She sounds very cross with you, Jimmy. Does she think you're responsible for the loss?

JIMMY: I'm gonna back up the goddam car. She did jump out before it stopped. Mad at me? Yeah, mad as hops! And I think I know why.

JULIE'S VOICE: Flashlight!

FISHER'S VOICE: I doubt somehow that it's going to be recovered.

37] EXTERIOR. NIGHT. FOUR-SHOT: JIMMY, FISHER, VINNIE, JULIE.

FISHER: You *did* back up the car.

JIMMY: You *did* jump out of the car before it stopped!

FISHER: Are you calling me a liar?

VINNIE: *I* saw her jump out of it, *too*.

FISHER: How about you, Julie?

JULIE: It's so terribly foggy, I just saw the car lights as you entered the drive.

FISHER: This young lady who says she's your cousin must have exceptional vision. *Jimmy?* I think I know what happened. —It fell in a pocket of your jacket.

JIMMY: Oh. You think I've got it on me? Yeah, yeah, you think I'm a jewelry thief!

[*He stalks rapidly away from her, the opposite way from the house.*]

143

FISHER: *Jim-meee!*

[*She draws a sharp breath and runs after him down the drive, overtakes him seizes his arm.*]

Where do you think you're going, Jimmy Dobyne?

JIMMY: If your accusation is right, to the county jail.

FISHER: What accusation, I made no accusation.

JIMMY: Here's my jacket, search the pockets!

FISHER: I will do no such thing! You misunderstood me. I only meant it could have dropped in your pocket by accident and you know it. Don't you remember? I—I leaned my head on your shoulder on the levee? —You suddenly started the car, and I felt my head jerk, that's probably when—oh, this is absurd! I'm ruining my slippers on this gravel drive. Come on to the house.

JIMMY: You go back and have a good time at the party, I couldn't now.

FISHER: I can't go back without a date!

JIMMY: Wouldn't it be better than going back to it with a suspected thief?

FISHER: You've got to go back with me! Think of the talk if you don't!

JIMMY: Look through the pockets of that jacket!

FISHER: All right, if you insist, for no other reason.

JIMMY: Of course I ought to be searched to the skin. That's what I'll demand if I go back there with you.

FISHER: You don't understand me yet, Jimmy!

JIMMY: Who does? Does anybody?

FISHER: Nobody I know of, to tell you the truth. I'm an only child which has the advantage of making me the heiress of two fortunes, my rich spinster aunt's in Memphis and also my parents'.

JIMMY: Do you always talk so much about your financial prospects? Depending on death?

FISHER: In Memphis it's not necessary, it's too well-known.

JIMMY: Has it made you popular there?

FISHER: —With some kinds of people, yes . . .

JIMMY: The kind of people you like?

FISHER: I don't like people but sometimes I like one person.

JIMMY: Do I have the honor of being one that you liked— till you lost the teardrop diamond?

FISHER: Why else would I be here with you? Come on! Please!

[*They start back up the drive.*]

38] INTERIOR. HALLOWEEN PARTY. ENTRANCE
HALL OF THE FENSTERMAKERS' HOUSE.
Fisher is confronted by a pair of spiteful sisters, twins but not identical—Esmeralda and Mathilde Bachelder. They have the

145

odd habit of completing each other's usually malicious laughter. Esmeralda goes "Ha-haa!" with a rising inflection and Mathilde goes "Haa!," an octave lower.

ESMERALDA: Haven't I seen you before?

FISHER [*coldly*]: Not that I recall.

ESMERALDA: Oh, I know. It was just a photo of you as a debutante of the season in Memphis.

FISHER [*calling out, retreating from the weird sisters*]: Jul—ie!

MATHILDE: We came out last season and still go to the important parties in Memphis such as Susie Bracken's.

ESMERALDA: Yais, her debut's tonight. We were invited, of course, but we—

MATHILDE: Didn't want to disappoint Julie.

ESMERALDA: You seem to be alone here. Did you come here alone?

FISHER: I don't see how that concerns you, but—

ESMERALDA: Ha-*haa!*

MATHILDE: Haa!

ESMERALDA: We just thought if you're here alone, we'd gladly introduce you to some of the—

MATHILDE: Guests—yaiss . . .

FISHER: Since I'm a close friend of Julie's, I'm sure she'll introduce me to anyone present that I care to know. —Excuse me!

[*The sisters utter their curious laugh. Fisher starts past them.*]

MATHILDE: May I touch that gorgeous coat?

ESMERALDA: Is it *real*?

MATHILDE: *Leopard*-skin? Coat? Like Elinor Glynn's?!

FISHER [*shrilly*]: Take your hands off my coat, get out of my way! *Julie! Julie!*

[*The camera follows her down the hall. Jimmy's voice is heard in the kitchen.*]

JIMMY'S VOICE: I wanted to walk home! She ran after me! I tell you that damn girl thinks I stole a diamond off her! That's why I've *got* to be *searched*! I'm gonna take off all my clothes and I want you fellows to go all through every pocket, any place that I could hide a goddam diamond on me!

MR. FENSTERMAKER'S VOICE: Now, now, son, everybody knows perfectly well that you never stole anything. Why, nobody that knows the Dobynes, and I had the honor of knowing your grand-daddy as well as I knew my own father, why, nobody with a grain of sense could possibly imagine a Dobyne stealin' a—

JIMMY'S VOICE [*cutting in*]: Mr. Fenstermaker, you just don't understand. My Father was accused of stealing by the *Hobsons* when he was workin' for *them*.

MR. FENSTERMAKER'S VOICE: Keep your clothes on, son. Just set down and have a drink with me, huh? You're all worked up over nothin', nothin'.

[*The camera has remained on Fisher, a fist pressed to her mouth as if to stifle a scream. She suddenly turns about and thrusts the Bachelder sisters roughly aside. She rushes up the winding staircase, calling* "Julie! Julie!"]

39] INTERIOR. NIGHT. THE LARGE OLD-FASHIONED KITCHEN OF A PLANTATION HOME.
Jimmy stands shivering in a suit of BVD's, the one-piece male underwear of the period, in front of the big woodstove; his clothes are lying over the back of a kitchen chair.

JIMMY: Mr. Fenstermaker, you haven't gone through the pockets of that tuxedo.

MR. FENSTERMAKER: No, sir, I haven't and furthermore I'm not goin' to, I'm not gonna search the pockets of a grandson of James Polk Dobyne, no, sir. Happy? Hand me a glass to pour Mr. Dobyne a drink. Son, get back in you' clo'se.

JIMMY: Happy, turn those pants pockets inside out, all of 'em, and put ev'rything you find in 'em on that table.

MR. FENSTERMAKER: Young man, drink your drink.

JIMMY: I—don't touch liquor, don't dare to. —Well—thanks [*He accepts the drink.*] but I shouldn't.

MR. FENSTERMAKER: Why's that, son?

JIMMY: My father—is a—notorious drunk. —But *honest.* And so am *I.* There was this scandal because Hobson's son Buster stole a bunch of old Liberty bonds, they called 'em, you know—

Well, Buster was the Hobson's only child if you'd call a two-hundred-fifty-pound thirty-eight-year-old half-wit man a child. My dad known Buster stole 'em, had caught him at it red-handed.

[*Vinnie and Julie appear in the kitchen doorway; Vinnie starts to enter.*]

MR. FENSTERMAKER: You girls stay out of here till we get Jimmy's pants back on him.

[*Vinnie remains in the door, Julie behind her. They whisper excitedly in the background.*]

JIMMY: But how the devil in hail was my old man going to convince the Hobsons that their son Buster'd stole off old T. J. Hobson? So my dad had to quit. He left the Hobsons with suspicion of robbery on him.

MR. FENSTERMAKER: We all know that story. Buster was caught attemptin' to sell the bonds in Vicksburg, son.

JIMMY: I never heard about that.

MR. FENSTERMAKER: It naturally wasn't advertised but Hobson got drunk one night at the Moose Lodge an' admitted his son had stole those Liberty bonds. And he'd put the blame on your dad.

[*Jimmy gets into his pants.*]

JIMMY [*in a choked voice*]: Then why'd he never clear my old man's name of the accusation?

MR. FENSTERMAKER: White trash, them Hobsons. Anyhow, T. J.'s daid and they tell me that Buster Hobson's gambled away all the place but the house and a few acres of ground.

JIMMY: And now this Fisher Willow has come down here from her social debut in Memphis to accuse me of stealin' a diamond. —I liked that girl, Fisher Willow, I really did like her. Whenever she came home from her Memphis parties she'd bring me some little present. Lately a wardrobe of clothes, this tuxedo, also white tie and tails so I—

VINNIE [*from the doorway*]: She was courtin' you, Jimmy?

[*Now dressed, he crosses to the doorway and takes Vinnie's hand in his.*]

MR. FENSTERMAKER: The search is completed. Here are the contents of Mr. Dobyne's pockets. Everything is listed.

JULIE: No teardrop diamond.

MR. FENSTERMAKER: Half pack Camel cigarettes, three sticks of chewing gum, three dollars and forty-seven cents. Take this list to her, one of you girls. Now, Jimmy, you can't go through life scared to have a drink. You're shakin' with understandable outrage. Get this down you and go back out to the party, your reputation is clear as the sky.

VINNIE: Clearer than the sky—the sky's full of river-mist . . .

[*Dissolve as she lifts the drink to Jimmy's lips and whispers something in his ear.*]

JIMMY [*raising voice*]: All those clothes, it was too much for me to accept from a girl. And I've gotten sick of receiving presents from people, given because the Dobynes have gone

150

downhill! Also, in the first place, I didn't know what I would do with a tuxedo, my crowd don't go with tuxedos! However! —Then it turned out that Fisher Willow had a plan in mind, a purpose fo' dressin' me up. She wanted me to take her to debut parties in Memphis because the men in Memphis had not cottoned to her, somehow.

40] INTERIOR. UPSTAIRS HALL.
Fisher is about to enter an open bedroom door when a nurse steps out of another room and stops her.

NURSE: Miss Willow?

FISHER: What?

NURSE: Julie's aunt wants to see you.

FISHER: Oh, please make some excuse for me, I can't stand t'see dyin' people. Say that—

ADDIE'S VOICE [*calling out from the bedroom*]: —Fisher? Fisher Willow?

FISHER: Oh, *Lord!*

NURSE: Just for a moment, Miss Willow, she's determined to see you. She won't take her sleeping medicine till she's seen you, Miss Willow.

FISHER: *Why?!*

NURSE: I don't know why, Miss Willow, but she positively refuses to go to sleep till she's seen you.

[*The cry within is repeated.*]

FISHER: —Well . . .

[*She enters the bedroom containing the terrible voice.*]

41] INTERIOR. UPSTAIRS BEDROOM, FIRE-LIT.
Fisher enters from the hall. The camera pans to a fierce, dying old woman propped up on pillows in a four-poster bed, then returns to Fisher.

FISHER: Hellow. How are you, Miss Addie.

ADDIE: Thank you for coming in. I know how unpleasant it is to enter this chamber of horrors!

[*Pause. Fisher blinks.*]

FISHER: Why do you call it a "chamber of horrors," Miss Addie?

ADDIE: Because that's just what it is. Will you please close that door? Is there a key in the lock?

FISHER: Yes. Why?

ADDIE: Will you please lock it? I want to have a completely private talk with you.

[*Fisher, after a slight hesitation, locks the door.*]

Now, then, come over here so I don't have to raise my voice. I have the use of my voice and my sight—too blurred for reading. My heart and lungs and the internal organs that one can't control—remorselessly continue! Oh, I attempted a hunger strike but people can be force fed. As for the rest of me, it's stone-dead Fisher. —Are you in a hurry to go back down there to the party?

FISHER: —No, I—feel more at home here with you . . .

ADDIE: We've met only once before, two years ago, when I was here for a short visit. Your Aunt Cornelia and I had a brief but memorable encounter in Hong Kong. She brought you along when she paid me a call at my—

FISHER: Of course I remember, you had a little—

ADDIE: Cottage on Sand Island.

FISHER: Yes, we went on a boat.

ADDIE: To that almost deserted island which—my habits required.

FISHER: Habits? Acquired?

ADDIE [*fiercely*]: Yes, acquired and required!

FISHER: When Aunt Cornelia and you had—

ADDIE: Completed our private discussion. Yes?

FISHER: She—she said you wrote travel books and stayed mostly in—

ADDIE: The very wide and tolerant Orient, Fisher. My base was Hong Kong. There is much tolerance there. And here?

FISHER: I would say none at all.

ADDIE: So I had elected to spend my life in the tolerant Orient. But things that one elects are often circumvented by others. I think you know about that. The game is the *double* game.

153

FISHER: Yes, I know about that.

ADDIE: I had a stroke—in China. Unfortunately it was publicized—I was brought home by force as I am kept living in agony by force . . .

[*A voice from downstairs calls "Fisher"?*]

—You're being called down, I must get on with this quickly. I had to stay in China because I'd become addicted to something that I could only have there.

FISHER: What to? To what, Miss Addie?

ADDIE: —To a drug that made it bearable for me to live after living became—unbearable for me, Fisher. You see, I had my first stroke five years ago, but that one was only a slight one, it only twisted one side of my face a little so it gave me a grin like a—tipsy pirate's! —I knew, I was told, there'd be others. So I quit my travels and settled down in one place, and needing something so badly to make life bearable for me, I found something, the poppy, the smoke of the burning poppy. D'you know what I mean? —I mean opium, Fisher. Well . . . early last summer the terrible thing that was coming, that the drug made me able to forget was coming—happened. —I had the stroke that caused my present condition. My brother Jack was told, and he came there and brought me back here, strapped on a stretcher, because I fought like a wildcat, and I was—withdrawn from my—comfort . . .

FISHER: Miss Addie, why are you telling me this story?

ADDIE: Because I remembered the impression you made on me when I last saw you. There was something hard and honest about you. I thought that maybe you could do something for me, the only thing that can be done for me, now. I see nobody but people that can't imagine. You can. You can imagine. Fisher, they give me something, but not enough of it, Fisher. See that little bottle on the mantel? I can't reach it. You could. You could give it to me. And I could—resume my travels! —Do you know what I mean? Have I made myself clear? —Nobody could know, nobody could possibly guess, you gave it to me, they'd just suppose I'd had a last stroke in my sleep . . .

FISHER: I think you mean this. . . . Yes, I know you mean it. [*She brings the pillbox to Addie.*] How many?

ADDIE: All—all . . .

[*Fisher closes her eyes tightly. Then opens the bottle and gently, tenderly, lifts the old woman's head and places several of the pills in her mouth.*]

ADDIE: Fisher, that's not all.

[*There is banging at door. Fisher removes her remaining earring and places it under the mantel clock, the pillbox beside it.*]

JULIE: Fisher! Open this door!

[*She does, and Julie enters with Vinnie.*]

FISHER [*to Addie*]: I'll come back later.

ADDIE: *Promise?*

FISHER: Swear on my word of honor. —I'll come back up for this other diamond earring and my leopard-skin coat.

JULIE: Fisher, Jimmy was searched to the skin before witnesses and here is all he had on him! Three sticks of peppermint gum, a few cigarettes, three dollars and forty-seven cents and—

FISHER: And? And what?

JULIE: Something in a small unopened package, almost completely flat. And the keys to your car.

ADDIE: What is this all about?

VINNIE: It's all about Fisher Willow's attempt to buy an escort for her to debut parties in Memphis, provide him with clothes—expensive tailored clothes—and now accuse him of stealing a diamond from her! Why? Not easy to guess!

FISHER: Oh! Have you guessed, Miss McCorkle? What have you guessed?

VINNIE: He hasn't responded to your courtship as you'd expected!

ADDIE: I must be getting drowsy. I don't understand all this. Julie, please take your loud-voiced cousin out so I can finish my little talk with Fisher. You know, excitement isn't allowed in sickrooms.

JULIE: Fisher, you will say the earring fell down your dress.

FISHER: I will say whatever I *can* without lying. I'm not a liar, Julie.

ADDIE: Julie, get yourself and that other girl out!

JULIE: Goodnight, Miss Addie.

[*She and Vinnie exit.*]

FISHER: —Miss Addie, you know I really did lose the other one of this pair of teardrop diamonds?

[*She holds up the one she had placed under the mantel clock.*]

ADDIE: Yes, Fisher. I know you lost it. But you have handled the situation in a terrible way.

FISHER: I merely reported that I had lost a teardrop diamond earring, Miss Addie.

ADDIE: You must have done it in a way that made the boy feel that you were accusing him of stealing it, Fisher, dear.

[*The fire crackles. The room has visual magic.*]

FISHER: Such a thought absolutely never entered my mind, till after I heard that he was telling them downstairs that I had— *you heard Julie!!* What she said he'd been saying? —That I asked him to drive me up on the levee in my car in order to get him to *kiss* me? What could be more insulting. A boy that would insult a girl like that would certainly not hesitate to steal a—*diamond earring worth five thousand dollars!* —I asked him to drive me up on the levee to see the mist rising off the river, because I love to see the river-mist rising! —Because I like nothing better! Nothing's more beautiful to me. —Of course *that's* peculiar of me . . . too, I suppose . . .

ADDIE: What did happen on the levee?

FISHER: *Nothing at all!* —To *speak* of. —We stopped there a while. —I leaned my head on his shoulder for a moment.

ADDIE: And he didn't kiss you when you parked on the levee to watch the river-mist rising?

FISHER: Now, Miss Addie. Do you suppose I have to BEG for kisses?

ADDIE: The boy is very attractive to you, is he?

FISHER: Some people find *me* attractive, *too,* Miss Addie! Can you believe it? It's *true!*

ADDIE: Fisher, of course you're attractive, but that's not the issue, is it?

FISHER: Hear that?

[*The hoot-owl calls out of the misty trees before the house.*]

Minerva's bird, the bird of the Goddess of Wisdom, has interrupted our conversation, Miss Addie! Ha ha ha . . .

[*She returns to the bedside.*]

I've made up my mind about something. Minerva's bird told me what I ought to do, now. I won't go back to Memphis to continue this ridiculous pretense of being interested in the society of that city, when it bores me to blazes! —I will catch the very next boat back to Europe, and I think that Aunt Cornelia will be glad to see me set sail from these shores! —I disgraced her in Memphis. Now I suppose I've disgraced the Willows in Mississippi! —Oh, well. I'm out of my element, here . . .

In Europe it isn't disgraceful to be interested in the arts! —It's considered a sign of—being a worthwhile person! Actually! Can

158

you believe it? You're not ashamed of having read—*Winesburg,
Ohio* by Sherwood Anderson, even!

—Yes, I'm going to catch the very next boat back to Europe
and take an apartment on the Rive Gauche in Paris and estab-
lish! —A salon! —Like Gertrude Stein's . . .

—I'll commission Pablo Picasso to do a portrait of me all in
—blue . . .

—I'm not going to lose my mind, not crack up again. —I'm going to develop my interest in the arts! —I'm going to, to, to!
—Do *sculpture*! Make beautiful things out of stone . . .

[*The owl hoots sadly and wisely outside.*]

—Because I don't belong here. I must be with people who DO
THINGS! —Paint, write, compose music! —And so forth.

ADDIE: You DO have CHARACTER, Fisher, and maybe
talent, but I *do* shudder for you.

[*The owl hoots. Victrola music is heard from the lower
floor.*]

FISHER: Why do shudder for me?

ADDIE: You want to be loved by somebody that you love but
you don't know how to arrange it. And not all the teardrop
diamonds, lost or found, in this world can arrange that for you.
Now go downstairs. And make an announcement to them. Say
that the teardrop diamond's been found, say that it fell down
your dress, say that it slipped down the low-cut front of your
gown! —So that the Halloween party can have a chance to be
fun.

159

FISHER: But I *haven't* found it, Miss Addie.

ADDIE: Say that you *did!*

FISHER: Why should I discard my honesty—all that I've got, really!

ADDIE: —Nonsense, Fisher! Strong people with character like you, Fisher Willow, don't care about losing a teardrop diamond. They've got more important problems. *Now, go!* But remember your promise to come back.

FISHER: Yes. *Soon,* Miss Addie.

42] INTERIOR. STAIR LANDING. FISHER AND JULIE.

JULIE: Are you going to make the announcement?

FISHER: YOU will make the announcement and I will not contradict it.

[*Fisher starts rapidly down the stairs, threading her way among the couples seated on the steps, saying, "Excuse me, Excuse me" in an icy voice. At the bottom she passes Mrs. Fenstermaker. The camera follows Fisher.*]

MRS. FENSTERMAKER: Are your slippers dry now, Fisher?

FISHER: Yes, sufficiently, thank you.

MRS. FENSTERMAKER: I know you'll be relieved that that nice young man was completely searched in the kitchen and nothing more incriminating was found on him than—

FISHER: I know all about that.

JULIE'S VOICE [*above*]: *HEY, EVERYBODY! Isn't it wonderful? Fisher's found her diamond!*

[*There is an indifferent reaction to the news. Julie descends the stairs, entering the shot.*]

ESMERALDA: Where'd you find it, Fisher?

[*Fisher ignores the question.*]

JULIE: She found it inside her dress; it had slipped down the front of her dress.

BOY: *That* dress?

MATHILDE: It must have been one of those tiny little chip diamonds.

[*They laugh. Fisher threads her way coolly between them. Vinnie and Jimmy Dobyne are dancing in the downstairs hall.*]

FISHER: Jimmy?! May I speak to you a minute? Will you excuse him, Miss McCorkle?

[*Vinnie doesn't look at her but draws herself gently from Jimmy's arms. Another boy immediately takes her in a tight embrace. The victrola is playing "Dreamy Melody." Someone turns out the lights in the big parlor and there are loud "Ahs," and gay laughter.*]

FISHER: Did you really have yourself searched in the kitchen, Jimmy?

JIMMY: Yeah. What do you want now, Fisher?

FISHER: —Don't talk to me like that!

[*He stares at her blankly a moment, then walks away.*]

FISHER [*seizing his arm*]: DON'T TURN YOUR BACK ON ME! Don't you dare walk away from me like that!

JIMMY [*coolly*]: Excuse me, Fisher.

FISHER: You told them I bought you clothes! I want to know why you told them I bought clothes for you!

[*She has drawn back against the wall, speaking in a shrill whisper. He leans the palm of his hand against the wall. They are partially screened by a potted palm tree in the hall.*]

JIMMY: Why *did* you, Fisher?

FISHER: Because I—felt *sorry* for you!

JIMMY: Oh . . .

FISHER: And because you're a gentleman, grandson of a governor of the state, and you dressed like a—colored fieldhand!

JIMMY: —I'm not so much of a gentleman that you wouldn't suspect me of stealing.

FISHER: Stand up! Or are you too drunk to?

JIMMY: I had some liquor while they were searching my clothes for your teardrop diamond.

FISHER: Are you going to drink like your father?

[*He starts to walk away from her.*]

FISHER: Jimmy! Don't walk away when I'm talking to you.

JIMMY: The talk, isn't it finished? What do you want now, Fisher? You say you've found your diamond!

FISHER: I did *not* say I'd found it. Julie said that I did. I agreed to let her say it so there'd be no more talk.

[*He stares at her a moment, then whirls about so violently that the potted palm is overturned. He enters the parlor and shouts above the victrola.*]

JIMMY: HEY, TURN OFF THE VICTROLA!

[*Nobody complies but all stare at him. He rushes to the machine and turns it off himself.*]

I wanna make an announcement, very important announcement. Fisher Willow did not find her diamond, never said she found it, had Julie say it for her! Truth is—it isn't found but still lost.

JULIE: Oh, Jimmy, you misunderstood. Why, I was there when she found it.

FISHER [*advancing to Julie*]: Under the circumstances, I think I'd like to go home. I—don't feel well. —I don't want to stay and spoil the party.

MATHILDE [*in a stage whisper*]: I don't hear any loud objections to that.

JULIE: Mathilde, will you hush up!

FISHER: Let's not suppress freedom of speech—no matter how crude and—

JULIE [*cutting in*]: Fisher, stay. It's all forgotten now. I'm going to get Mama to bed so we can play post office.

FISHER: Play what?

VINNIE: Your Mama's guarding the punchbowl like a hawk. Nobody's had a chance to spike it so the boys are drinking straight moonshine in the yard.

JULIE: They show it already.

VINNIE: I'll get Eddie Peacock to dance your mother away from the bowl.

[*She puts a lively two-step on the victrola and whispers to Eddie. He goes up to Mrs. Fenstermaker and pulls her on to the floor.*]

JULIE [*to a boy*]: Tommy, dance with Fisher. She's decorating the wall.

TOMMY: She'll decorate walls all her life.

FISHER [*shrilly*]: Not the walls at this party!

ESMERALDA: Walls in Memphis?

FISHER: *No, much, much further than Memphis!*

[*She starts to the front door.*]

JULIE: Fisher, don't go out, not without a coat; it's turned so chilly outside.

FISHER: I don't feel the outside temperature will seem different to me, with a coat or without one.

[*The camera follows her outside. Some drunk boys are clustered about the front steps under which bottles of moonshine are hidden.*]

BOY: Mike, I dare you to go up to her and ask her if she'd like a good lay.

[*Mike laughs drunkenly and crosses to Fisher standing under a tree. His question is indistinct.*]

FISHER [*distinctly*]: How dare you, what a—! —You?!

[*He persists, his hands clutching her spare body. She slaps him fiercely.*]

BOY: Haul her back of the bushes!

FISHER: WHOEVER APPROACHES ME WILL BE SORRY THEY DID!

[*Julie comes out on the porch.*]

JULIE: Mama's gone upstairs!

VOICES: Good for Mama! Mama's a good sport!

[*The camera follows them back into parlor.*]

VINNIE: Julie, your mother's gone to bed, we can play post office now!

[*There is an excited reaction.*]

JULIE: *SSHHH!* —Be very quiet moving the furniture!

[*Fisher has crossed to Jimmy.*]

FISHER: Are they going to play another kid's game?

JIMMY: Yeah. Post office.

FISHER: What kind of game is that?

JIMMY: Haven't you ever played post office?

FISHER: Why, no, I've never even heard of a game by that name.

JIMMY [*without attention to her*]: —Honestly?

[*He is looking at Vinnie.*]

FISHER: Yes, honestly, I haven't. What kind of a game is post office?

JIMMY: —It's a kissing game.

FISHER: Oh? You mean we're all going to kiss each other like, like—New Year's Eve?

JIMMY: No. More private.

FISHER: I don't understand this game.

JIMMY: Watch it. You'll catch on.

FISHER: It sounds *nice*! But I'd like to have it explained.

JIMMY: Just watch it. You'll catch on.

FISHER: I'd rather take part if it's fun, watching's no fun, just—watching . . .

JULIE: Jimmy, don't be so lazy! Bring in some dining-room chairs to make the circle.

[*He moves into dining room.*]

FISHER: Julie, what's this game? I never heard of it before.

JULIE: You'll catch on to it quick. Fisher! Have some *fun*!

[*She rushes off again. Fisher remains alone and, ignored, wanders along the hall, pausing before a pier glass.*]

JULIE'S VOICE: FISHER? FISHER?

FISHER [*turning back to the parlor*]: Yes, Julie?

JULIE: Why do you keep straying off?

FISHER: I don't know what's going on . . .

JULIE: We're dealing the cards for post office! —Take *this*! [*She thrusts a card into Fisher's hand.*] Keep it out of sight. Here, here, wrap it in this napkin! [*Then, she turns to the party guests.*] Awright, we're ready to start. Hank, close the hall door. And ev'rybody talk quiet.

FISHER: —How d'you *PLAY* post office, I don't know the game!

JULIE: Oh, Fisher, you do!

FISHER: Oh, Julie, I don't!

JULIE: You'll catch on very quick if the right boy sends you a letter.

FISHER: Will I? All right. I'll sit down and give my undivided attention . . .

[*She has suddenly gathered up an air of confidence and power. She takes a straight-backed chair and looks out at the parlor with the bright, unblinking eyes of a bird, her face wearing a brilliant, set smile. The victrola is playing a duet of "Kiss Me Again."*]

JULIE: Turn that record off, it's too appropriate, Mama might catch on!

[*The record is changed to "Whispering."*]

That's too soft! Something louder!

[*A loud and lively record of the period, such as "Collegiate" or "Yes, Sir, That's My Baby!" is put on the victrola.*

[*A record is dropped and broken.*]

What record was that you broke, Hank Ellis, you fool!

HANK: Oh, just some old one. Blues.

JULIE: The "Basin Street Blues"? Why, that's a *class*-ic!

HANK: Julie—a classic is by Beethoven or Brahms or—

JULIE: Naturally I meant a *modern* classic and I don't retract my statement that *you* are a *fool*!

FISHER [*imperiously*]: Will somebody please explain post office or do you prefer to leave me in total dark about it.

[*Esmeralda runs about the room extinguishing lamps. Another blows out the candles in the jack-o'-lanterns.*]

JULIE: Esmeralda, Mathilde! —If you all go on like this I'm going to call off the game!

ESMERALDA: I thought Fisher wished to be left in total dark!

[*There is general mocking laughter.*]

JULIE: You thought no such thing! Turn those lamps back on!

MATHILDE: Just the jack-o'-lanterns!

JULIE: It appears that boys can handle spiked punch better than some of you girls can.

[*Julie lights a floor lamp. Fisher laughs with a choked sound and goes into the hall.*]

Now, where is Fisher? Where is Fisher Willow gone?

ESMERALDA: She's gone to blow up the south end of a levee!

JULIE: Ezzie, you are making me very annoyed with you! S'pose Fisher heard you say thaa-at?

FISHER [*returning*]: She *did*.

JULIE: Fisher, you know better than to pay any attention to silly, vicious little remarks of that kind?

FISHER: Yes. I consider the source. She has an unfortunate dental problem and it's too late for braces to do much good, I'm afraid.

MATHILDE: I don't think Esmeralda made a silly, vicious remark since it concerned the murder of seven innocent people for personal profit.

FISHER [*eyes wild*]: I! —I—do not reply to—slander—beneath contempt!

[*She starts out again, followed by Julie.*]

MATHILDE: Who does she think she is!

FISHER [*at parlor door*]: I have the advantage of *knowing* who I am! I hope that you have the same.

MATHILDE: What *am* I, in your opinion?

FISHER: Someone surprisingly common to be at Julie's party. I don't like making remarks like that, but sometimes—one is compelled to. —Sorry, Julie. Perhaps I really ought to go home now! —Alone. [*She and Julie continue out into the hall.*]

JULIE [*in Fisher's ear*]: Fisher, forget it! Both those girls are bitches.

FISHER: Female dogs in heat? Good lawd, Julie, what's become of your taste in company lately?

JULIE: Mama! She insisted I ask them because, well, they have just lost their mother!

FISHER: Probably murdered her! —What is this card that you told me to hide?

JULIE: Highest one in the deck, the ace of spades! —So you can deliver a letter to your date!

FISHER: Julie, that is cheating! —I don't intend to use this card for such a purpose.

[*But she follows Julie back into the parlor, the ace of spades in the napkin.*]

43] INTERIOR. PARLOR.

JULIE: Fisher! Take a chair!

FISHER: Thank you, Julie, but I think I'll just watch the game.

JULIE: You will not! You are going to play it! Please *don't* be a killjoy, Fisher!

FISHER: Can I *help* it, Julie? [*Fisher stays in the doorway.*]

JULIE: Yes, you can! [*She whispers.*] You're going to send a letter to Jimmy!

FISHER: Julie, *really*! —Isn't this sort of silly?

JULIE: No more than—life is, Fisher. Seats, ev'rybody! Has everyone got a card?

JIMMY [*turning from Vinnie in a corner*]: We don't have any cards, Julie.

JULIE: Take 'em, draw a card, each, and go sit down so we can start the game. Will somebody put another dance record on the victrola so Mama doesn't catch on to what we're playin' down here?

[*The victrola is wound up.*]

44] CUT TO: CLOSE TWO-SHOT OF JIMMY AND
VINNIE.

VINNIE: It's turned so chilly in here. I'm going to spread
Uncle Freddy's coat over my lap.

[*She spreads the coat over both her lap and Jimmy's.*]

JIMMY [*whispering*]: Careful, they're going to notice.

VINNIE: Turn out the floor lamp again.

[*Fisher has retreated behind the door drapes, and stands motionless. Jimmy rises with the coat held in front of him and
turns out the floor lamp, an old-fashioned one on a stand with
a pink silk shade.*

[*The group laughs and applauds as Jimmy makes his embarrassed cross to the floor lamp. Somebody jerks the over-
coat away from him. The parlor rocks with laughter.*]

FISHER [*flinging the door curtains open*]: Well, really, I thought
you said this was a kissing game but it appears to be as sophisticated *and* primitive as *The Rite of Spring* which would be a
perfect selection for the victrola—if among your record collection, Julie!

[*As Jimmy returns to the dark corner with Vinnie, Fisher
turns to the hall.*]

JULIE [*seizing Fisher's wrist*]: Fisher, you've got the—

FISHER: Please let go of my wrist.

JULIE: Highest card! All you've got to do—!

FISHER: If I wished to descend to her level. Look. They've spread that coat over both their laps.

JULIE: Vinnie, give me that coat! *And whoever turned that floor lamp off again, turn it back on!*

[*Spontaneously as a fire springing out in dry brush, they all start singing, led off by Hank, "Shine On, Harvest Moon." The camera goes in and out of focus.*]

FISHER: Julie, may I have a word with you in the hall?

45] CUT TO: CLOSE TWO-SHOT OF FISHER AND JULIE IN THE HALL.

FISHER: Either you separate my escort from that little drug-store tramp who claims to be your cousin—

JULIE: She *is*! —First cousin once removed.

FISHER: I would not admit any kinship no matter how far removed!

JULIE: Oh, Fisher, all you've got to do is—

FISHER: Excuse me, but I don't want to take part in this, Julie.

[*She crosses on to the downstairs verandah and slams the door. There is a sudden muting of interior sound. The owl hoots.*]

FISHER: Is that your message to me? —I think I understand it . . .

[*Julie comes out quietly and places an arm around Fisher's waist.*]

173

JULIE: Fisher, what are you doing out here in the cold and damp?

FISHER: Receiving an excellent piece of advice from the Bird of Minerva.

JULIE: I wish you'd talk a little more simply for us country folks, honey.

FISHER: I was referring to that hoot-owl. See it? That white thing with big, big luminous eyes in the tree there?

JULIE: Then say hoot-owl.

FISHER: *HOOT-OWL!*

JULIE: I'm outdone with you, Fisher. You're not like this.

FISHER: Just you watch me, I'll show you what I'm like. I'm cold, I'm going back in!

[*She enters the house. Julie follows.*]

ESMERALDA [*shrilly*]: Why, Fisher Willow has returned from Paris with the latest style hair and evening gown to go with it!

MATHILDE: I thought she'd just come down to help her father blow up another levee!

[*Fisher rushes toward the girl and slaps her. There is confusion in the parlor. Fisher rushes into the arms of Julie and sobs uncontrollably.*]

FISHER: *What did I do? I want to go home, I want to go home but I can't drive, I've gone all to pieces!*

JULIE: I'll tell Jimmy to—

FISHER: Not him, not him, anybody but him, deliberately insulting me, even worse than that—than those—two—tramps! Is there a downstairs bathroom?

46] CUT TO: FISHER ALONE IN A DOWNSTAIRS BATHROOM.

This should not look like an ordinary bathroom of any specific period. Color gives it a curious muted and melancholy radiance. Could it suggest a small apothecary shop near Verona at the time of Romeo's exile from that city? Many glass objects in different colors catch flickering points of light. A transformation is immediately apparent in Fisher; she becomes beautiful and other-worldly—a sorceress of sorts . . .

The music from the party should be chosen appropriately. It should be somewhat stylized to fit the key of the room.

Fisher stares at herself in the mirror of a cabinet, then opens it and discovers a strange bottle.

FISHER [*aloud*]: "Warning: contains a small quantity of opium and—could be—habit-forming. Adults: One or two teaspoons at bedtime . . ."

[*She lifts the bottle to her mouth and takes a swallow. Her attention is caught by the owl's hoot through the open, mottled in color, windows.*]

—What shall I do, Bird of Wisdom? I am madly in love!

[*The owl hoots in response to this question. She goes to the double windows, gothic in shape, and leans out.*]

175

Stop making fun of me! —You're alone, too! —Surely you understand . . .

JULIE'S VOICE: Fisher! Fisher!

[*Fisher turns and leaves the bathroom with the opiate bottle still in her hand.*]

47] CUT TO: THE HALL. TWO-SHOT: JULIE AND FISHER.

JULIE: My heavens! What are you doing with that bottle?

FISHER: Oh—I noticed it in the—what is it?

JULIE: It's one of Aunt Addie's fake remedies with opium in it.

FISHER: It had rather a—nice—bitter taste . . .

JULIE: You took some of it? Oh, Fisher. Let me put some ice on your forehead at once.

48] DISSOLVE TO: THE PARLOR AS FISHER RETURNS.

GIRL: Why, Fisher, we thought you'd *go-one*?

FISHER: I am not in the habit of retreat. . . . Has the game started? Oh, yes, I see it has. —I hope you'll all excuse my—fit of nerves; I've served some time in a mental clinic in Zurich and you never completely—return . . .

49] CUT TO: JULIE ENTERING THE PARLOR.

JULIE: Mama's sound asleep. —Change the record to something more romantic. —Has everyone got cards?

VINNIE: Everyone has cards, now.

JULIE: Jimmy, would you mind hanging daddy's coat back on the coatrack by the front door.

[*He rises slowly, holding it against him. Giggles, etc.*]

VINNIE: Jimmy has an ace.

JULIE: What of? Spades?

VINNIE: No. —Hearts.

JULIE: That can only be beaten by the ace of spades. Has anybody got the ace of spades or is it still in the deck?

[*There is a slight pause.*]

Well, you're the postman, Jimmy. Go out to the post office on the verandah and deliver someone a letter. The time limit is three minutes, remember.

[*He rises and passes Julie who whispers: "Be smart!" —He ignores this admonition and goes out on the verandah.*]

[*Now everyone chatters.*]

JULIE: WILL YOU ALL HUSH? SO I CAN HEAR WHO THE LETTER IS GONNA BE *SENT* TO!

[*Jimmy's voice from the verandah, through the half-open door.*]

JIMMY: *I have a letter for Miss Vinnie McCorkle!*

JULIE: Oh!

177

VINNIE: For *ME*?

FISHER [*speaking up shrilly*]: Julie, put a different record on the victrola. Play something *very romantic*!

JULIE: Remember: just three minutes, that's the strict time limit . . .

[*Vinnie crosses out in a grave, portentous silence.*]

FISHER: —*May I supply the music on the piano?*

[*She crosses to piano and plays* Liebestraum.]

JULIE: *Who's got a watch?*

50] DISSOLVE TO: THE VERANDAH.
Jimmy takes Vinnie's hand as she comes out of the house. For a moment they just look at each other. Then he draws her very sweetly into his arms and presses his cheek to hers.

VINNIE: Your eyelashes! —I feel 'em on my cheek.

JIMMY: We've only got *three minutes*?

VINNIE [*in a low, breathless voice*]: According to Julie's kissing game. Kissing is where I start. Follow me, hurry!

JIMMY: Where?

VINNIE: A parked car down the drive!

[*They dissolve into the mist of the drive. The sound of the piano playing* Liebestraum *fades.*]

51] SHOT OF A PARKED CAR DOWN THE DRIVE.

178

52] TRACKING MEDIUM SHOT OF JIMMY AND VIN-
   NIE APPROACHING ALONG THE DRIVE TO THE
   HOUSE.

VINNIE: Many men—of course, some were just kids with
pimples but others were responsible men with positions—have
said to me, "I love you, Vinnie!" —But only one has ever said to
me "Will you marry me, Vinnie?"

JIMMY [*his arm around Vinnie*]: You turned down the proposal? From the responsible man?

VINNIE: Yes. He had a position, a good one, an officer of the
Delta Planters Bank!

JIMMY: Gosh. And you turned him down?

VINNIE: It was just—well, I couldn't consider marriage with
a man I wasn't attracted to—physically, Jimmy. —Like back in
the car back there? It took my breath away, it did! Didn't you
hear me? Gasping for breath?

JIMMY [*solemnly*]: Yes. So was I.

[*They hear calls from the house.*]

VINNIE: Not as loud as me. —Jimmy, I don't want to keep any
secrets from you. None, ever. Something happened tonight and
I want to tell you about it. —I want to show it to you. —Follow
me! Quick! Don't answer those calls!

[*They dissolve into mist for a moment.*]

53] CLOSE TWO-SHOT: JIMMY AND VINNIE BY A
   FLOWER BED AT THE SIDE OF THE PLANTA-
   TION HOUSE.

Vinnie is crouched, digging carefully in the earth.

JIMMY: What're you digging for, Vinnie?

VINNIE: Oh, my God, I wonder if it was here. I counted down five bushes. This is—oh, this is the fourth—it's the next one!

[*She rushes to the fifth bush and resumes her digging.*]

Ah, now, here! Here it is!

JIMMY: What?

VINNIE: Release—release! *Release!*

[*She rises, extending her cupped palm toward Jimmy. Light from a window glistens on the lost diamond.* Liebestraum *is still heard on the piano.*]

JIMMY: God—why, that's the—

VINNIE: Shh, don't say it! This is our secret now!

JIMMY: Vinnie, you ain't serious, are you?

VINNIE: Course I'm serious!

JIMMY: Why, that's worth five thousand dollars, five thousand each, her aunt says!

VINNIE: And I know where the other one is. I saw Fisher take it off in Aunt Addie's bedroom and put it under the clock on the mantel. I'm going up there and get it, too. Ten thousand is a fortune. —A pretty girl with a fortune is more than just sexually desirable; she is someone that even a Dobyne the Fifth might—accept as a wife!

JIMMY: You must be—you must've—gone crazy . . .

VINNIE: To love you, to want you, to run away with you anywhere, for life!

JIMMY: This is all wrong, Vinnie. This is a terrible—mistake. Think about—honesty and—pride!

VINNIE: A girl that works at the cosmetic counter of Liggett's Drugstore on a sidestreet between Main and Front Streets in Memphis does not think about honesty and pride standing between her and—RELEASE! TO LIFE AND TO LOVE!

JIMMY: All I can say is—give it back to her, Vinnie.

VINNIE: Not on your life, boy! —Name of a soap, huh? But I mean it, not on your life, I mean not on *mine*! Finders are keepers, losers are weepers, if she's human enough to weep. —Anything but more diamonds. . . .

Diamond teardrops! Isn't that what she said "I've lost my diamond teardrop earring!"

Go back in the parlor. I'll run upstairs and get the other one under the clock.

[*He seizes hold of her wrist. He is trembling.*]

JIMMY: Vinnie, I'm poor, you're poor. That's hard, especially for a, for a—beautiful girl. But—Vinnie, you've got a—you've got a moral decision to make about this, you know.

VINNIE: Don't talk to me like a preacher! Why, just a minute ago you were having me and we were gaspin' for breath.

JIMMY: That's not the point, that's—

VINNIE: Common, in your opinion? All right, I'm common as dirt, but I'll wash myself clean.

JIMMY: By giving that diamond back to her.

VINNIE: Oh, no. These diamond teardrops will wash me clean as the sharecroppers that her father drowned last spring when he blasted the south end of his levee! —Let go of my hand!

54] CUT TO: MEDIUM CLOSE ONE-SHOT OF JULIE OPENING THE FRONT DOOR ONTO THE VERANDAH.

JULIE: Vinnie, is that you and Jimmy?

JIMMY [*huskily*]: —Yes.

JULIE: My heavens, you two have been out here half an hour at least!

VINNIE [*her eyes wide on Jimmy's*]: Yes, Jimmy sent me a very long letter, Julie, a—declaration of—love.

JULIE: Vinnie, you're talkin' crazy. The game's broken up, and Fisher—I don't know what's happened to her. She's kept playing the piano louder and louder, the same piece over and over, till Mama woke up and called down, "Quiet down there!" And still Fisher—she kept on playing, louder. I think she's having another breakdown, Jimmy. After all, you're her date to the party, you brought her!

JIMMY [*eyes moist*]: Julie, call Fisher out here.

VINNIE: For *what*?

JIMMY: Vinnie's got something to give her, something she just now accidentally found.

VINNIE: Why, what are you talking about?

JIMMY: FISHER! —FISHER!

55] MEDIUM CLOSE SHOT INCLUDING FISHER COMING ONTO THE VERANDAH, JIMMY AND JULIE BY THE STEPS.

FISHER [*wild-looking*]: What's going on? Why did you all interrupt my piano recital?

[*There is an awkward silence.*]

JULIE: —When the three minutes were up, I—we expected you back, so I dealt the cards out again. —This time Fisher received the highest card in the deck.

FISHER: Oh yes, but a little too late.

[*Vinnie breaks free of Jimmy's grasp and rushes into the house. Fisher goes down the gravel drive and disappears in the mist.*]

JULIE: Jimmy! Call her!

[*Jimmy calls "Fisher! Fisher Willow" several times, and is answered by the hoot-owl in the misty trees. Then—suddenly—a clear voice comes from the mist.*]

FISHER: Does somebody want Fisher Willow?

JIMMY: *Hey!*

[*He crosses toward the voice. The Pierce Arrow becomes visible through mist and Fisher is sitting at the wheel of it. Her necklace, her rings catch the light from the house.*]

JIMMY: Why didn't you answer me, didn't you hear me shouting?

FISHER: You call that shouting? Ha-ha. It sounded to me like a scared little boy in the dark.

[*He rests a foot on the running board of the car.*]

Well, what shall we do? Go now? I'm ready to go if you are; it's an awfully dull party. Of course, I don't like parties anyhow, much. But this one seems especially idiotic, all these games, these silly little kid games. Shall we run away, now?

JIMMY: I'd like to stay a while longer.

FISHER: Would you, really?

JIMMY: Yes.

FISHER: Why? You're grown-up, Jimmy!

JIMMY: I like the people at it.

FISHER: Especially one of the people? Julie's poor little cousin that works in a drugstore?

JIMMY: What's that against her?

FISHER: Nothing, not a thing in the world. You want me to leave you with her?

JIMMY: —You know if you go I will have to go with you, don't you?

FISHER: Don't be so conventional. It doesn't suit you, or me! —I swallowed my pride, I—called you!

[*Pause.*]

JIMMY: Fisher, I don't think you ever had to swallow your pride.

FISHER: Oh, no? You really don't think so?

JIMMY: Pride is something that *poor* people have to swallow.

FISHER: How naive you are! I don't think anyone's ever had to swallow their pride or choke on it as often as I have! For instance, it wasn't easy for me to come back downstairs to that party after you insisted on being searched in the kitchen.

JIMMY: It wasn't easy for *me* . . .

FISHER: Well, that's over, that's over! Shall we forget about it? Let's get in the car!

JIMMY: Let's go back to the party.

FISHER: I'm not going back to the party, get in the car!

JIMMY: —*I'm* going back to the party!

FISHER: Are you?

JIMMY: Yes, I am, Fisher. I've got to. There's an important reason.

FISHER: You mean you'd go back to the party when I asked you not to?

JIMMY: You're going back to it, too.

FISHER: Are you telling me what I'm going to do, Jimmy Dobyne?

JIMMY: Yep! Come on! Get out of that Pierce Arrow!

[*He opens the door.*]

FISHER: I believe you're serious!

JIMMY: *Get out! Get out of your Pierce Arrow car!*

FISHER: *Make me! Make me, I dare you!*

JIMMY: *You dare me?*

FISHER: *Yes, you heard me, I dare you!*

JIMMY: *Come on, get out, Fisher Willow!*

[*He has seized her thin arm.*]

FISHER: *You better let go of me or you'll get kicked!*

JIMMY: *Kick! Kick!*

FISHER: You don't think I will? Oh, Jimmy, you don't know the Willows! I think they invented kicking! And also scratching! I think you'd better let go of my arm, now, Jimmy!

JIMMY: Come on, get out of that car.

[*She kicks him, but he keeps hold of her arm. She suddenly leans against him.*]

FISHER: Weren't we—playing—post office?

JIMMY: This is not the post office.

FISHER: —Where is the post office?

JIMMY: On the front porch.

FISHER: Oh—on the dark verandah? —Is that where you were with the drugstore girl half an hour?

JIMMY: Yes—no . . .

FISHER: Or maybe! —The third possibility's always maybe, you know. Listen!

[*The owl hoots directly above them. She catches his hand.*]

Minerva's bird again!

JIMMY: Whose bird?

FISHER: The Goddess of Wisdom's bird is a hoot-owl! Didn't you know?

VINNIE [*from steps*]: *Fisher? Fisher Willow?*

FISHER: Who's that?

VINNIE [*advancing to them*]: —I've found your teardrop diamond!

[*Fisher and Jimmy get out of car.*]

FISHER: What did you say?

VINNIE: I found the teardrop diamond that you lost!

FISHER [*fiercely, coldly*]: Oh? Where did you find it?

VINNIE: —I—found it—on the—verandah!

FISHER: How could you find it on the verandah when I discovered I'd lost it before I got to the verandah? When I was in the drive?

VINNIE: —It probably fell out of your dress, or—something . . .

[*Her pleading eyes are on Jimmy.*]

Will you please take it back, it's burning my hand like a hot coal, Fisher Willow!

FISHER: You won't take a reward?

VINNIE: I just want to forget it, if you will *let* me!

FISHER: That's very—magnanimous of you, or something, I'm not sure what!

[*Jimmy grabs Fisher's hand and slaps the earring fiercely in Fisher's palm.*]

JIMMY: NOW!!! SHUT UP ABOUT IT, WILL YOU? YOU'VE GOT IT BACK!! Now, will you get in your car?

FISHER: Without my coat? I left it upstairs.

JIMMY: I'll get it. Where'd you— ?

FISHER [*running back to the house*]: Never mind. Tell Miss McCorkle good night while I—

[*Her voice fades as she disappears in the mist. Jimmy and Vinnie face each other in tortured silence.*]

JIMMY: —Thanks for doing that, Vinnie.

VINNIE: Did I have any choice? —Since I'm going to marry that officer in the bank, I don't suppose we're likely to meet again. —Are we?

[*Jimmy draws her hard and quick into his arms.*]

56] CUT TO: AUNT ADDIE'S ROOM. FISHER ENTERS.

FISHER: Miss Addie?

ADDIE [*hoarsely*]: I knew you'd come back, Fisher.

FISHER: I promised I would.

ADDIE: Lock the door. —Till you've fulfilled the promise completely. You know what I mean.

[*Fisher locks the door, then crosses to the mantel for the pillbox. She carries it to Addie's bed.*]

FISHER: All?

ADDIE: All.

[*Fisher empties the contents of the pillbox into Addie's mouth—draws a deep breath and presses the glass of water to it.*]

ADDIE: You are honest and brave. Put the box back where it was, and—collect your things.

[*Fisher picks up her leopard-skin coat and the other earring.*]

Now go quick—with God . . .

FISHER: —With Jimmy Dobyne.

ADDIE: Isn't he—?

FISHER: Yes. The same . . . to me . . .

57] CUT TO: CLOSE TWO-SHOT OF JIMMY AND
VINNIE EMBRACING IN THE DRIVE.
They draw quickly apart at the sound of Fisher's footsteps running on gravel.

VINNIE: Good-bye, Jimmy.

JIMMY [*in a choked voice*]: Good-bye—Vinnie.

FISHER [*appearing*]: Miss McCorkle, please tell Julie good night for us. Explain I had to rush away.

[*Slowly Jimmy opens the car door for Fisher.*]

58] CUT TO: CLOSE TWO-SHOT: FISHER AND JIMMY
IN THE CAR.
It turns out of the drive.

FISHER: Turn up the road to the levee.

JIMMY: Again?

FISHER: It's so lovely up there with the moon on the river.

[*He draws a deep breath, and exhales it, then slows the car at the road to the levee, and turns slowly up it.*]

JIMMY: Fisher, the moon is not on the river, the moon is in the sky—

FISHER: Which is reflected on the river.

[*They arrive at the height of the levee.*]

Turn out the lights so we can see it better.

[*With a set, determined face, she waits till he has turned the car lights out then moves close to him.*]

Jimmy, have you forgotten that I am the postman and have a letter for someone?

[*He is silent, staring straight ahead.*]

—The letter is for you.

JIMMY: Fisher, I think you could do better than me.

FISHER: —I don't agree, since it's only you that I want. I still hear that owl. It's such a wise bird, Jimmy, it gives such good advice.

[*Pause.*]

Jimmy, your mother could be removed from that dreadful place called the Drum to a nice private asylum. And your father, he could remain in charge of the commissary for as long as he lives, no matter how drunk.

[*The owl's hoot is distant, sad.*]

And as for me, well, no one will ever love me. But you could get used to me, Jimmy, and—may I deliver the letter to you now?

[*There is a slight pause. He turns his face towards hers. She catches her breath and presses her mouth to his with a longing almost ferocious.*

[*Music from the party is heard as the camera draws back and the scene dissolves.*]

THE END

ONE ARM

||||||||||||||||||||||||||||||||||||||||||||||||||||||||||||||||||||||||||||||||||||||||||||||||||||||||||||||||||||||||||||||||||||||||

PRINCIPAL CHARACTERS

(in order of appearance)

OLLIE, *a male hustler*

NARRATOR *(off-camera)*

SAM, *a hot tamale vendor*

WILLY, *another male hustler*

A MIDDLE-AGED HOMOSEXUAL

SAILORS

A STRIPPER

NURSE

THE YOUNG MAN IN THE PARK

THE YACHTSMAN

THE GIRL ON THE YACHT

ANOTHER MIDDLE-AGED HOMOSEXUAL

A QUEER

THE QUEER'S COMPANION

KEWPIE, *a young effeminate hustler*

A DRUNK

A GYPSY WOMAN

THE GIRL IN THE FRENCH QUARTER

MRS. WIRE, *the proprietress of a boarding house*

SEAN, *a young writer*

LESTER

THE GIRL ON THE STEAMER

CLAUDE, *a male masochist*

CHERRY, *an old queen*

THE SOLDIER ON THE BUS

DETECTIVES

THE QUESTIONER AT POLICE HEADQUARTERS

THE PRISON GUARD

THE PRISON CHAPLAIN

THE DIVINITY STUDENT

THE ANALYST

THE WARDEN

AUTHOR'S NOTE

Perhaps this film-play is in a somewhat experimental form, so much of the visual action being combined with spoken narration which is taken nearly exactly from the short story *One Arm*. I don't believe that the impact of the film will be at all lessened by this circumstance: I think, more probably, it will be increased. I have conceived of the film as a dark poem whose theme is the prevalence of mutilations among us all, and their possible transcendance.

A producer must offer me a choice of the few directors who would be right for this script. I don't think I'm mistaken in thinking that he should be an American. There is so much of (allegorical) American life in the script, whose story, basically, is not a limited one.

T.W.
c. 1972

ONE ARM

1] EXTERIOR. CLOSE-UP OF OLLIE. DAY.

Ollie, a male hustler, rather scantily dressed for winter, shivers on what seems to be an anonymous street corner.

NARRATOR [*voice-over*]: The young man on the corner, so young you could call him a boy, is an actor, of course, and in the part that he's going to perform, when the screenplay begins, he's supposed to have only one arm. He's supposed to have only one arm except in a few short scenes that will show how the arm was lost, in the time before he became a hustler. In the film you'll notice that one of his arms is never lifted, never used, that it always hangs motionless at his side. Think of it as an arm that doesn't exist.

2] EXTERIOR. STREET CORNER. DAY.

The camera view widens and it becomes clear that Ollie is standing on the corner of Canal Street in downtown New Orleans.

NARRATOR'S VOICE: Now the screenplay begins. . . .

OLLIE [*calling to someone in the street*]: Hey, Sam!

[*A hot tamale vendor enters the frame and rolls his steaming cart to the curb where Ollie stands.*]

Gimme half-a-dozen. Need something hot in my belly. Whoever said you don't freeze y'r balls off in this town never hit it in winter.

SAM: Whyn't you wear somethin' warmer?

WILLY'S VOICE [*off-screen, a bit "nelly"*]: Ollie's gotta show his merchandise.

OLLIE [*grinning bitterly toward the voice*]: Unpeel these fo' me, Willy.

[*Willy enters the frame. He is a comparatively ordinary hustler, somewhat on the "femme" side.*]

WILLY [*unpeeling a tamale*]: I seen a guy with no arms in a sideshow that could cut and butter a piece of toast with his toes.

OLLIE: I ain't in no sideshow. What the fuck you—?

[*Willy is eating the tamale himself.*]

WILLY: Took a percentage for labor.

[*He has unpeeled the second tamale; he tries to stick it in Ollie's mouth.*]

OLLIE [*abruptly savage*]: *Quit clowning!*

[*He seizes the tamale from Willy, wolfs it, then another; he grimaces.*]

This stuff's rat meat an' pepper but it warms your stomach. You can have the rest.

[*A sea gull's thin, anxious cry is heard. Ollie lifts his large, lost, pale blue eyes to watch its flight with envy.*

[*The camera closes on Ollie's lean, Gothic face.*]

Somebody tole me that if you stand in one place long enough near the sea or the Gulf— [*He grins slowly.*] —a sea gull will fly over and shit a pot of gold on you. [*He laughs harshly.*] Is that a fact or a fiction?

[*Willy laughs bleakly.*]

You scored yet today?

WILLY [*shaking his head*]: This is a bitch of a day.

OLLIE: 'Still too early for action. Work that other corner and tell your sister Kewpie to work on Bourbon, up, down, and sideways. She needs t' walk some of that baby fat off her ass an' git an ID card so she can operate in gay bars. If she could grow a little mustache or beard she'd pass for seventeen maybe. Does Kewpie shave yet?

WILLY: Once a month.

OLLIE: She might be a morphodite but she could attract older johns that dig chicken. She needs a faked ID card to get her in places like Mona's, some new clean threads, and you ought to separate when you're workin', you camp an' giggle together, come on like a pair of sisters.

WILLY: Voice of authority?

OLLIE: Voice of three years' experience, enough t' know.

WILLY: That Kewpie, shit. [*He grins.*] Father Rogers from Saint Jude just now talked a man out of jumpin' off a tenth floor windowledge at the Père Marquette building. The Father held up a cross an' shouted through a megaphone, "Christ loves you. Don't jump." An' that Kewpie, he hollers back, "Christ don't *know* you! Jump!" —Got kicked in the ass by a cop.

OLLIE: Guys that jump out windows mess up streets.

[*Willy grins widely at this.*]

You oughta see a dentist. That missing tooth makes you look morbid.

WILLY: You got to pay for a tooth that ain't your own. . . . I see an old john I blown for five bucks back of the Pirate's.

[*He crosses quickly out of the frame.*]

3] **CLOSE ON OLLIE'S FACE.**

OLLIE [*directly into camera*]: That's the name of the game.

4] **EXTERIOR. STREET CORNER. MEDIUM CLOSE SHOT. DAY.**
A middle-aged homosexual has stopped on the walk a few yards from Ollie and is pretending to be deeply concerned with the contents of a shop window.

NARRATOR [*voice-over*]: Ollie shows no sign of having noticed the unknown somebody he was waiting for on the corner. The somebody passes him again, for a closer inspection, or you might say appraisal. Still Ollie appears not to see him, you'd think he was looking at a sea gull in the sky.

[*There is a background of rock/soul music as the action is described by the narrator.*]

The middle-aged homosexual stops, now, closer to Ollie and looks in another shop window with blinded eyes. His appraisal of the boy has been more than satisfactory, it's overwhelming. But he's in town for business other than this dangerous business of cruising. He argues with himself. Maybe the boy is employed by the police to attract imprudent homos. The boy doesn't look it, though, no, and he has one arm missing. Yes, he's almost certainly a male prostitute, yes, but this nervous john is still waiting for the boy to give him a sign of interest.

Perhaps if he goes by the boy again, a little more slowly, the boy will give him the sign. All right, he'll pass him again, this time very slowly.

[*Now the title and credits are superimposed on the film as the middle-aged man passes Ollie repeatedly, stopping each time a little closer to him.*

[*When the credits of the film are finished, the man interested in the boy with one arm stops right beside him, but also appears to be looking at a sea gull in the sky.*]

Now Ollie gives him, at last, the sign that the cautious "john" was waiting for. Ollie still doesn't look at him but he jingles a bunch of keys and coins in his pocket. The middle-aged man with a hunger for boys is as reassured as he can be in a city, a world, so dangerous to the pursuit of his kind of pleasure, which is an ancient pleasure, but never out-of-date.

5] CLOSE TWO-SHOT: OLLIE AND ADMIRER.

MIDDLE-AGED MAN: If I'm not being too personal, you've got a wonderful build.

OLLIE [*with no perceptible reaction*]: Thanks.

MIDDLE-AGED MAN: Do you, uh, work out in a gym, or—

OLLIE: No, sir. [*Then, he continues with a quiet, sad pride.*] —I used to be light-heavyweight champion of the Pacific Fleet.

MIDDLE-AGED MAN: Before you—

OLLIE: Yes. Before I lost one arm.

NARRATOR [*voice-over*]: Of course the actor has not lost an arm. Its loss is represented only by the fact that he doesn't use it in the film.

6] DISSOLVE TO: BOXING ARENA.
Ollie's opponent is being counted out; there is a background of cheering and a blaze of light.

7] EXTERIOR. STREET. NIGHT.
Five or six sailors are in a convertible on a downtown street of some city that has a naval base, such as San Diego. The driver is parking the car.

OLLIE: Drinking and driving is a bad combination, y'know. Do one or the other, not both.

FIRST SAILOR: Some nights are a celebration.

OLLIE: I'll go in with you and have a Coke or Pepsi, but when we hit the road again, I'll drive, it's me that'll drive this wagon.

[*The car is parked and they are already entering a strip-joint that says in diamond-white bulbs ALL NITE and GLORY BLAZE.*]

8] INTERIOR. STRIP-JOINT. NIGHT.
The group of sailors is at the bar. A stripper is on the runway, tiredly but shrilly performing to brassy music.

STRIPPER: Slam, bam, alla kazam, out of an orange-colored sky!

9] EXTERIOR. SIDEWALK. NIGHT.
The sailors are returning to the car.

SAILOR: Some Glory Blaze! Older'n my mother.

ANOTHER SAILOR: A pig.

OLLIE: Slam, bam, alla kazam, out of an orange-colored sky!

ANOTHER SAILOR: All night! Imagine all night.

[*He starts to get behind the wheel.*]

OLLIE: Didn't you hear me say I drive if you drink?

ANOTHER SAILOR: Shit, come off it, git in.

OLLIE: I'll drive this heap or go back to the base in a cab. [*He speaks vehemently, above the riotous laughter and singing of his companions.*] You guys don't value your lives? I value *mine*! I got one hell of a good life to live and I value it too much to put it in the hands of a drunk at a car wheel!

SAILOR: Okay, Eagle Scout, catch a cab!

[*Ollie vaults the side of the car and starts shouting, "Cab, cab!"*]

ANOTHER SAILOR: Ollie thinks he's ape-shit t'night, let him go!

SAILOR: Where's your cab, Ollie?

[*No cabs. Glowering, Ollie vaults back into the backseat of the car. The altercation has not been too serious and in a moment the sailors are all singing a reprise of "Slam, bam, alla kazam, out of an orange-colored sky."*]

10] DISSOLVE TO: EXTERIOR. HIGHWAY. NIGHT.
The car, driven at high speed, is approaching an underpass. All the boys are singing, "Slam, bam, alla kazam, out of an orange-colored sky!"

The car screeches and disappears in front of a truck. A few seconds later there is a violent crash in the underpass.

11] **EXTERIOR. HOSPITAL ENTRANCE. MEDIUM CLOSE SHOT.**
The camera pans onto the sign "HOTEL DIEU."

NARRATOR [*voice-over*]: The hospital is called God's Hotel in French—a language that Ollie doesn't know.

12] **INTERIOR. HOSPITAL SOLARIUM. ROOFTOP. NOON.**
Ollie is seated on this rooftop with a number of more or less spectral-looking patients. He is in a wheelchair. All the blaze of light that characterized his young face before the accident has disappeared from it now. He has a slight growth of blond beard; his stare, straight up at the noonday sun, has the fixity of a catatonic's. A nurse enters the frame and approaches him; she is baffled but sympathetic, more than professionally.

NURSE: Ollie, do you want to get sun wrinkles at your age?

[*There is no response.*]

We have sunglasses. Would you like a pair?

OLLIE [*without inflection*]: No, thanks—Miss . . .

NURSE: You know, that wheelchair isn't necessary, Ollie. —If you have trouble with balance, you should use the crutch for a while.

OLLIE: Don't want a crutch at my age neither.

NURSE: A wheelchair is worse, it suggests—

OLLIE: Both of 'em suggest a cripple.

NURSE: Ollie, you're being too bitter about that—accident, that—loss; you're not being grown-up about it. Think ahead of it. You'll adjust to it, Ollie, someday you'll even—accept it so much you'll ignore it . . .

OLLIE: Adjusting, accepting, ignoring, you mean throwing in the towel. —I asked somebody what's the name of this hospital and they said it was Hotel Di-err. They said that was French for God's Hotel. I never known he was in the hotel business.

NURSE: Ollie, not so loud. A lot of the patients out here are terminal cases.

OLLIE: I noticed they don't look good. Well. When I leave God's Hotel, it ain't gonna be in a wheelchair or on a crutch. I'm gonna walk out balanced on my feet, that's how. Wheelchair, fuck it—excuse me. . . . You know why they want me in it? So they can roll me anywhere they want me when they want to.

NURSE: "They, they," who are "they"? Ollie, we're just nurses and orderlies and we entered the profession, most of us, because of wanting to offer assistance to—

OLLIE [*cutting in sharply*]: How many floors up is this roof?

NURSE: —Why—thirteen.

OLLIE: But you all don't call it thirteen, you call it 12A.

NURSE: —Some people, especially old people, are superstitious.

OLLIE: Fuck superstition—excuse me.

NURSE [*abandoning her effort to reach him*]: The orderly Jimmy says you refuse to let him shave you, and, Ollie, he says you're going to stay in your room till you're shaved.

OLLIE: I don't give a shit where I stay. I was wheeled out here, I didn't ask to come out here or nowhere, and put this on your chart, too. That goddam orderly that bathes me, that Jimmy, he tries to play with my—

NURSE: Please, Ollie, keep your voice down.

[*Ollie shrugs and stares speechless into the sun's glare.*]

You want to be wheeled back into your room?

[*Ollie shakes his head slightly.*]

We know the strain you're under, how hard it is to accept the loss of an arm.

OLLIE [*tonelessly*]: Do you?

[*She draws up a chair beside him and touches his shoulder.*]

I don't want nothing.

NURSE: Don't want recovery of interest in—?

OLLIE: Boxing? —Life?

NURSE: Of course boxing isn't life for you, now, Ollie. You've got to face that loss. Everyone out here is adjusting to losses, some of them worse than yours. I could point out to you old and hopeless cases that are adjusting to their condition bravely, cooperating, you're not.

OLLIE: Thanks for the professional sympathy.

NURSE: It's—personal.

OLLIE: I'll cooperate better, I'm just planning how.

NURSE: I hear the lunch trays. I'll wheel you back.

OLLIE: Thanks but I ain't hungry.

NURSE: You want a little more sun?

[*Ollie nods. The nurse crosses out of the frame. Ollie pushes his chair slowly forward; it approaches the edge of the roof. Then, with a rapid, unsteady lunge, he springs from the chair and clambers onto the low ledge. People cry out. Before he can leap, arms draw him back. He crumples onto the floor of the rooftop solarium. A shrill bell is ringing. Two orderlies force him, struggling, cursing, back into the corridor.*]

13] EXTERIOR. PARK. NIGHT.

Out of swirling mist, Ollie becomes visible. He is seated on a bench in Pershing Square, Los Angeles, and is eating a hot dog that's dripping with chili. Just behind the bench stands a youngish man with an apparitional quality: hair dyed flaxen, pale eyes outlined with eye pencil, lips unnaturally distinct. After a moment or two, he moves around to the front of the bench and speaks to Ollie.

YOUNG MAN: I haven't seen you in the park before.

OLLIE: That might be because I ain't been in it before.

YOUNG MAN: Mind if I sit down?

OLLIE: You're already sitting.

YOUNG MAN: I hope you don't object.

[*He has seated himself very close to Ollie, who slides a foot or two away. Ollie devours the last bit of the dripping hot dog and licks the fingers of his one hand, an animal gesture that's natural.*]

YOUNG MAN: Handkerchief?

OLLIE: No, thanks.

[*The young man startles Ollie by applying the handkerchief to Ollie's chin.*]

What're you—?

YOUNG MAN: You spilt some of the chili on your chin, which, incidentally, needs shaving. A boy with your looks shouldn't neglect them, you know. I'll tell you something else. You ought to be having sirloin steak for dinner instead of a greasy hot dog. I have a feeling that you don't know the score. I don't think you're even aware that four johns in this park are watching you like bird dogs watching a game bird. [*His speech is rapid.*] That one, that one, that one, and that one.

OLLIE: Why?

YOUNG MAN: Your innocence would be incredible in anyone but you. Those johns are hungry, they're ravenous for you. Let's break their hearts by walking around the fountain together, huh?

[*The apparitional young man rises from the bench.*]

OLLIE: G'night.

[*He starts away.*]

YOUNG MAN: Not that direction. The other. I want to treat you to a thick malt, and give you a quick education in the mysteries of the park . . .

[*The swirling mist begins to dim them out.*]

Come on. It won't take long.

[*Ollie hesitates a moment more. Then he accepts the indicated direction.*

[*The scene dissolves in mist.*]

14] INTERIOR. BAR. NIGHT.
The camera lens clears. We see the interior of a bar that attracts various offbeat characters—hippies, a few hustlers and "johns," some gray-faced lushes and addicts.

The camera faces the entrance. Ollie enters. Now his face is smoothly shaven. He wears a skivvy shirt and dungarees, a costume that holds as closely to his body as the clothes of antique sculpture.

He slides onto a barstool.

BARTENDER: What's yours, Ollie?

OLLIE: Bourbon an' Coke. Open a fresh Coke for me. I don't like one that's dead. I like a Coke to spit at me. Fzzzz, fzzzz!

[*A man effetely dressed for yachting emerges from one of the booths along the opposite wall and sits on the stool next to Ollie's. (Since the style of the filmplay is not realistic, shouldn't there be a momentary hush in the bar as the yachtsman emerges from his booth and crosses to the stool beside*

211

Ollie? It would suggest a significance—ominous—in the encounter.)

[*The camera closes on the man and Ollie.*]

MAN: Young man, you have a wonderful voice.

[*His face turned abruptly "cagey," Ollie glances at the man.*]

MAN: How'd you like to make two hundred dollars?

OLLIE: —Well, I'd be int'rested in knowing how to make it.

MAN: Something very simple.

OLLIE: Simple like what?

MAN: Appearing in a short movie I'm making on my yacht.

OLLIE: I'm not an actor.

MAN: Doesn't matter. All you have to do is—

[*The voice fades out.*]

15] INTERIOR. YACHT. CLOSE-TWO SHOT: OLLIE
AND A GIRL. NIGHT.
*Cabin of a large and luxurious yacht, perhaps in Venice or
Balboa, California. Ollie and the girl are both in men's dress-
ing robes.*

VOICE OF THE YACHTSMAN: You get the idea now?

OLLIE: Yeah, I get the idea, but do you? Can't you see I only
got one arm?

VOICE OF THE YACHTSMAN: That doesn't matter. You have all the qualifications necessary.

[*Several people are heard laughing.*]

OLLIE [*with fury*]: I get it. I understand it. The fact that I have one arm is the reason you wanted me for this freak show. You wanted a man that was *mutilated!* That was the qualification that you wanted. A beautiful girl doing things to a mutilated man, a man with one arm and the other a stump, a flipper. What you want is this girl's humiliation. Shove it. I want out of this job. I want your launch to put me back on shore. Now! Meaning now!

VOICE OF THE YACHTSMAN: You don't have to do anything. She does it all. You just lie still and twist and moan a little. Can't you do that? Lie still and twist and moan like you were out of your skull? For two hundred each?

[*The girl helps Ollie reluctantly remove his robe. She removes her own.*]

OLLIE: You didn' hear what I said? You thought I wasn't serious about it?

[*The girl tries to encourage Ollie.*]

VOICE OF THE YACHTSMAN: Lie there like that. The camera is rolling. Lila, start with his toes.

16] INTERIOR. YACHT CABIN. NIGHT.
Ollie suddenly springs from the cot, kicks the camera over, and tears down lights.

OLLIE: Now is it still rolling, is it still rolling now?

[*A silk robe is tossed at him.*]

VOICE OF THE YACHTSMAN: Go up on deck and think it over, while we set the lights up again. [*Then he speaks to the girl.*] Go up on deck with him, honey. Explain how simple it is.

17] EXTERIOR. DECK OF THE YACHT. NIGHT.

GIRL: Honey, you shouldn't have done that. It could have cost us two hundred dollars each.

[*There is a background of guitar music.*]

OLLIE: When he told you to—

GIRL: I know, but, honey, it didn't matter to me.

OLLIE: I used to respect myself. Didn't you? Didn't you, ever?

GIRL: Never much.

OLLIE: I respected myself until I lost one arm.

GIRL: Let's not talk about self-respect, or losing it, or how.

OLLIE: It's something important. It's important to have it and a sick thing to lose it.

GIRL: Would it make it easier for you if we—

[*She kisses him lingeringly.*]

OLLIE: They want to put us both down.

GIRL: I don't think of it that way.

214

OLLIE: Then what way do you think of it?

GIRL: A way to make two hundred dollars.

OLLIE: Even with one arm I could drive his launch back to shore. Let's get the hell off this yacht, and out of this dirty business.

GIRL: Ollie? I need the two hundred dollars.

OLLIE: I'm scared to stay here.

GIRL: Scared of what?

OLLIE: I'm scared that I might kill him. I could with just one arm and I might do it.

GIRL: You know what you ought to do, baby? Don't think of it as anything but a job, a night job that you can forget in the morning.

OLLIE: Can't we still have a little self-respect? Just a little?

GIRL [*slipping a hand inside his robe*]: Self-respect can be put away for a while.

OLLIE: I never thought the lights on a shore could semaphore to you: "Come back, hurry, quick, before you—"

GIRL: Ollie, go through it for me and two hundred dollars and then we'll go back to the shore.

OLLIE: You don't feel disgust?

GIRL: With you, no, I feel pleasure, which is a rare thing for me.

215

OLLIE: I hate hearing him tell you to do unnatural things to me like he tells you in his oily voice with his fat wet-mouth grin.

GIRL: Two hundred dollars is two hundred dollars and I need it bad.

OLLIE: What are we?

GIRL: —Don't think about it. It's me that does it to you. I like doing it, so you don't have to think.

OLLIE: Maybe not think, but feel.

GIRL: Just think of it as a thing that you can wash off your memory in the morning and that pays you two hundred dollars that maybe you can use as much as I can, which is a hell of a lot.

OLLIE: I can't wash things off my memory that easy.

GIRL: Come on. Please. For me. Let's get it over with. Quick!

[*He finally shrugs and follows the girl back down to the cabin.*]

18] **INTERIOR. CABIN. CLOSE-UP OF OLLIE. NIGHT.**
We hear the sound of the motor launch departing from the yacht. Ollie listens, apprehensively.

19] **CLOSE-UP OF THE YACHTSMAN.**
He looks sickeningly corrupt.

YACHTSMAN: The launch will come back for you later. You have the privilege of getting to know me better.

OLLIE: I think I could live without that. When do I get paid?

YACHTSMAN: Don't sweat it, baby. What's your drink?

20] INTERIOR. CABIN. NIGHT.
The cabin seems to be whirling in mist. Then Ollie is seen standing over the yachtsman's lifeless body. He drops the copper bookend he is holding, and slowly, dazedly, stoops over the dead body and takes money from the wallet. Then he leaves the cabin.

21] EXTERIOR. DECK OF THE YACHT. NIGHT.
Ollie appears on deck, looks around in the heavy fog, then plunges into the sea.

22] EXTERIOR. THE SEA. NIGHT. HEAVY FOG.
The camera is very close on Ollie as he struggles to swim a sidestroke.

NARRATOR: He swam to shore, collected his things and disappeared from the city.

[*Ollie reaches the shore and lies exhausted on the sand.*]

23] EXTERIOR. STREET CORNER. DAY. RAIN.
The rainy New Orleans street corner, as in the opening scene, with Ollie standing on it quite impervious to the weather. Again a middle-aged man strolls back and forth past him, then stops.

MAN: Aren't you afraid of catching cold, young fellow?

OLLIE: No. I never catch cold.

MAN: But you feel cold, don't you?

OLLIE: Yes, I feel cold. I'm not unconscious.

MAN: You ought to go in somewhere and get warmed up.

OLLIE: Such as where, for instance?

MAN: I have a nice apartment, and a good supply of liquor.

OLLIE: Which way?

MAN: A few blocks, in the Quarter. We'll take a cab.

OLLIE: —Let's walk and you give me the cab fare.

24] DISSOLVE TO: EXTERIOR. STREET. DUSK.
Another queer is admitting Ollie to his premises. The queer is almost breathlessly aesthetic. They are just on the street side of a wooden gate which the queer is unlocking.

QUEER: When you pass through this gate you enter another world.

OLLIE: Hah, I've gotten used to that.

QUEER: Now. Enter my garden.

25] EXTERIOR. GARDEN. WIDE SHOT OF A FAC-
SIMILE OF A JAPANESE GARDEN. DUSK.

OLLIE: Aw. Everything's Chinese.

QUEER: No, no. Japanese. I'll light it for you.

[*Lanterns are lit in the garden. We return to a medium two-shot as the queer and Ollie enter this fantasy.*]

QUEER: The pool is lovely, don't you think?

OLLIE: I've never seen nothing like it.

QUEER: The bottom of it is all mother-of-pearl—the inside of shells. —The pool, it's heated, is full of tropical fish.

OLLIE: It's something else, like they say.

QUEER: You wouldn't expect to find a garden like this in the city, would you?

OLLIE: All of you queers—excuse me, I mean gay guys—are artistic in some way. Work in antique shops and things like that. But this is something else. —Hello, fish. How's tricks?

QUEER: Now walk over the bridge to the house.

[*Ollie complies with this suggestion, but at the center of the little bridge, it collapses. The queer utters a stricken cry.*]

OLLIE [*wading across the pond*]: That bridge was too flimsy for me.

QUEER [*recovering*]: I'll repair it this weekend. I have some friends that will help me.

OLLIE: I'm wet up to my knees.

QUEER [*skirting the pond*]: I'll give you a silk robe in the house.

OLLIE: Uhh.

26] INTERIOR. THE JAPANESE HOUSE. NIGHT.

QUEER: Every morning, before I go to work, I make a new flower arrangement for this table.

OLLIE: You do what?

QUEER: Arrange fresh flowers to put in the lovely blue, Japanese vase.

OLLIE: Everybody has to do something besides his regular work.

QUEER: What do you do besides your regular work?

OLLIE: I guess I've got no regular work, unless hustling is regular work. I think it's irregular work. Oh, I keep busy at it but it's not a thing that you could call regular work. It's too irregular from a society point of view to be called regular. It's an illegal, outlaw occupation, so I got to be well-paid for it. You can understand that. I used to think nobody would want a hustler with one arm. But I was wrong. It don't throw them off me. [*Then, bitterly.*] A mutilation attracts them.

QUEER: You've got a beautiful face and such a fine body.

OLLIE: A body mutilated.

QUEER: Why don't you forget about that?

OLLIE: Have you ever tried forgetting about a thing like that when you'd wanted to be a athlete?

QUEER: No, well, of course, I never was an athlete.

OLLIE: I didn't think you was.

QUEER: I think you should have a drink.

OLLIE: I like to keep pretty sober when I'm working.

QUEER: I wish you wouldn't think you were working now.

OLLIE: Yeah, but I'm going to work, now, and I think we ought to discuss how much you pay me for it.

QUEER: When a young man leaves, I put a bill in his pocket, so there's no need of discussion.

OLLIE: I'd like to know the amount, the size of the bill.

QUEER: I spend so much on my place.

OLLIE: I reckon you do, but that means nothing to me.

QUEER: The collapse of the bridge over my pond is going to set me back a pretty penny.

OLLIE: I didn't collapse it on purpose. You said walk over the bridge.

QUEER: I'm not arguing that, but—

OLLIE: There's nothing to argue about. I got a certain price and it don't change if a Japanese bridge collapses and I fall in a pond. You see, hustlers are not unionized. Each of 'em has his own price and if he don't stick to it, he's screwin' himself. Can he go to collect unemployment when he's not approached on his corner or in his—whatever's his hangout? Can he say to an unemployment clerk, I'm a hustler that johns pass by? Figure the answer to that in Japanese. No. I have a price and stick to it. And I want to know in advance if I'm gonna get it or not.

QUEER: —Five?

OLLIE: Maybe five years from now, but now I don't accept nothing less than twenty.

QUEER: Did you say plenty?

OLLIE: Is your bad hearing on purpose or is it a real affliction?

QUEER: You said—?

OLLIE: I said *twenty*.

27] INTERIOR. JAPANESE HOUSE. NIGHT.
*The house-companion of the queer bustles in, a fussy man
about fifty.*

COMPANION: The bridge is broken!

QUEER: This young man walked across it and it collapsed.

OLLIE: I've heard enough about the Japanese bridge collapsing.
My pants are dry now, and I'm going.

QUEER: Oh but—

COMPANION: Who is this very attractive young man?

QUEER: Isn't he? Yes! We met each other downtown.

OLLIE: I'm heading back there now.

QUEER: Oh, no, no!

OLLIE: Yes, yes. I want to stop by the White Castle and get a
hot cup of coffee and a bowl of chili.

QUEER: It would take me no time to make you coffee and
scramble you some eggs.

OLLIE: I have to get back to work.

COMPANION: Little disappointments happen in life.

OLLIE: Where's the front door, for instance?

QUEER: I won't hear of you going!

OLLIE: You do seem to have ear trouble. [*He turns to the companion.*] I want out some way.

QUEER: Stay! Please! Your price!

OLLIE [*to the companion*]: Front door?

COMPANION: Yes, I'll let you out it.

[*He conducts Ollie from the room. A door is heard closing. He returns to his stricken companion.*]

QUEER: Your sarcasm drove him away! You love this to happen to me.

[*The companion crosses to a shelf of phonograph records.*]

QUEER: After twenty-five years you still resent it when I bring home a boy.

[*The companion puts a record on the phonograph. It is* Un bel di—*loudly vocal.*]

QUEER: You'll have to prepare dinner for yourself this evening. I am going to bed and I am going to lock my door.

28] DISSOLVE TO: INTERIOR. TABLE IN A "NEVER CLOSED" CAFETERIA. NIGHT.

OLLIE [*to Willy and Kewpie*]: You complain all the time, you kids, about how you don't make enough to suit you. I can tell you why. If you want to know. You're too anxious, too active, you're like a couple of sparrows on the street. Look. I been hustling three years and maybe I can give you some advice. You notice a john look at you. Don't look back. Look somewhere else. Anywhere else. A sea gull. A store window. Or nothing. Most important, more important than that, don't change your position, don't move. You kids chase after a john. Follow him. Wrong. Let him come up to you and if he wants you, he will. Stand there, just stand there, that's all, till he comes up besides you. Then if you got some keys in a pocket, jiggle the keys a little.

WILLY: I got no keys to nothing.

OLLIE: For this purpose, they don't have to be keys to anything. They don't even have to be keys; you can go out to the lake an' scoop up a handful of pebbles to jiggle in your pocket. And listen, listen to your johns. They're well-educated, most of 'em. Improve your vocabulary. I bet you don't even know what vocabulary means. What's it mean, the word vocabulary?

WILLY: They want to get your ass in a hotel room and soon as they've had you, they want you out, faster'n they wanted you in.

OLLIE: Possibly in some cases. But like I said—if you listen to them and improve your vocabulary, the price of your ass'll go up. Of course you shouldn't hustle your ass but you do, you're what they call "gay trade." I'm not an' never will be. If they try to get in me, I dress an' walk out. Politely.

KEWPIE: She likes to be—

OLLIE: Don't say "she." Say "she" and you turn to "she." It shows in your face an' you walk with a wiggle.

WILLY: Ain't that what they—

OLLIE: No, that ain't what they're after.

KEWPIE: They're after a one-arm hustler, is that it?

[*Ollie pushes his chair over and Kewpie sprawls to the floor.*]

OLLIE: Sorry, beg your pardon, I was reachin' for the ketchup.

[*Ollie rises from the table.*]

There's a short limit on our time, yours, mine, Kewpie's, and it's a hell of a lonely business if you operate right. You choose your corner and stand on it alone. Kewpie, you keep scratchin' like you had crabs. Get a bottle of Kuprex and rub it all over. Take care of your merchandise or you'll get no buyers. Drop in the free clinic once a week to see if you've picked up the clap, front or back. Don't kid yourself it's a non-specific infection. You got a room for the night?

KEWPIE: No, I ain't.

[*Ollie hands him some bills.*]

OLLIE: Get one. And the Kuprex. The wind out there is blowin' garbage pails over. Sounds like someone had dug up some ole graveyard. Ha!

[*He picks up the check on the table. The camera follows him out of the cafeteria.*]

29] EXTERIOR. SIDEWALK. NIGHT.

Ollie is lighting a cigarette under the cafeteria sign which alternates between ALL NITE and ALL RITE. An overturned garbage can is blown to his feet.

OLLIE: Hello, buddy-oh.

[*He kicks the pail before him a few paces down the walk. A girl on the opposite sidewalk shrieks as her hat is blown off. Her escort starts to chase it. Ollie chases it faster and returns it to the girl. Ollie continues down the street. Jazz piano music drifts out from a bar. Then from another bar, a Negro is heard singing blues. Ollie grins. A newspaper is windblown off the street and for a moment it covers Ollie's face. He tears it off. He reaches a narrow building with mysteriously emblematic signs on its window. A drunk collides with him and inquires thickly—*]

DRUNK: Where's Salvation Army?

OLLIE: Never made that scene. You're walking but you can't talk. Check in at the Silver Screen before you're hauled into the house of detention.

DRUNK: —Silver?

OLLIE: Screen, next turn to the left.

[*He gives the drunk a dollar.*]

Stay off bright streets my advice.

[*The drunk stumbles off.*]

OLLIE [*continuing, loudly, like a circus barker*]: FREE ADVICE TO EVERYBODY TONIGHT.

[*A gypsy woman appears in the door of the building.*]

GYPSY: Boy! Boy!

OLLIE [*turning*]: Huh?

GYPSY: I tell your fortune. Come in.

OLLIE: How much?

GYPSY: Whatever you want to give me?

OLLIE: When you hear that, you know it'll be expensive.

30] INTERIOR. GYPSY PARLOR. NIGHT.
In the garishly bizarre room, Ollie sits across a small table opposite the gypsy. The gypsy reads his palm or a crystal ball.

GYPSY: You sell something.

OLLIE: That's right.

GYPSY: It isn't a thing, that you sell.

OLLIE: Yes, it's a thing, that's broken.

GYPSY: What you sell is yourself.

[*Pause.*]

OLLIE: Broken.

GYPSY: Yes, broken, but still wanted by many.

OLLIE: I'm doing okay for awhile.

GYPSY: I see a shadow behind you.

OLLIE: A natural place for a shadow to be.

GYPSY: Be serious, please.

OLLIE: Okay, mama. Don't you see a shadow in front of me, too?

GYPSY: You live between two shadows.

OLLIE: The one in front of me, when do you see it coming?

GYPSY: This shadow in front of you is not in front of you far.

OLLIE: I been expecting it and I don't understand the delay.

GYPSY: It's almost like you wanted it to come.

OLLIE: I'm tired of waiting.

GYPSY: You don't have long to wait. Maybe a month, maybe a week, maybe only a day. This shadow in front of you is closely connected with the shadow behind you. The shadow behind you is dark as a crime.

OLLIE: You're pretty good.

GYPSY: The shadow in front of you is payment for the shadow behind you. You stay in crowded places. That's a mistake. You should not be exposed. To crowds.

OLLIE: In my business, my line, I got to be exposed in crowded places.

GYPSY: Give me something personal on you, like a ring or a watch.

OLLIE: What for?

GYPSY: To hold and feel and know you.

OLLIE [*laughing a little*]: There's nothing personal on me but four five-dollar bills and keys and coins.

GYPSY: Two five-dollar bills will be okay.

OLLIE: One five-dollar bill is personal as two.

[*He hands her a bill.*]

GYPSY: The shadow in front of you, I will tell you how to avoid it. Don't follow your plan to go to a city that's north. Go south till you're out of the country. Now, you disappear now. Walk home on a dark street, and if you have a suitcase, pack it quick. The shadow before you is close unless you do what I tell you.

[*She rises from the table and holds out her hand.*]

GYPSY: Give me now whatever you want to give me.

OLLIE: I given you five and I'll give you another five if you'll tell me one thing more.

GYPSY: What is this thing more?

OLLIE: The shadow in front of me, why don't I run away from it?

GYPSY: The other five, please, and I tell.

[*He hands it to her.*]

You despise yourself and you are more like the shadow of a man than like a man, and for another five I will answer another question. A man has many questions.

[*He shakes his head. There are tears in his eyes. Ollie is leaving the gypsy.*]

It is no good, no use, to say to you "Good Luck."

[*Ollie exits.*]

31] EXTERIOR. THE FRENCH QUARTER. NIGHT.
Ollie and a thin, nervously chattering girl in her late twenties enter a courtyard by a narrow, wooden, gatelike door. It has just stopped raining: the girl juggles a wet umbrella as she fumbles for her keys; Ollie's thin clothes are soaked.

GIRL [*unlocking the gate*]: There, now! The key was the last thing I could locate in my bag! Watch your step on these bricks, they're the original bricks of the patio—which is called the slave quarters, you know.

OLLIE: Slaves used to live back here?

GIRL: Yes, there were slaves in all these old houses in the *Vieux Carré* which is also called the French Quarter, you know.

OLLIE: Yeah, I know about that. It's quiet here, not a sound.

GIRL: Now I have to locate another key, and I hope I'll be luckier this time.

OLLIE: Want me to do it for you since you've got shaky fingers?

GIRL: Found! Found!

OLLIE: GOOD.

GIRL: When I was looking for a little apartment in the Quarter, there were two vacancies here. One was very inexpensive in spite of having much better facilities, even a rotisserie in it for cooking at home, but the other apartment we'll soon be in— I really couldn't afford it—I chose it for a particular reason you'll see in just a moment.

[*She gets the door open.*]

GIRL: There, now! Who enters first?

OLLIE: You better, I don't know the place.

GIRL: You go in first. I want to see if you see the particular reason I took it.

OLLIE [*entering*]: Okay, I'll go in first.

32] INTERIOR. APARTMENT. NIGHT.
Ollie strikes a match.

GIRL: No, no, no, no match!

OLLIE: I think you took it because of the skylight.

GIRL: That's the reason, exactly. —Shall I turn on a lamp or is the skylight enough?

OLLIE: Enough for me.

GIRL: Enough for me, too. There aren't any chairs in the room, not a single chair, so you have to choose between the

floor and the bed under the skylight. But the first thing I want
you to do, if you'll oblige me, is get out of those wet things and
rub yourself dry with a towel. Do you want to undress in the
room or in the bathroom? No, no, do it in here, and then, after
that lie down on the bed under the skylight and look up at
those low clouds running over like a parade of enormous roses.
They're lighted by the neon signs downtown. But I'd rather
think that they had the light from inside them. Get out of your
almost no clothes and I'll rub you dry with the towel.

OLLIE: I can do it myself, even with one arm.

GIRL: I know you could, but don't deprive me of—the enjoyment, please.

OLLIE: What?

[*They turn to shadow figures.*]

GIRL: The enjoyment, please. I'm a trained nurse so you
mustn't feel any embarrassment with me.

OLLIE: I don't feel any. There aren't many things I feel. As a
trained nurse, could you explain that to me?

GIRL: Lie down under the skylight and I'll try to explain it to
you. I think it has something to do with—before you lost one
arm did you feel things more?

[*Ollie speaks an indistinct syllable.*]

GIRL: Did you say yes or no?

OLLIE: Yes. Naturally.

GIRL: How recently did you lose it?

232

OLLIE: Three years ago. I was an athlete then.

GIRL: And since that time you've felt—

OLLIE: Less and less and less all the time.

GIRL: You feel less because you feel that you're mutilated. What you should feel is the truth. The loss of one arm makes you look like a—piece of antique sculpture.

OLLIE: Is that good?

GIRL: It makes you—more attractive.

OLLIE: Some people are maybe attracted by mutilation but the person that has the mutilation, he isn't attracted by it, and that's for sure. Sometimes it—in my own case, it fouled up my life. I live a fouled-up life and I'm disgusted with it.

GIRL: —What do you do?

OLLIE: —I—live.

GIRL: I mean what for a living.

[*Pause.*]

OLLIE: That corner where we met, I stand on that corner from ten in the morning till midnight.

GIRL: Doing what?

OLLIE: All right. Waiting to be picked up.

[*Pause.*]

233

Well?

GIRL [*rising from the bed*]: You have a place to stay, somewhere to go to?

OLLIE: Yes. I have a room.

GIRL [*coldly*]: It's three a.m. and I go on duty at the hospital at seven a.m. I ought to sleep now instead of shacking up with a male prostitute.

OLLIE: You mean you want me to go.

GIRL: I'm afraid that's just what I mean.

OLLIE: —I'll go. I'll go right away . . .

33] DISSOLVE TO: EXTERIOR. ROOMING HOUSE. NIGHT.
The camera approaches the entrance to a French Quarter rooming house through mist faintly permeated by the light of a street lamp halfway down the block. The tall double doors are scarred as if by many battles. The paint is peeling. On one of them is carved crookedly the word "Bitch."

The camera closes on this inscription, hesitates momentarily, and then is inside the tenebrous hallway.

34] INTERIOR. ROOMING HOUSE. NIGHT.
The camera, with some caution, approaches a cot beside the staircase. On it, beneath a wrinkled blanket, rests the proprietress of this low-grade establishment, a creature whom we will call Wire—for the benefit of the typed pages of this scene. She is muttering in her always fitful sleep. The camera is able to exhibit her because a dim, naked light bulb is suspended several feet behind the landlady's cot. In the scene it

will be explained that Wire sleeps by the staircase so that no tenant will enter or leave without her grim awareness.

The camera lingers only a moment on Wire, long enough for her to writhe on the cot and mutter "deadbeats."

35] INTERIOR. ROOMING HOUSE. A BEDROOM. NIGHT.

A wide shot of a bedroom of the rooming house. At a wobbly table is seated a young (about twenty-five) writer, Sean. He is working but the wobbling of the table distracts him. He gets up, furiously, and stuffs a matchbook under a leg of the table, then he resumes work. But the wobbling is worse than ever. As he rises again, a shower of small coins strikes the glass panes of the double doors to the balcony.

The camera narrows on Sean as he crosses—pacified—to the balcony doors and opens them.

36] EXTERIOR. BALCONY. NIGHT.

A medium close shot of Sean on the grilled balcony. He is enveloped in the mist of the night.

We hear a soft whistle. Then, from Sean's POV, the camera peers down at Ollie on the walk below. Ollie smiles up at his friend gravely.

Sean nods and returns quickly to the bedroom.

37] INTERIOR. ROOMING HOUSE. NIGHT.

Barefooted, Sean is stealing down the creaky stairs. Wire mutters loudly in her sleep. Sean freezes on the stairs till the muttering turns back to snoring. Then he runs down the stairs to the bolted entrance. As he draws the bolts open, a loud muttering from Wire.

38] EXTERIOR. ROOMING HOUSE. NIGHT.
Framed by the Gothic entrance, stands Ollie.

OLLIE [*in a whisper*]: I come to say good-bye.

SEAN [*in a whisper*]: —Come in with your shoes off.

[*Ollie nods and removes his shoes.*]

39] INTERIOR. ROOMING HOUSE. NIGHT.
*The two young men are stealing upstairs over the coiled,
muttering figure of Wire.*

WIRE: Can't run a clean house in the Quarter. Bunch a crack-
pots and deadbeats— [*She snores.*] —degenerates . . .

40] CUT TO: INTERIOR. SEAN'S BEDROOM. NIGHT.
*There is a wide shot of Sean's bedroom as he enters with
Ollie. The shot is a little cloudy as if the night mist had en-
tered the room.*

SEAN: That witch of a landlady, she sleeps on a cot in the hall
so no one can come or go without her knowing it.

OLLIE: I wouldn't have come this late if I wasn't leavin' town
so early.

SEAN: —You're leaving New Orleans?

OLLIE: Yep. At seven a.m. I made my bus fare t'night.

[*There should be no suggestion of homosexuality in this scene
between the two young men. It should contain, though, an
intense, shy feeling of comradeship.*]

SEAN: —I'll—

OLLIE: Huh?

SEAN: Miss you, Ollie.

[*They smile at each other sadly and shyly.*]

SEAN: —Well, sit down. I'm sorry I've got no liquor.

OLLIE: I don't need no drink. [*He sits in the other straight chair.*] —Were you writing?

SEAN: I was trying to write with a pencil. You know, when I work with my typewriter, it makes so much racket that I don't notice the creaking of the table. I think one leg of this goddam table is shorter than the others but I couldn't discover which leg it was, and—I was relieved when you interrupted the—

[*Ollie rises quickly. He snatches the matchbook from under one leg of the table and inserts it beneath another.*]

OLLIE: There, now.—Where's your typewriter?

SEAN: —On vacation.

OLLIE: You mean in a Rampart Street hock shop. What did you get for it? Ten bucks?

SEAN: Five. He said it had deteriorated in value. From use and abuse.

OLLIE: Fuggin' sharks.

[*He digs a roll of money from his pocket, peels off a ten spot and puts it on the table.*]

Write up my life story.

SEAN: You can't write up a life story till the subject is dead.

OLLIE: I been dead three years.

SEAN: You can't afford to—

OLLIE: If I couldn't afford to, I wouldn't. I—made fifty bucks t'night from a single john. Jesus. I never known a morphodite with a perversion like he had.

SEAN: Oh?

OLLIE: He ast me to—

[*Pause.*]

SEAN: What did he ask you to do?

OLLIE: —To—

[*Pause. He goes out on the balcony. After a few moments, Sean follows him out.*]

41] EXTERIOR. BALCONY. NIGHT.
In the bar, half a block away, a piano is playing blues.

OLLIE: Human perversions. There's no limit to them. This lunatic I went with t'night, he wasn't unusual lookin'. But on the way to his pad, he kept bringin' up the subject of— "Do you feel like takin' a pee?" Well, I did. I said— "Wait a minute for me outside the next bar we pass." "No," he said, "no. Hold it till we're home."

SEAN: Oh. He wanted what is called a golden shower.

238

OLLIE: I'd never run into a thing like that before. He got onto his knees with his arms around mine and—I kicked his mouth to break away from him.

WIRE'S VOICE: Somebody's sneaked somebody up there.

SEAN: He was indulging himself in a fit of *mea culpa.*

OLLIE: What's that mean?

SEAN: *Mea* is Latin for my and *culpa* is Latin for crime.

OLLIE: Lately I've thought of goin' north. This thing t'night convinced me it's time to.

WIRE'S VOICE: Everybody will stick to house regulations or get the hell out!

OLLIE: I've valuated your friendship because it was always decent.

WIRE'S VOICE: I'll open the doors and howl for the police if this goes on!

OLLIE [*extending his hand*]: Good luck, Sean. Write good an' take care.

[*Ollie snatches more money from his pants' pocket and tosses several bills inside the room. Then he swings himself over the balcony and slides down a rail to the pavement.*]

OLLIE: Take care.

SEAN: Take care.

OLLIE: Take care.

[*Ollie vanishes into the mist that always precedes his appear-
ances and his departures. Why? It makes him seem more like
a mythical character.*

[*The scene dissolves completely.*]

42] EXTERIOR. MANHATTAN. NIGHT.
*Ollie comes out of what seems like the same mist he disap-
peared into when we last saw him. A wind seems to disperse
the mist. We see a bench in a New York park. The focus is
still soft. Street lamps have an ethereal appearance. Oc-
casionally, a human figure passes behind the bench. The
occasional figures are tenuous as shadows.*

*Ollie seats himself on the bench and stares straight at the
camera. It closes on him. Ollie begins to speak.*

OLLIE: I spent a month here looking for employment, I mean
legitimate jobs, you know. Nobody wanted to hire a man with
one arm. Well, I'd hit this city with money, but—

[*Fade in soft guitar music.*]

—money moves, and the way it moves is away in my case. Yeah,
the direction it takes is away. Oh, I—I'd go to Nedicks for
dinner. "Gimme a hot dog, with ev'rything on it, please, and a,
and a—glass of milk" . . . Gradually I begun to notice where
hustlers make out in this—imperial city. Yeah, and by the end
of the month, when Nedick's become too expensive, yeah, even
Nedick's too extravagant for me, I—

—I took up the old occupation, and I don't mean boxin'.

—I met this ole queen that runs a call house for boys. We call
him Cherry. Fat, motherly. You check in about eight o'clock an'
sit around playin' poker, exchangin' jokes an' stories of your ex-

240

periences in— The phone rings ev'ry coupla minutes. Cherry says to you: "This john wants you, or you." —"This john is good for whatever you're good enough for. Pretend you don't notice the yellow toupee on his head. Go in your best suit. Tell him you just come in town from Idaho or somewhere. I think you're right for him, Ollie. Here's the address. It's the penthouse apartment. His name is Lester Dubinski. He likes to talk, you know, to come on intellectual. Get the picture, Ollie?" —Hell. —I painted the picture! [*He glances at his watch.*] —I guess I've kept him waiting long enough.

[*Ollie rises from the bench. Mist is blown around him again as he walks off. The guitar continues a minute as an old woman roots in a wire trash can for something.*]

43] CUT TO: INTERIOR. LESTER'S LUXURIOUS PENT-
    HOUSE APARTMENT. NIGHT.
    The camera faces Ollie sitting on a sofa.

OLLIE: I been in town just three days, Les.

LESTER'S VOICE: But you've already met Cherry.

OLLIE: Yes, accidentally, yes. I was comin' out of the library.

LESTER'S VOICE: With a book?

OLLIE: Yeah, with a book.

LESTER'S VOICE: What was the title of it?

OLLIE: —The name of the book?

LESTER'S VOICE: Yes, its title. I'm interested in your taste in reading matter.

OLLIE: —It was—

[*Pause.*]

LESTER'S VOICE: —You've forgotten the title of the book?

[*He laughs a bit shrilly.*]

OLLIE: I ain't forgotten.

[*The camera draws back to a medium two-shot. Included in the shot is a suit of armor.*]

OLLIE: It was named *The Care and Preservation of Male Hair.*

[*Pause. Lester—his back is still to the camera—laughs uncomfortably.*]

LESTER: Why would that subject interest a man with such crowning glory as yours?

OLLIE: I thought sometime in the future my hair might start to go on me.

LESTER: —Oh.

OLLIE: Yes . . .

[*Slight pause. Ollie points a thumb at the "suit of armor."*]

Does that outfit have a name?

LESTER: You mean my suit of armor?

OLLIE: Yeah. When do you get in it? Like for what occasions? Or what situations?

LESTER: Never, never, of course. A suit of armor is the battle dress of medieval knights. —Would you like a little more brandy?

OLLIE: My mother, back on the farm in Idaho, the last thing she said to me was, "Son, watch out for liquor." —I guess she meant I should keep an eye on it so it wouldn't escape me.

[*Lester turns to the camera as he approaches his bar.*]

LESTER: Courvoisier again, or Remy Martin?

OLLIE: Two jiggers of Five Star Hennessy in that fish bowl, please.

LESTER: I'm literally astounded that an Idaho farmboy would know the names of brandy.

OLLIE: Well, the Idaho farm was a swinging place. My father played a harpsichord and mother doubled in brass.

LESTER: What did you play?

OLLIE: I had those gourds that you rattle.

[*Lester hands the brandy to Ollie.*]

LESTER: *Voici!* —Idaho farmboy.

OLLIE: Thanks.

[*A phone rings.*]

Your phone's ringin', Les.

LESTER: I have an answering service.

[*The phone rings repeatedly.*]

Someone is ringing through.

OLLIE [*broadly naive*]: D'ya mean through a telephone wire?

LESTER: Cherry should have told you that pulling my leg is totally impossible, since I—

[*His voice fades out as he leaves the room.*]

44] EXTERIOR. TERRACE. NIGHT.
Ollie goes out on the terrace. He casually plucks a blossom from a potted plant and puts the blossom in the fly of his pants.

LESTER'S VOICE: Not tonight, Artie. A lot of work's piled up on me and I'm devoting myself to, uh, nocturnal, uh, labor. How were exams at? —F in three courses, you're kidding! —A state of nerves, I suppose. —Well, I'll have to consult my date book.

[*The camera is on Ollie. Lester's voice fades out as Ollie strolls down the terrace away from the camera.*]

LESTER [*in the living room and then on the terrace*]: Where are you, where are you, where—

OLLIE [*calling back from a cloud of mist*]: Takin' a little stroll on your groovy terrace.

[*Slight pause. The distant sound of a siren is heard.*]

LESTER: —Do you have impulses of self-destruction?

OLLIE: —Why'd you ask me that?

LESTER: —Ask you what? Oh. Yes. Because, yes—I have them. I suppose that's why. Listen. The inimitable Dietrich, imperishable as the sky. . . . Let's go back in. Even in summer, I shiver on this terrace.

45] INTERIOR. LIVING ROOM. NIGHT.
They return to the living room. Lester slides a hand down Ollie's back. The hand stops at Ollie's buttocks.

LESTER: Mmm. Classic callipygean. Did they teach you what that means in Idaho? It means narrow hips with high, prominent buttocks.

OLLIE: Les, you're out of bounds. Know what that means, Les?

LESTER [*reluctantly dropping his hand*]: Yes. —Sorry. —What a pity!

[*Another distant siren wails.*]

OLLIE: How much do you pay a month for this apartment?

LESTER: Nothing at all, this apartment is a co-op.

[*The Dietrich record ends.*]

OLLIE: Is a what did you say it was?

LESTER: Cooperative apartment.

OLLIE: Cooperating with what?

LESTER: Shall we have some more of the inimitable Dietrich?

[*Lester goes to the stereo and turns the record over.*]

245

OLLIE: You walk around like a pigeon. Why don't you light somewhere?

LESTER: Light?

OLLIE: I mean sit down somewhere since we've got to discuss the deal. We ain't discussed it yet.

LESTER: I discussed the deal with Cherry.

OLLIE: The deal has to be negotiated again, now that I've seen your elegant penthouse.

LESTER: Oh, but a deal is a deal.

[*Lester nervously runs his hands through his toupee, and it falls to the floor.*]

OLLIE: Your hair come off.

LESTER [*picking up his toupee*]: I'm not bald.

OLLIE: Neither is a hen's egg.

LESTER: I had a little eczema on my scalp so I was advised to wear this hair piece till the condition cleared up. It will.

OLLIE: My price is a hundred, Les.

LESTER: Cherry said fifty.

OLLIE: Cherry hadn't seen your luxury penthouse, either, I reckon.

LESTER: Listen to her. The inimitable Dietrich.

246

OLLIE: Never mind Dietrich right now. Do you want me for my price? Or do I go?

LESTER: Cherry would be displeased. He doesn't like his boys to make separate deals.

OLLIE: Cherry's attitude don't always concern me much.

LESTER: I wouldn't dream of paying a hundred dollars to a—

OLLIE: Don't dream of it, just do it.

LESTER: —May I enquire what special endowments you have that are worth this exorbitant price?

OLLIE: I have the special endowment of a mutilation.

LESTER: —You have—

OLLIE: One arm. I have one arm, Les.

LESTER: —It's fortunate for you that I can afford to satisfy your demand.

OLLIE: Les, I have one arm.

LESTER: Dear boy, you said that before. I saw it. I didn't mention it, did I?

OLLIE: It don't hurt to repeat it.

LESTER: —I'm a lonely man.

OLLIE: I got one arm. I just have one arm, Les.

LESTER: Try to forget it, Ollie. I don't think about my hair piece.

OLLIE: It took me a while to find out that johns like a mutilation, as long as it's above the belt. One arm. I got one arm.

LESTER: You have—remarkable beauty.

OLLIE: When I walk down a street and look in a store window, if I doubted the fact, the fact that I have one arm, it's visible to me. Not that I ever forget it. Les, put the hundred where I can pick it up when I go, like on the mantel.

LESTER: You're not leaving before—?

OLLIE: No. Not before. Not till after.

LESTER [*taking out his wallet and removing a hundred dollar bill*]: I can see that you wouldn't. Put it in a pocket now.

OLLIE: Thanks. You see I'm not leaving before. But time passes in this city faster than any I know. The clocks take Dexedrine and bennies. Speed!

LESTER: A wild idea occurred to me just now. Stay with me on a permanent basis. A while.

OLLIE: Les, I like you, but dismiss that idea.

LESTER [*sorrowfully*]: Impermanence is the—order of civilization as I've observed it.

[*Ollie yawns.*]

—Stretch out on that long sofa and let me undress you, Ollie.

OLLIE: Even with one arm, I can dress and undress without assistance, Les.

LESTER: But to undress you would increase my pleasure.

[*Ollie kicks off his shoes, stares at Lester a moment, then stretches out on the sofa.*

[*Lester kneels beside the sofa, and the camera goes into clouded focus. The undressing of Ollie is like a church ceremony. When it's completed, Lester bends to kiss him.*]

OLLIE [*covering his mouth quickly*]: Les, I'm not gay trade. In three years of hustling I've never let a man kiss me.

LESTER: Oh, but—

OLLIE: No personal offense.

LESTER: —May I touch your lips with a finger?

OLLIE: —Yes, Les . . .

46] DISSOLVE TO: INTERIOR. LESTER'S APART-
    MENT. NIGHT.
    Almost nothing is visible. A Dietrich record is playing.

LESTER: Music may be the food of love, but on this occasion, love required no nutrition. Oh, but she's a miracle. The inimitable Dietrich . . .

[*Ollie sits up, dressed.*]

LESTER: A grandmother. Can you believe it?

OLLIE: I never made her acquaintance.

LESTER: Phenomenal.

OLLIE: Would you give me half a—what do you call it?

[*He raises a glass.*]

LESTER: Snifter. I'll put the bottle between your feet.

OLLIE: That'll spare the carpet.

[*The Dietrich record stops. A "country" singer comes on.*]

OLLIE: I heard that song before.

STEREO: I took provisions with me,
     Some for hunger, some for cold,
     But I took nobody with me,
     Not a soul, no, not a soul.

     Buildings seem much taller
     When you're going from a town.
     You see peculiar shadows
     But don't let 'em bring you down.

     If you had a buddy with you,
     I mean one that's tried an' true,
     I can tell you 'cause I know it,
     Shadows wouldn't be so blue.

OLLIE: Country music. Les, put the miracle grandmother back on, huh?

[*As Marlene Dietrich begins to sing again, the scene dissolves.*]

47] EXTERIOR. BRYANT PARK (BACK OF THE MAIN PUBLIC LIBRARY). NEW YORK CITY. DUSK.

The camera, briefly, kaleidoscopically, explores the little park which seems strangely dead at this hour of a hot summer day's exhaustion. The trees look worn out, so do the benches, and the round concrete basin of water, meant to decorate the place, is full of sodden litter: tokens of human pollution such as burnt matches, candy bar wrappers, paper spoons smeared with mustard for hot dogs, etc.

NARRATOR'S VOICE: This is Bryant Park just behind the main branch of the public library system. It is dusk; it is the hour of the day's exhaustion, a day in steaming late summer, yes, still summer and for some the last one . . .

[The camera closes on a derelict man in late years. He is dressed with a pitiful effort at neatness and respectability. He is wandering about the concrete basin of fouled water as if dazed. He suddenly stops, starts forward again, and stumbles to his knees. There are people in the frame but they only glance at him as he kneels by the basin. Then—

[Ollie enters the frame and assists the old man to his feet.]

OLLIE: What's the matter, Pop?

[The old man stares at him blindly, dumbly.]

Are you okay, Pop?

[The old man first shakes his head in negation, then nods it slightly and starts on, continuing his way to—]

Where you going now, Pop? —Sure you know where you going?

[The old man produces, fumblingly, a cheap hotel key.]

251

Aw. Hotel Ritz. Men only. Hah! Some Ritz. — okay, Pop. The Ritz Men Only is right over there where I'm pointing. See? See?

[*The old man again shakes his head in negation, then in tentative "yes."*]

Naw, you don't, Pops, come along with me, I'll get you to your stall in that damn stable. When you get there, Pops—

[*He's leading the old man out of the park, now.*]

—Take this five dollars and rent you a 'lectric fan. This'll cover the deposit and a week's use. Understand?

[*The old man again shakes his head, then nods it slightly.*]

Naw, you don't, Pops. Pops, you are suffering from heat prostration. LOOK. FIVE BUCKS. E-LEC-TRIC FAN! They rent 'em there, I know, I been there once before I got into business in this city. Can you see light? There's a blue neon sign on the corner there. RITZ. Men only. $1.50. Okay. Toddle on, Pops, you're gonna make it . . .

[*The old man shakes his head, then nods it with a tentative smile, turns, and starts off as directed. He disregards an amber sign that turns red; a siren is shrilling, brakes SCREECH. There is a quick, short cry of anguish and terror, then a babble of people. The old man has been run down; the incident is masked by a crowd of people.*]

Run down by an ambulance, Jesus. It run him down and now they've put him in it. Some Pops! —Some fuckin' town . . .

[*The camera closes on his face. Tears well into his lost pale eyes; he squeezes them fiercely shut. A furtive-looking middle-aged man stops in front of him.*]

MIDDLE-AGED MAN: Terrible, huh?

OLLIE: Yeah. Including you . . .

[*He grins at the man and crosses to a bench.*]

NARRATOR'S VOICE: There were so ma*.y of them, the queer, the mutilated, the not-so-young-anymore with their loneliness a terrible cry in their throats, muted, or stifled to dumbness by the iron hand of bigotry and law. We can't play back all their voices or deal out all their photos like a gypsy's deck of filthy, dog-eared cards, telling always almost the same fortune both to them and the boy. You've seen how the boy still defends with fierce pride the surrounded, constantly assaulted citadel of his manhood, his virility. Oh, he must have known, he must have realized with God knows how much—dread? Yes, dread, even terror—that the game could only be won the way that he played it for a little while and then—well, he'd have to surrender a bit, and then a bit more, and more and more and more, till finally—well, he couldn't think about that without feeling sick to his stomach. Solution? Well . . .

—Surely there'd be another head-on crash in his life and this time he'd not just lose one arm but—*win*! The stake that he was unconsciously playing for, the one which his buddies had at once in the underpass . . . oblivion!

And yet there was this time when—

48] DISSOLVE TO: EXTERIOR. DECK OF AN EXCURSION STEAMER. DAY.
   The steamer is circling the Island of Manhattan.

BARKER'S VOICE: You will soon have an excellent view of the world's most famous statue, the Statue of Liberty, presented to our country by the government of France in—

[*The voice fades out.*

[*The camera closes on Ollie and a girl in her late twenties. They are standing a little apart at the rail of the steamer. Without turning his head, Ollie appraises the girl.*]

OLLIE'S VOICE: Not a pig. Definitely not a pig. I'll say something to her like how she's enjoying the trip.

[*He moves closer to the girl and speaks aloud.*]

OLLIE: Are you enjoying the trip?

GIRL: Oh, why, yes. Aren't you?

OLLIE: It's a, you know, it's a relief from the heat.

GIRL: Isn't it, though! According to the paper I read this morning, a lot of people have fainted on the streets.

OLLIE: Yes, some of 'em permanently fainted.

GIRL: It's heat prostration.

OLLIE: Uh-huh. These elderly persons, you notice 'em leaning out of their windows to avoid suffocation in their rooms.

GIRL: Do you live here or are you just visiting here?

OLLIE: Oh—I'm here on business. Do you live here or are you just visiting here?

GIRL: I, uh, work here. I'm employed by the World Wide Moving firm. A small job in a big concern.

OLLIE: Who're you with?

GIRL: In the city?

OLLIE: On this boat ride.

GIRL: I—went on it alone. Mainly to escape the heat, you know.

OLLIE: Can I offer you to a drink?

GIRL: A little later I would like one but not right now. I'm waiting for a good view of the Statue of Liberty.

OLLIE: There it is, right out there. It's smaller than what I expected and it's green as a frog, but I like what it represents. The freedom of a man, and of a girl, too. But the freedom's a secret now.

GIRL: Would you mind—taking a picture of it with my Kodak for me to send home?

OLLIE: It looks better on a postcard.

GIRL: I suppose it would, but—

OLLIE: It would mean more to your folks if it was a Kodak picture of you and—

GIRL: I, uh, I guess that that's what I mean. Oh, but—

OLLIE: Yeah, it's a little tricky takin' a Kodak picture with one hand, but I'll manage. Turn around, honey. Face me.

255

[*He draws back from the railing of the steamer as she turns. Her smile is tremulous. Ollie takes the picture.*]

GIRL: Could you get the Statue and me both in the—?

OLLIE: You and Miss Liberty are both in the picture, honey, and you ain't green.

[*He returns to the railing. After a moment she joins him but stands a foot apart from him. He closes the gap.*]

OLLIE: You can't buy a camera better than an old-fashioned Kodak. —Over there is—

GIRL: What?

OLLIE: Nothing. We've passed it now. I reckon I've took this boat trip about fifty times.

GIRL: You're in New York for the summer?

OLLIE: For the summer and fall and winter and spring.

GIRL: Oh. You work here?

OLLIE: Yep. —On the graveyard shift.

GIRL: —Is it, do you think it's fair of you to press against me like this?

OLLIE: Honey, close human contact won't hurt you on this boat. Would you like that drink now?

GIRL: Yes, now it would be nice, now.

[*As they enter the steamer's interior . . .*]

49] DISSOLVE TO: INTERIOR. BEDROOM. NIGHT.

This is the girl's bedroom in a building that borders upon a slum area. The only light comes from a radio dial. We see two figures on a bed, and hear the girl sighing with pleasure, panting, gasping. Then, abruptly, two stories below, window glass is shattered, a policeman's whistle is blown, voices rise in fury. We hear a police car siren. The voices become demoniacal.

OLLIE [*quietly*]: What's going on out there?

GIRL [*quietly, too*]: Another riot. —Looting.

[*In the dark room Ollie crosses to the window.*]

—The second time this week. —*Don't look out!*

[*He does.*]

OLLIE: I've never seen nothing like this.

GIRL: I wish you wouldn't lean out the window, Ollie. Sometimes they shoot over the heads of the crowd.

OLLIE: —If the world had a mouth with a tongue it would shout like this, yeah, this is how it would holler . . .

[*He leans farther out. The revolving red light on a squad car lights his face flickeringly. Accidentally, he knocks a potted plant off the window sill.*]

GIRL [*crying out*]: My plant!

OLLIE: —Sorry, honey. I'll get you a new one tomorrow.

GIRL: *Please*, will you *please* come back here! A bullet went through the window of the—

[*A bullet shatters the upper glass of her window. She screams.*]

OLLIE [*returning to the bed*]: Okay, baby. We'll read about it tomorrow, but let's forget it tonight.

GIRL: —I think they're—I can't catch my breath!—breaking up now!

OLLIE: Lie back in my arms. I mean against me. Don't be scared. The gang is breaking up now. We're perfectly safe together.

[*She is sobbing.*]

OLLIE: Hush, now. Shhh. I'm gonna sing you a song. You can't hear the song if you cry like that.

GIRL: Sing to me. I'll be still.

[*He sings* Kentucky Babe.]

OLLIE: "Fly away. Fly away and stay away, Sweet Kentucky Baby Babe." —Tomorrow I'll go to a flower shop an' get you a new geranium plant—two of 'em. Three!

GIRL: A plant that you've lived with, that you've gotten used to, it—almost seems to speak to you when you come in the room, you know.

OLLIE: It won't take long for the new ones to speak to you, too. See how much quieter it is? Except for you cryin'? Lie back down, now, with me.

GIRL: —I was so ashamed to take you to this ghetto, and—

258

OLLIE: Honey, being with you has made me forget everything I'm ashamed of, and that's a lot. —Lemme put my tongue in your sweet mouth so you'll stop cryin'.

50] DISSOLVE TO: EXTERIOR. STREET. EARLY DAWN.
Ollie emerges from the rooming house. It is ghostly, misty daybreak and all about him is the debris, the tokens of violence, the shattered glass catching early light so that it looks like a motionless river. After a moment, he moves and the glass breaks, crunches under his feet with a crunching sound.

OLLIE [*aloud to himself*]: I'm glad I have on shoes—she was a sweet girl—I never had a happier night in my life.

[*He is in the middle of the street, on a corner. He turns about indecisively to discover the direction in which to move, and all about him, the shattered glass, catching the dawn light, refracts fragmentary pieces of his body in brightening silver. He shrugs and turns the corner in the direction he knows no better than the other. The camera stays on the broken glass, which still brightens.*]

51] DISSOLVE TO: INTERIOR. APARTMENT. TWO-SHOT: OLLIE AND A MALE MASOCHIST NAMED CLAUDE. NIGHT.
They are entering a severely furnished bedroom.

OLLIE: I never seen a room decorated with such a lot of helmets.

CLAUDE [*proudly*]: There's fifteen of them.

OLLIE: It looks like you're on a military kick.

CLAUDE: I can hardly wait till seven when the news comes on.

259

OLLIE: Such as how many were killed yesterday?

CLAUDE: The world has to be corrected.

OLLIE: Let's get down to business right away. All I do is lie on the bed face up, and my price is a hundred.

CLAUDE: You don't have to lie down.

OLLIE: Then why did you call for me?

CLAUDE: The walls of the room are soundproof.

OLLIE: What's that got to do with it?

CLAUDE: Open the closet door there.

OLLIE: Why? What's in it?

CLAUDE: Nothing dangerous to you.

OLLIE: I wasn't afraid there would be.

[*He crosses to a door and opens it.*]

52] CLOSE SHOT: THE CONTENTS OF THE CLOSET. *The closet is filled with uniforms, some plain leather ones, others military, a policeman's uniform, a fireman's, etc. There are also straps and whips, some of them studded.*

CLAUDE [*falling to his knees*]: I need to be corrected. I need correction.

OLLIE: Pitiful. Pathetic. I see how you need correction but I'm not giving you none. You've taken up a good deal of my time. I told you my price. I want it now so I can go back to Cherry's.

CLAUDE: I haven't been corrected. I've been a very bad boy.

OLLIE: Peel it out now. The hundred.

CLAUDE: I never pay until I've been corrected. Cherry knows that.

[*Ollie seizes the collar of his jacket. Claude cries "Ahhhh!" with a note of pleasure. His arms are pinioned. Ollie snatches his wallet and crosses to the door with it.*]

OLLIE [*as he goes out*]: Corrected?

CLAUDE [*rushing to door*]: Take the money, all of it, but throw the wallet at me, it has addresses in it!

OLLIE [*removing a bill from the wallet*]: I'm taking out the price of—disgust.

CLAUDE: Throw the wallet at me, hit me in the face with it!

OLLIE [*dropping the wallet on the floor*]: Be sick with somebody else.

[*We hear the crash of a drum and there is an instant blackout of the scene.*]

53] INTERIOR. CHERRY'S PLACE. NIGHT.
Some boys are playing poker, but Ollie is staring at Cherry with a ferocity that is very thinly disguised. The phone rings, of course. Cherry (drunk) speaks into it.

CHERRY: —Oh. You want Ollie. When? Immediately. Well, he's here. Ready to go right over. Bye-bye.

OLLIE: Cherry?

CHERRY: Huh?

OLLIE: You need correction, Cherry.

[*Ollie rises and gives Cherry a series of slaps, each harder, and after each slap Cherry gasps. The boys playing poker are strangely inattentive.*

[*The scene dissolves, and mist envelops the camera lens.*]

NARRATOR'S VOICE: Summer and fall and winter and spring, yes, time has a habit of passing . . .

54] EXTERIOR. BUS. NIGHT.
The camera faces a bus. On the front of the bus is the name of the line: PATHFINDER, then, beneath, LOS ANGELES.

55] INTERIOR. CLOSE TWO-SHOT: OLLIE AND A YOUNG SOLDIER. NIGHT.
Ollie is drinking from a pint bottle. He offers it to the youth beside him.

SOLDIER: Yeah, thanks.

OLLIE: I like to get paralyzed on a bus. People snorin', babies cryin'. You start to catch a little shut-eye and the driver hollers out: "Ten minute stop here, folks."

[*The brakes squeal as the bus stops.*]

DRIVER [*loudly*]: *Ten minute stop!*

56] EXTERIOR. BUS. NIGHT.

Sleepy passengers shuffle off the bus. The last is Ollie. The camera follows Ollie inside the terminal then faces Ollie and the soldier. They are having coffee at the counter.

SOLDIER: Why're you goin' to L.A.?

OLLIE: Oh, I got a letter of introduction to this movie producer out there that's int'rested in guys with one arm.

SOLDIER: For any particular reason?

OLLIE: Yeah. He makes a lot of war pictures.

SOLDIER: —Oh . . .

[*Unconsciously, he runs his hand down his right arm.*]

OLLIE: Excuse me. That was tactless of me to say that.

[*A shadow is cast over Ollie's section of the counter. A voice speaks just behind him.*]

VOICE: Turn around, Bud.

OLLIE [*turning only slightly*]: Huh?

ANOTHER VOICE: That's him. Put the lock on him.

57] EXTERIOR. BUS TERMINAL. NIGHT.

We see Ollie emerging from the terminal between two detectives. He is handcuffed to one of them; his face is expressionless. The bark of a coyote is heard.

OLLIE: —That's the only coyote I've heard outside of TV and movies . . .

FIRST DETECTIVE: He's a cool one.

SECOND DETECTIVE: Not too cool to burn.

OLLIE: —We gettin' back on the bus?

FIRST DETECTIVE: We're driving you into Albuquerque. From there you'll travel by plane.

OLLIE: Sounds like an improvement in transportation . . .

58] CUT TO: INTERIOR. A ROOM IN POLICE HEAD-QUARTERS. CLOSE ON OLLIE. DAY.

NARRATOR [*voice-over*]: Yes, he made no effort at all to dodge their questions. He gave them—after they'd given him half a tumbler of whiskey to loosen his tongue—an exact account of the crime that he'd committed three years ago.

OLLIE: —We didn't finish the picture.

QUESTIONER: The film wasn't finished.

OLLIE: No, sir. Then people started leaving.

QUESTIONER: The guests of—?

OLLIE: Yes. His guests. I said, "I want on the launch." There was a launch going to shore. The man that was makin' the picture come up beside me and said, "You stay. I'll pay you a hundred more dollars." I reckon that I knew then that if I stayed on the yacht I'd kill that man, I had that feeling in me that I'd do that if I stayed.

VOICE: Premeditation.

OLLIE: I knew when they left me alone with him, he'd be sorry . . .

59] INTERIOR. COURTHOUSE. DAY.
Ollie is led down a corridor. Spectators and newsmen follow.

NARRATOR [*voice-over*]: Everything went against him at the short trial. Did he want it that way? His testimony, if you could call it that, it was really just an exact account of what had happened on the yacht, was ineffectual as opposed to the prestige of the party that had been on the yacht that night. [*The narrator continues speaking as the scenes change.*]

60] EXTERIOR. COURTHOUSE STEPS. DAY.
Ollie and the group surrounding him exit the building and descend the steps. Ollie is put into a police car and driven away.

NARRATOR'S VOICE [*continuing*]: They all declared that nothing irregular had occurred, and the girl who had participated in the blue movie could not be located, and, of course, the guests had no recollection of her presence at the occasion.

61] INTERIOR. PRISON CORRIDOR. DAY.
Ollie is led to a cell and locked in it. The cell is the "bird cage" reserved for the soon to be executed—no windows and a single naked light bulb that burns continuously.

NARRATOR'S VOICE [*continuing*]: The defense of Ollie, if it could be called a defense, was particularly hopeless when he admitted that he had removed from the dead man's body a wallet containing several hundred dollars. These things assured the conviction of Ollie and doomed him to the chair.

265

62] INTERIOR. PRISON CELL. DAY.

A guard stops at Ollie's cell. Ollie is now in prison garb. The guard passes a big batch of letters to him.

GUARD: Letters for you.

[*Ollie takes the letters, pretending an indifference that he may not feel.*]

OLLIE: I been all around the country and made lots of friendly contacts here and there.

GUARD: Want to keep 'em or have 'em burned?

OLLIE: I want to keep them. They're mine.

[*The guard walks off. Ollie opens one letter almost mechanically. Ollie continues, reading aloud.*]

"I have never stopped thinking of you and I doubt that anyone who knew you could forget you either."

[*Ollie lets the letter drop to the floor. After a moment he picks it up and reads the first phrase aloud again.*]

"I have never stopped thinking of you and I doubt that anyone who knew you could forget you either."

[*A change occurs on Ollie's face. He goes to his cell door and shouts to the guard.*]

Hey. Can I have me a pencil and paper?

GUARD: Going to write your mother?

OLLIE: What goddam mother!

63] INTERIOR. PRISON CELL.
Ollie is writing a letter.

NARRATOR [*voice-over*]: Ollie began to answer some of the letters. It wasn't easy for him. Having no family or close friends to write to, this was his first attempt at writing letters and he wrote them, at first, with a laborious stiffness. The simplest sentence, at first, would knot up the muscles in his one arm, and he found that printing was easier for him than ordinary writing. [*The narrator continues speaking as the scenes change.*]

64] INTERIOR. PRISON CELL.
There is a rapid montage of Ollie writing letters.

NARRATOR'S VOICE [*continuing*]: But as he went on—notice the stiffness going?—soon the printed sentences gathered momentum just as springs clear out a channel for themselves after heavy rain. The sentences began to flow out of his less and less cramped fingers almost—yes, expressively after a while, and to ring with the backwoods speech of the underprivileged South, to which had been added salty idioms of the underworld he had moved in, and the road and the sea. Goddam it, he'd say, because he had to write with his left hand and he'd been right-handed. But into the letters went the warm and vivid talk that liquor and generous dealing had brought from his lips on certain occasions, the sort of talk that American tongues throw away so casually in bars and hotel bedrooms. The cartoon symbol of laughter was often used, that heavily drawn, "HA HA," with its tail of exclamatory punctuation—stars, spirals. And setting that down on paper—the "HA HA" bit—was what gave him most relief, for it had in it the boiling intensity that a boy feels on Death's Row.

65] SHOT OF A SKETCH FROM ONE OF OLLIE'S LETTERS.

NARRATOR'S VOICE [*continuing*]: Sometimes the letter would contain a "HA HA" illustration such as this. . . . Sometimes, bearing down so hard on the pencil would break its point . . .

66] INTERIOR. PRISON CELL.
Ollie springs to the bars of his cell and shouts.

OLLIE: Hey! Hey! I need another pencil!

GUARD: Sure, you got to keep up with your correspondence.

[*The guard passes a pencil to Ollie, who immediately continues to write.*]

OLLIE'S VOICE [*as he writes*]: Yes sir! I remember you plain as day in spite of its being midnight when I met you.

[*Guitar music comes up as Ollie continues.*]

It was last spring or summer of— Am I right or wrong about that? You stand out plain as day in spite of the many, many, many people I've met since I lost one arm, for some reason. Yes, I remember. Don't think I don't remember. You give me a look as we passed in opposite directions on Canal Street and I said to myself, "He wants me." I stopped on the sidewalk and looked in a window and in less than a minute you was looking in the same window and I was jiggling keys in my pocket which is my way of saying "Okay, if you want me."

67] A CRUDELY DRAWN SKETCH OF THE CHAIR.
A sketch of the chair is projected on the screen.

NARRATOR'S VOICE: In these letters Ollie would often enclose a sketch of the chair to which he was condemned. . . . Yes, the chair reserved for Ollie . . .

68] VERY CLOSE SHOT: OLLIE'S FACE.
*Ollie's face is far from expressionless, now. The camera shot
goes into blurred focus.*

69] DISSOLVE TO: BLURRED FOCUS, GRADUALLY
CLEARING.
*The camera settles on the huge collection of letters stacked
against one wall of Ollie's cell.*

NARRATOR'S VOICE: The number? It was hard to count them,
but during the last few days of his life, Ollie counted the letters he had received . . .

70] CUT TO: INTERIOR. THE WINDOWLESS PRISON
CELL. CLOSE ON OLLIE.
*Ollie is counting the letters, his voice hushed and almost
breathless.*

The shot widens to include a guard in the corridor.

OLLIE [*in a low whisper*]: Seven thousand eight hundred and
five. Seven thousand eight hundred and—

GUARD: How many come to you, Ollie?

OLLIE: Don't interrupt me, I'm counting.

[*The guard chuckles and pushes a plate of food through a
narrow opening in the bars. Then passes on.*]

Seven thousand eight hundred and — seven . . .

NARRATOR'S VOICE: —Not all of the letters have come from
people who knew him. A good number have come from people
who have only seen his picture in a newspaper. An ordinary
newspaper photograph of Ollie is a photograph of a legend . . .

269

71] INTERIOR. THE CELL AND CORRIDOR.
The guard moves again into view.

OLLIE [*screaming to the guard in crescendo*]: Is it day or night? Night or day? Day or night! Day or night!

GUARD: It's February fourteenth—Valentine's Day.

OLLIE [*exhausted, panting for breath*]: Day or night. I got no way to know, no window to look through, have I? In this bird cage you took me to from the row. And this electric bulb that hangs over me all the time. Can't it be turned off?

GUARD: I put your supper through the slot.

OLLIE: A paper plate of slop with a paper spoon.

GUARD: You tryin' to starve yourself to death before you go to the chair?

OLLIE: What do I need with food?

GUARD: If you go on not eatin' you're gonna git fed through a pipe in a vein.

OLLIE: Isn't there nobody human in this place? Nothin' human in it but letters from people known and unknown?

GUARD: Don't they sign the letters?

OLLIE: They're naturally scared to have their names connected with mine. —Why can't you turn that big, enormous light off when it's night so I can sleep?

GUARD: You're in the bird cage now, and it's always lighted.

OLLIE: Can't I have something to tie around my eyes?

GUARD: It's night. When I say here's your breakfast, you'll know it's morning, when I say here's your supper you'll know it's night.

OLLIE: What kind of clock is that?

GUARD: A clock has sharp parts in it that you could cut yourself with.

OLLIE: Jesus.

GUARD: We have rules we're given, not made up.

OLLIE: Ask the warden.

GUARD: The warden has rules, too.

OLLIE: Screw the warden.

GUARD: The best thing you could do is see the chaplain.

OLLIE: Screw the chaplain.

GUARD: You're not gonna screw nobody.

OLLIE: Just cut off the big, enormous light bulb.

GUARD: Against the rules. The light's got to stay on till you go to the chair and the next lucky occupant of the bird cage takes your place.

OLLIE: Jesus, Jesus, not human.

GUARD: He wasn't supposed to be human but the son of God. Why don't you lie on your stomach if you don't like the big light.

OLLIE: Even then I'd, even if I closed my eyes, I'd know the big, enormous light was still hangin' there.

GUARD: Ollie, you got to live with it, till you die.

OLLIE: Turn off the light, you bastards! Turn off the light! Nobody can live day and night under a light like a sun that don't set!

[*Abruptly a terrific stream of water strikes him and hurls him back from the bars. He continues to shout. The stream crushes him to the floor of the cell. Ollie, overcome, falls silent, then says, hoarsely . . .*]

The bastards. . . . They soaked my letters.

72] INTERIOR. CELL.
Ollie's wet body shudders on his cot, his hand knotted over his eyes. He rises, paces the cell.

NARRATOR'S VOICE: Restlessness possessed him, the sort of restlessness that must possess a jungle animal in a cage. He would pace continually about the cell, stopping only to eat a bit of food so they wouldn't tie him in a straitjacket and feed him through a vein. The light, the fierce overhead light, never went out and the guards stopped telling him if it was night or day. Of course the guards were men selected and trained to feel no sympathy, not even for a condemned youth with one arm. There was the prison chaplain . . .

73] INTERIOR. CELL. MEDIUM TWO-SHOT: OLLIE AND THE CHAPLAIN.

The chaplain is in the corridor outside the cell, Bible open.

CHAPLAIN [*reading tonelessly*]: "Yea, though I walk through the valley of the shadow of death, I will fear no evil, for thou art with me; thy rod and thy staff they comfort me," etc.

OLLIE: Shut up and get the hell away!

[*The chaplain moves out of the shot.*]

OLLIE [*continuing; panting, speaking aloud to himself*]: Is it night or day?

74] INTERIOR. A DIVINITY STUDENT'S ROOM. DAY.
The camera comes in for a close shot of a newspaper picture of Ollie.

NARRATOR [*voice-over*]: The city that had appointed his death could not be oblivious to Ollie, and so the next day his picture, the picture of a legend, appeared again in a newspaper. [*The narrator continues speaking through the next scene.*]

75] CLOSE ON THE STUDENT.
The divinity student picks up the paper and again studies the picture, then places the paper face down on the table. He walks around the room, disturbed, always returning to take another glance at Ollie's haunting photograph.

NARRATOR'S VOICE [*continuing*]: A copy of the paper was delivered to the home of a divinity student. Ollie's face looked at him, above the caption: "Condemned Youth Refuses Consolation of Faith." Was it the caption or the face that disturbed the student so much? It was probably both. His rather austere living room, appropriate to his Protestant faith, was certainly not as small as Ollie's cell, under the scrutiny of the large electric bulb. What was the bulb? An eye without mercy? Yes. But the

273

divinity student paced about his living room as if it were that small. And the center of it was the newspaper with the picture of Ollie.

76] INTERIOR. A PSYCHOANALYST'S OFFICE. DAY.
There is a fairly close shot of the divinity student stretched out on the couch. The camera moves back to reveal the analyst with an open notebook.

ANALYST: Have you had any dreams lately?

DIVINITY STUDENT: —Yes. One.

ANALYST: Ah? Will you tell me about it?

DIVINITY STUDENT: I don't understand it at all. It's a mysterious dream.

ANALYST: Perhaps we can discover its meaning if you tell me about it.

[*There is a pause. The analyst drums his notebook with his pencil.*]

DIVINITY STUDENT: I've had it several times. It's a recurrent dream.

ANALYST: That makes it more important.

DIVINITY STUDENT: —It's about myself and a jungle beast.

[*The dream is obviously hard for him to tell. He twists about on the couch and takes two quick sips of water.*]

ANALYST: Go on, please. The dream.

DIVINITY STUDENT: The jungle beast is a golden panther.

ANALYST: Can you think of any particular reason why the jungle beast should be a golden panther?

DIVINITY STUDENT: —No, no, no, I don't know, except that when I was a child there was a golden panther in the zoo, and every day in summer I went to see it.

ANALYST: You were strongly attracted by this golden panther.

DIVINITY STUDENT: Attracted, but—frightened, too.

ANALYST: To fear a thing to which you're attracted is a frequent misfortune of yours.

[*The analyst looks at his wristwatch and stifles a yawn. Beads of sweat appear on the face of the patient, and his voice is somewhat strangulated.*]

DIVINITY STUDENT: The animal was supposed to be unusually savage; it had a sign on its cage that warned visitors at the zoo to keep a safe distance from it. However, you see, it had a—

ANALYST: It had a what? Your face is perspiring and there is a box of disposable tissue on the table right beside you. Wipe your face, take a deep breath, stop twisting about, and tell me about this panther.

DIVINITY STUDENT: It had a—radiance in its eyes as if it—*loved! Me!*

ANALYST: Would you like a mild sedative?

DIVINITY STUDENT: Oh, yes, please. Please! [*The divinity student takes the pill supplied by the analyst.*] Most people get over the timidities of their childhood, but I never did.

ANALYST: What does that statement have to do with the recurrent dream of the golden panther?

DIVINITY STUDENT: Despite the danger sign on the panther's cage, I would look into its eyes, and when I closed my own eyes, before going to sleep, I would see the panther's eyes.

ANALYST: Go on. We have twelve minutes.

DIVINITY STUDENT: I'd—sometimes—cry myself to sleep—with pity for the animal's imprisonment and—

ANALYST: Was the panther male or female?

DIVINITY STUDENT: Oh, it was male.

ANALYST: Go on.

DIVINITY STUDENT: Was I—could I—have been in love with the panther?

ANALYST: You were a child.

DIVINITY STUDENT: One night I dreamed of the panther in a way that was shameful. Its eyes appeared to me in a forest at night and I thought, "If I lie down very quietly it will come near me."

ANALYST: You wanted the golden male panther to approach you in the forest?

DIVINITY STUDENT: —Yes!

ANALYST: Go on. Did it approach you? Ever?

DIVINITY STUDENT: I took off all my clothes.

ANALYST: With the intention of having sexual relations with this golden male panther in the jungle?

DIVINITY STUDENT: A wind, a chilly wind, began to stir in the forest where I lay naked. Then—fear! The panther was not in a cage. I reached about me and noiselessly as possible covered myself with the fallen leaves in the forest and lay under them, curled up, breathing as quietly as I could. But the forest wind became stronger; it blew the leaves away, and then, and then—

ANALYST: And then?

DIVINITY STUDENT: I felt warm and I knew that the warmth meant that the golden panther was coming near me. Oh, then, it was no use trying to hide myself from it. I spread out my body, arms, legs, all. Something began to stroke me. It was liquid. I knew it was the tongue of the panther. [*He is now sobbing a little.*] The golden panther was licking me as animals lick their infants. It would start at my feet but its tongue would go up my legs till—

ANALYST: It was licking your groin?

DIVINITY STUDENT: Yes! And I had—I had an orgasm and it woke me.

ANALYST: The dream is recurrent?

DIVINITY STUDENT: —I had it again last night. Could it have been because of—?

ANALYST: Because of what?

DIVINITY STUDENT: This newspaper photograph that I cut out of the paper.

[*He removes a clipping, with very tremulous fingers, from his wallet and passes it to the analyst.*]

77] CLOSE-UP OF OLLIE'S PICTURE IN A NEWS-PAPER.
Under the photograph is the caption: "Condemned Youth Refuses Consolation of Faith."

ANALYST [*rising*]: I'll put this in your files. I understand.

DIVINITY STUDENT: No, no, please, I'd like to have it back.

ANALYST: You want to go on having this childish dream?

DIVINITY STUDENT: What I want to do is to visit the young man about to be executed, and offer him, persuade him, to receive the only comfort left him, which is faith—belief!

78] DISSOLVE TO: INTERIOR. OLLIE'S CELL.
Ollie is seated in a pair of shorts on the edge of his cot when the nervous, heavily sweating but well-groomed young divinity student is admitted by a guard, who returns to his post out of sight. The visitor has a wheezing sound in his throat.

DIVINITY STUDENT: Is there—do I—can I—a place to sit down?

OLLIE: Sit on that stool there.

DIVINITY STUDENT: Oh. Yes. Thank you.

[*He sits and immediately removes a small paper box from a pocket. From the box he takes out several little white tablets that he stuffs in his mouth.*]

I have come to see you.

OLLIE: I reckon you have. What did you take out of that box?

DIVINITY STUDENT: Pills for a—condition.

OLLIE: What's the condition?

DIVINITY STUDENT: A little on-again-off-again functional disturbance of the heart.

OLLIE: Oh.

DIVINITY STUDENT: In this condition my mouth turns very dry. Could I have some water?

[*Ollie fills an enameled tin cup at a tap in a corner of the cell.*]

Thank you.

OLLIE: You don't have to whisper. The guard is at the end of the corridor. What have you come here for?

DIVINITY STUDENT [*still whispering*]: Why, uh—just for a talk.

OLLIE: I got nothing to say except—tomorrow they say I go.

DIVINITY STUDENT: Go where?

OLLIE: To the chair.

DIVINITY STUDENT: —Oh. It takes a minute or two for the, uh, condition to, uh, subside.

279

OLLIE: Lemme see the box you took the tablets out of.

[*The student hands it to him.*]

In hot weather like today you shouldn't keep the box in your shirt pocket. The box is melted by sweat and the tablets are glued together.

DIVINITY STUDENT: I'll—remember not to—after today. [*Pause.*] May I—I'd like to—read you something.

OLLIE: What?

DIVINITY STUDENT: The Twenty-first Psalm.

OLLIE: I tole 'em I didn't want no chaplain in here.

DIVINITY STUDENT: Oh, I'm not a chaplain, I'm a seminary student. And also a stranger to you with sympathy for the mis-understood in the world.

OLLIE: Then you got sympathy for a good many people. Huh?

DIVINITY STUDENT: Yes, I have, I'm afraid so. . . . Are you prepared for tomorrow?

OLLIE: I'm not prepared for the hot seat but the seat is pre-pared for me.

DIVINITY STUDENT: I'm talking about eternity that waits for us all.

OLLIE: It can afford to wait as long as it wants to. Eternity. A man can't wait that long. Can he? No, he can't. Especially when he's got a date with the chair tomorrow. Not day after tomorrow but early tomorrow. Look. I got a cell-mate.

280

DIVINITY STUDENT: —Do you mean me?

OLLIE: I was talkin' about that fly that's buzzin' around in here. He's got more eternity going for him than I have going for me. Ha?

DIVINITY STUDENT: Would you like me to try to swat it with one of these magazines?

OLLIE: No. A fly as a cell-mate is better than nothing at all. I'll tell you something. I've been lonely in here, and the loneliness don't get lesser, it gets bigger. Now it's the size of a mountain and it's built on me.

DIVINITY STUDENT: Would you let me give you a cross to carry with you?

[*Pause.*]

OLLIE: That's a nice offer but the prison chaplain will have a cross.

DIVINITY STUDENT: Please take it from me. I want to give it to you. Afterwards it would be returned to me. That is, if I ask for it. Look at it. A gold cross with an amethyst in the center.

OLLIE: I would take it if I was able to hock it, but the offer was nice.

DIVINITY STUDENT: This world of ours—

OLLIE: It's no world of mine.

DIVINITY STUDENT: —This world of ours, yours, mine, everybody's—this transitory existence is just a threshold, a stepping stone to something immense beyond.

OLLIE: Yes. Death is immense but there's no stepping stone to nothing but a plain, unvarnished pine box.

DIVINITY STUDENT: Try to meet your Savior in a state of grace— You're still holding my pillbox.

OLLIE: The pills are melted to paste.

[*He tosses the box back to the student but it falls to the floor.*]

DIVINITY STUDENT: I'll put just a little bit of the paste on the tip of my little finger, and—

[*He does this and Ollie fetches him another cup of water.*]

Yes. Thank you. The paste is bitter. . . . You are face to face with the last and greatest adventure.

OLLIE: Bull.

DIVINITY STUDENT: I wish that you would believe me.

OLLIE: I was a boxer. A good one.

[*Then with the sad, quiet pride that always accompanies this statement, he continues.*]

I was light heavyweight champion of the Pacific Fleet. Then I lost one arm.

DIVINITY STUDENT: It could be that you were in error.

OLLIE: No, that's what I was—till I lost one arm.

DIVINITY STUDENT: I think that you were in error and didn't know it and persisted in error.

OLLIE: I wasn't driving the car. I yelled at the kid that was drivin', "Slow down, you fucker." We entered an underpass. The underpass of my life. The kid that was drivin' was drunk. Not competent to drive. Then came, in the underpass of our lives, the crash. They never came true. I mean to. Skulls busted wide open. Like a bean is busted when you're shellin' beans. I was what they call the survivor. What sort of survival? A boxer with one arm torn off him. All right. I mean all wrong. Can you explain that to me?

DIVINITY STUDENT: It—

OLLIE: —It?

DIVINITY STUDENT: It gave you the chance of a lifetime.

OLLIE: Chance for what? Being reduced to a hustler?

DIVINITY STUDENT: A chance to grow your spiritual arms and reach for God.

OLLIE: I reach for nobody till they reach for me.

[*The student leans forward and grips Ollie's knees.*]

DIVINITY STUDENT: Don't think of me as a man but as a connection.

OLLIE: Shit! A connection is a man pushing dope.

DIVINITY STUDENT: I am—

OLLIE: You are what? What are you? Now, you see, I'm whispering like you. Is this conversation a secret?

DIVINITY STUDENT: It's a private communion between you and me. What I am, what you must let me be, is a wire plugged in your heart and charged with God's message to you.

[*Pause. Ollie stares at his visitor.*]

I see that you've received a great many letters.

OLLIE: I been all over this country and gotten to know many people. I've forgotten most of 'em but they've remembered me. For a long while in here I paid no attention to the letters. Now I answer them. I try to remember each one as best as I can and if I had a little more time before tomorrow, yes, I think it's tomorrow, they don't give me the time here, I think I'd answer them all.

[*The scene tightens to a one-shot, close on Ollie.*]

Would you like to hear it and see if the grammar's okay? —I'll read it to you out loud. [*He reads the letter.*] "Yes, I remember you plainly. I met you in the park in back of the public library or was it in the men's room of the Greyhound Depot? I met so many, sometimes I get them mixed up a little. However, you stand out plainly. You said to me, son, can you direct me to the art museum and then we got to talking and the first thing I knew we was in your duplex apartment on the lake front and you offered me to a drink. I asked for my favorite drink which is Five Star Hennessy and you had some. And how is the Windy City of Chicago now that it's summer again? I sure would appreciate feeling those cool lake breezes and pouring down a few shots of that Five-Star Hennessy where we shacked up that day. I tell you it's hot in this cooler and it's going to get hotter before it gets cooler again. Do you get what I mean? Here's a picture of it as I imagine it looks."

79] **CLOSE TWO-SHOT.**
He shows the student a picture of the electric chair.

80] **CLOSE-UP OF THE PICTURE.**
Pulsating flashes of light create an electrifying effect on the sketch.

81] **REVERT TO ONE-SHOT.**
Ollie resumes the reading of the letter.

OLLIE: "I mean the chair on the wire that is anxious for me to set down on it. My date with it is tomorrow? And you are invited except you couldn't get in. The room is exclusive. I guess you would like to know if I am afraid. The answer is yes. I don't look forward to it a bit in the world. I was a boxer till I lost one arm and after that happened I seemed to go through a change which I can't account for except I stopped caring what happened to me. That is to say I lost my self-respect. I went all over the country without any plans except to keep on moving. I picked up strangers in every city I went to. I had experiences with them that only meant money to me and a place to shack up for the night—liquor, liquor—food. I never thought it could mean very much to them. Now all these letters like yours have proved it did. I meant to them something important, yes, to hundreds of people whose faces and names had slipped clean out of my mind almost as soon as I left them. (Now I feel like I have run up a debt of some kind to all these people. Not money but feelings. Sincere appreciation.) I would leave them sometimes without even saying good-bye. I can't imagine how these men could forgive me. If I had known then, I mean when I was outside, I guess I would have felt there was more to live for. Anyhow now the situation is hopeless. All will be over for me in a very short while. Ha ha! Tomorrow?

[*Pause.*]

82] CLOSE TWO-SHOT.

OLLIE: Letters. Words. How long will they remember Ollie Olsen?

DIVINITY STUDENT: —I doubt that—don't think that—they will ever forget you.

OLLIE: Wet that towel, will you?

DIVINITY STUDENT: I don't see any towel.

OLLIE: You're sitting on it. That's why you can't see it. Explanation.

[*The student rises and lifts a towel from the stool.*]

DIVINITY STUDENT: It's not a very clean towel.

OLLIE: Clean enough.

DIVINITY STUDENT: What do you want to do with this towel?

OLLIE: I don't want to do nothing with it. I want you to do something with it.

DIVINITY STUDENT: What?

OLLIE: Rub the sweat off my back.

[*He rolls on his stomach. Pause. The student is swaying a little.*]

Do I smell bad to you or something?

286

DIVINITY STUDENT: No. —No.

OLLIE: I am clean. I was given a shower.

DIVINITY STUDENT: Yes. Yes. Yes, but—

OLLIE: I have always been careful to keep myself clean. I was a very clean fighter—and a very clean whore— Did you know that I was a whore?

DIVINITY STUDENT: —No.

OLLIE: Well, that's what I was all right, and all those letters are from people that had me as a whore on the street. After boxing was finished by having one arm, my second profession was whoring.

[*The student approaches him as if he were a dangerous animal and begins to rub Ollie's back.*]

NARRATOR'S VOICE: An invisible drummer seemed to be advancing from the end of the corridor to the locked entrance of the cell and then to come through the bars and stand directly above the prison cot. It was the heartbeat of the divinity student. Now it was becoming irregular and his breath could be heard. He dropped the towel and took out of a pocket the box of sedatives that had turned to paste.

OLLIE: Go on. Why'd you stop?

DIVINITY STUDENT: I—I—

OLLIE: If you don't like the towel, you can rub with your hands.

NARRATOR'S VOICE: He arched his body a little and pulled his shorts further down his back. The narrow and sculptural flanks were exposed.

OLLIE: Now, then. Rub with your hands. They're cleaner than the towel.

DIVINITY STUDENT: No, no, please, I can't, no!

[*He seems to be in a kind of agony.*]

OLLIE: Don't be a fool. There's a door at the end of the hall. It makes a noise if anybody comes in it.

DIVINITY STUDENT: I'll go, now. Yes, I'll go now.

[*Quick as a panther, Ollie springs up and catches his wrist.*]

OLLIE: You've seen the pile of letters sent to me. They're bills from people I owe. Not money but feelings. For three whole years I went all over the country stirring up feelings without feeling nothing myself. Now that's all changed and I have feelings myself. I'm lonely and bottled up the same as you are. Oh, I know you, your type. Everything is artistic or else it's religious or talk too educated for Ollie Olsen. Come off it. Get with it. All that stuff's a pile, a mountain of bullshit. I don't buy it. I'm clean. And you? Aren't you clean? Take me so I can pay back. Hell, man, little man, all you need like 'em all needed, if they needed, is less than a push on the head . . .

DIVINITY STUDENT: Guard! Guard! God!

83] DISSOLVE TO: INTERIOR. CELL. GROUP SHOT: OLLIE, WARDEN, CHAPLAIN, AND GUARDS. EARLY MORNING.

OLLIE: Warden, the letters, I want to take them with me.

WARDEN: A few of the letters?

OLLIE: All of 'em. I want 'em with me.

WARDEN: In the room?

OLLIE: Some of 'em in the chair with me.

WARDEN: Son, they'd burn.

OLLIE: That's all right. Me and the letters together.

84] LETTERS.
A shot of the immense pile of letters. Early morning light touches them.

85] TWO-SHOT: OLLIE AND THE WARDEN.

OLLIE: It's a request, the last one.

WARDEN: The newspaper people will wonder what they're—

OLLIE: Newspaper people wonder, let 'em wonder. I want all my letters with me.

WARDEN: Where do you want them, Ollie?

OLLIE: Some of 'em in the chair with me and the rest where I can see 'em.

86] THREE-SHOT: INCLUDING THE CHAPLAIN.

CHAPLAIN: It would distract him from prayer.

OLLIE: I'm not gonna pray or lissen to you praying.

WARDEN: I'll have them carried in.

OLLIE: Let me carry some.

WARDEN: Which ones?

OLLIE: Any.

[*The warden places some letters in Ollie's one hand.*]

OLLIE: Thanks.

87] CLOSE ON OLLIE APPROACHING THE CHAIR.

NARRATOR'S VOICE [*accompanying the visual action on the screen*]: He carried them with him as a child carries a doll or a toy into a dentist's office to give him the protection of the familiar and loved. . . . He showed no fear; he showed only what he had shown on street corners waiting to be solicited. When he sat down in the chair his hand deposited the letters between his legs, near the crotch. At the last moment a guard reached out to remove them. But Ollie's thighs closed on them in a desperate clutch that could not have been easily broken and the warden gave a sign to let them stay there. Then the moment came. The atmosphere hummed and darkened. Bolts from across the frontiers of the unknown, the casually named and employed but illimitably mysterious power that first invested a static infinity of space with heat and brilliance and motion, were channeled through Ollie's body for one instant, a second, and a third . . . and then swept back across those immense frontiers, having claimed and withdrawn whatever was theirs in the boy whose lost right arm had been known as "lightning in leather."

88] GROUP SHOT OF MEDICAL STUDENTS IN A LABORATORY FOR THE DISSECTION OF UN-CLAIMED DEAD BODIES.

A shaft of intense light shines momentarily upon the dissecting table and on the body of Ollie covered with a white sheet. As the sheet is drawn away the camera lifts to the heads of the medical students.

Quick glances of something needless to define are exchanged between two of the students.

NARRATOR'S VOICE: —The body, unclaimed after death, had been turned over to a medical college to be used in a classroom laboratory.

The young men who performed the dissection were somewhat abashed by the body under their knives. It seemed intended for some more august purpose, to stand in a gallery of antique sculpture, touched only by light through stillness and contemplation, for it had the nobility of some broken Apollo that no one was likely to carve so purely again. —But death has never been much in the way of completion.

[*The scene dissolves.*]

THE END

STOPPED ROCKING

for Maureen Stapleton

PRINCIPAL CHARACTERS

(in order of appearance)

OLAF SVENSON

SISTER GRACE

ALICIA TROUT

SISTER GRIM

SUGAR, *a patient*

JANET SVENSON

STUART, *a student*

SOPHIE, *the patient in the rocker*

MADGE, *a patient*

GLORIA, *a patient*

TINY, *a patient*

DR. J. PLANTER CASH

EMILY, *the uncooperative patient*

GEORGE

THE CLERK IN THE GENERAL STORE

THE APPARITION OF FATHER O'DONNELL

AUTHOR'S NOTE

A piece of writing for the screen or television is never complete in its existence on paper but must be transfigured by the exceptional sensibilities and talents of such performers as Maureen Stapleton (for whom I created the part of Janet) and Anne Meacham whom I see so clearly as Sister Grace, and whatever other gifted artists, especially the director, become my collaborators in the bringing of what is written into what is seen and spoken, and is heard and felt by the waiting audience. I say "waiting audience" with full confidence that one is, indeed, waiting for *Stopped Rocking*. This confidence is secure in me because I know that the "dark" of the work is more than balanced by its humanity, and that this light of humanity will tip the balance favorably, as a natural act of grace.

T.W.
1977

STOPPED ROCKING

||||||||||||||||||||||||||||||||||||||||||||||||||||||||||||||||||||||||||||||||||||||||||||||||||||||||||||||||||||||||||||||||||||||||||||||||||||||||||||||||||||||||||||||

1] EXTERIOR. DAY.

A long shot from St. Carmine's—a Catholic sanitarium—of a camping vehicle drawing up before the institution. The door explodes open and Olaf springs out. This initial alacrity is almost immediately slowed: the camera closes on Olaf. He is tall, much younger looking than his age. His face, especially now that his approach slows almost to a halt, is curiously void of expression: its blondness seems bleached (not artificially: he is athletic director at the local community college) and his features appear to be sculpted from stone.

When the camera has closed upon his face it then shifts its POV to Olaf's and we see what has halted his approach to the mental hospital.

2] ONE-SHOT: A PATIENT IN A WHEELCHAIR.

A patient "in restraint" is being rapidly wheeled out of a side entrance to a waiting ambulance marked STATE HOSPITAL FOUR. Two orderlies and a nun in nurse's costume attend the transference to the ambulance. There are dreadful strangulated cries from the patient as she observes the inscription on the ambulance.

3] ONE-SHOT: OLAF.

The camera returns to the face of Olaf or "Stone Man" and it draws back as he now slowly, and then more rapidly, continues his approach.

OLAF: Nurse. Sister!

4] MEDIUM TWO-SHOT: OLAF AND SISTER GRACE.

Her face is wet with tears. He ducks his head in perfunctory acknowledgment of her grief.

OLAF: A patient was removed and I—thought for a moment it was my—wife—Janet . . .

SISTER GRACE: Oh, you're Mr. Svenson. [*She dismisses her involuntary moment of grief and smiles at him cheerfully.*] Yes, of course. You're bringing her Easter flowers. She'll be so excited.

OLAF: Isn't it better for Janet to avoid excitement?

SISTER GRACE: Not *good* excitement.

OLAF: I don't think any excitement is good for Janet.

SISTER GRACE: Mr. Svenson, you know she lives for your visits.

OLAF: Surely in five years' time she's formed other attachments.

SISTER GRACE: Among the patients, oh, yes, she's friendly with other patients if they're at all responsive. Of course, some are withdrawn. Janet isn't. Plays bridge every evening, has animated conversations with those that are talkers. Some aren't. She's quite active in recreational and occupational therapy. All in all, I think you can be quite pleased, quite happy and proud of her adjustment. No, no, I don't mean adjustment. Adjustment isn't desirable always to a place of confinement. What I meant is her progress toward conditions for release.

OLAF: Sister, I don't think this is the time to discuss Janet's condition.

SISTER GRACE: Certainly not. This is the time for your visit.

OLAF: No. That's not what I meant. I haven't come for a visit.

SISTER GRACE: Today of all days, Easter Sunday? But you're here with the flowers.

OLAF: Would you please just give the flowers to her. You see, in five years' time, I've formed other attachments if she hasn't, I have—other commitments.

SISTER GRACE: But you wouldn't, you mustn't, allow that to prevent the visits that she lives for?

OLAF: Just, just give her the plant!

SISTER GRACE: How will I explain, what can I say to Janet, that you delivered a plant but wouldn't come upstairs to—

OLAF: Wouldn't, couldn't! Say that—

[*He breaks away abruptly and starts rapidly down the walk with its regimental border of neatly trimmed shrubs.*]

SISTER GRACE [*calling after him*]: Say that love is perishable as flowers?

[*The camera closes on Olaf's face.*]

OLAF: *YES!* Say that or—

SISTER GRACE: *What?*

OLAF: Nothing, nothing!

SISTER GRACE: Mr. Svenson, it will break her heart!

5] MEDIUM LONG SHOT OF OLAF.
He springs into the cab of the camper which, unable to break old habits, he always calls the "trailer." Before gripping the

299

steering wheel, he lifts his hands: they vibrate with tension. He shuts his eyes tightly for a moment: then brings his hands down fiercely on the wheel.

We hear the motor starting. A woman's voice, fades in, purring to him.

ALICIA'S VOICE: Olaf, Stone Man, don't you know what it is? It's simply moral blackmail. You must have the strength to resist it, moral blackmail, resist it.

OLAF [*responding to the voice*]: It—*hurts* . . .

ALICIA'S VOICE: A temporary hurt necessary to—new life!

6] CLOSE SHOT OF SISTER GRACE.
The flowerpot of lilies trembles in her hands. She draws a breath, then crosses to the hospital entrance where she is encountered by Sister "Grim."

SISTER GRIM: When will you learn that emotional involvement is out of place in a mental institution?

SISTER GRACE: I hope never, never! Otherwise, I would be heartless and lifeless.

SISTER GRIM: And better able to function.

SISTER GRACE: *Then this is a cemetery?*

[*Dim out.*]

7] INTERIOR. DAY.
A fairly close shot of Sister Grace walking along a corridor of numbered cubicles, bearing the Easter plant. She encounters

300

a great, lumbering woman who stands in her way so that she must halt for a moment.

WOMAN: You so sweet, you just a lump of sugar, you sweet, sweet lump of sugar!

[*Then without warning she strikes at Sister Grace. The sister is not unaccustomed to such "surprises" and she evades the blow. The patient, called Sugar, thrown off balance, careens against cubicle number four. The door crashes open.*]

8] CLOSE SHOT OF JANET.
She is the occupant of cubicle number four.

JANET [*at the sight of Sugar*]: *Don't say it! Don't call me Sugar!*

[*Sister Grace enters the close shot. She catches fearlessly hold of the great, menacing patient's arm.*]

SISTER GRACE: Sugar! Back to the day room. Or would you like the tubs?

SUGAR [*the ferocity going out of her glare*]: Sugar, you so sweet, jus' a lump a—sugar . . .

[*She lumbers out of the cubicle entrance and down the corridor.*]

SISTER GRACE: Janet, you're all dressed up for—Easter Service?

JANET: Sister Grace, today *Olaf* will visit! I've got a beauty appointment, shampoo, rinse! trim! Oh, I—hope I—will make a good impression on him this time, Sister. Excuse me, I'll see you at Service, after my beauty appointment!

301

SISTER GRACE: Janet, look! [*She extends the potted flowers.*]

JANET: Beautiful! For Chapel? [*Her tremulous hand touches the lilies a moment. Then she gasps and rushes out of the shot.*]

[*Sister Grace, her face irresolute, starts to say something— then enters cubicle four and sets the potted lilies on the tiny bedside table and withdraws. The camera remains on the lilies. Chapel music: "Angels of Light." But light is seen to be fading about the lilies.*]

[*Dim out.*]

9] INTERIOR. NIGHT.
We see Janet's cubicle. There is a close shot of the potted lilies on the bedside table. We hear her outcry and see her violently trembling hand snatch up a card.

10] CLOSE ONE-SHOT: JANET.
The camera draws back to include her full figure as she rushes to the doorway, shouting, "Olaf! Olaf!" as if she thought he might be within hearing.

Sister Grace rushes into the frame, pressing a hand to Janet's mouth.

SISTER GRACE: Janet, please, the night nurse will *report*!

JANET: —How—were the flowers—delivered?

SISTER GRACE [*hushed, tightly clasping Janet's hand*]: By hand. Your husband delivered them to me.

JANET: Olaf wouldn't come in? Just, just delivered the lilies?

SISTER GRACE: Your husband seemed to be—overcome with emotion. —I think he didn't want you to see him in that—condition, Janet.

JANET: What does it say on the card?

SISTER GRACE: "Happy Easter, Janet."

JANET: —Not? —*Love,* Janet, from—*Olaf?*

11] A CLASSROOM IN PHYSICS AT THE COMMUNITY
COLLEGE. MORNING.

A bell has just terminated the period. There is a medium shot of students trooping out the door, including the teacher who is not trooping out but loitering by a window through which radiant spring sunlight is not adequately excluded from her rather sheer blouse. The effect is a bit more provocative than seems altogether unplanned. She is a mathematical bombshell. Her name is Alicia Trout.

ALICIA: Stuart, I asked you to erase the blackboard.

STUART: You've got a free period now so there's no hurry, is there?

ALICIA: My husband Mr. Svenson, the athletic director, visits me at this time.

STUART: In that corner? Not visible from the hall?

[*He has approached within reach of her, sweat on his tawny skin. He extends a hand, automatically, shakily, toward her bosom. She cries out histrionically.*]

ALICIA: *OLAF!*

STUART [*backing away*]: Sorry, Miss Trout. No offense intended but—that blouse is—transparent.

[*He turns to erase the equation from the blackboard. She leans out the half open window and repeats her cry "OLAF!" He enters, at this moment, the classroom door.*]

STUART: Erased.

[*He nods to Olaf and exits from the shot.*]

12] CLASSROOM. DAY. CLOSE TWO-SHOT: OLAF AND ALICIA.

ALICIA: I've had a very upsetting experience with that student who just walked out. He—attempted to—place his hand on my—

[*She touches her bosom.*]

OLAF: Better report that. But, honey, that blouse, well, it's spring and a slight see-through blouse with a lace bra—I'd say the kid was offered some provocation.

ALICIA: What a contemptible—insinuation! Provocation? Yes, he did have that. He knows that I am unmarried. But living with you.

OLAF: Please, not that again in the year seventy-five.

[*He shrugs, grins, clasps her in his arms.*]

ALICIA: That door has glass panes; there are students in the corridor grinning in at us!

OLAF: Oh, want me to let you go?

ALICIA: —No, Stone Man. I want you to let *her* go.

OLAF [*releasing her from embrace*]: You know what Janet means to me.

ALICIA: Exactly. Moral blackmail. Accept it. But prepare yourself for the natural, normal woman's retaliation against this five-year insult! You must not go out there again! —Easter Sunday you came back enveloped in her shadow like a—an eclipse of the sun.

OLAF: You know I didn't visit her last Sunday.

ALICIA: Oh, yes, you did, with flowers!

OLAF [*in a strange, strangulated voice*]: I went—to the asylum—but did not make a visit.

ALICIA: Even your voice is affected! What are you trying to tell me that's so difficult to say?

OLAF: I delivered the flowers to a nun called—Sister—Grace. Just delivered. No visit. I said—"Just give her the flowers." She said, "With what explanation, what message—"

[*With a vehemence that makes Alicia gasp, he flings himself violently into a chair, clutching his head.*]

ALICIA: Now you see what it's doing to you—it's making you crazy as Janet. Olaf, a clear-cut decision has to be made.

[*A bell rings. He rises slowly, exhausted.*]

OLAF: Got another class waiting. "Clear-cut decisions"—they're a mathematical possibility, maybe, but in life? See you.

305

[*He gives her a hard kiss and runs out of the classroom. She goes to the window. Olaf blows a whistle on the playing field below the window.*]

ALICIA [*shrilly, from the window*]: Are you blowing that whistle on me?

13] INTERIOR. THE "DAY ROOM" OF ST. CARMINE'S. AFTERNOON.

A very wide shot establishes the day room of St. Carmine's. It is about 5 P.M., the dinner hour at the place; the afternoon is fair and summery. This wide shot should have the appearance of a canvas by a master painter. I think of early Van Gogh and of the early Dutch schools—the emphasis on light and shadow. A poetic tristesse, *on the surface, a stark desolation of the spirit under . . .*

The asylum is superior to ordinary public institutions of its kind only through the rather formalized humanity of the sisters who are its attendants.

The light is smoky as even fair summer light is often smoky in St. Louis, at least as I recall it. Through grated and screened windows, fast shut, the light slants, now, toward early dusk. The sisters move almost choreographically about the bleakly undecorated, the sparely furnished room, serving the evening meal from large metal carts on wheels; most of the patients are assembled at the bare-looking tables. There is no glassware since glass is a possible means of attack on the self or another; the film is in black and white or very, very unobtrusive color.

14] THE SAME.

The camera approaches four women seated about a card table. A nurse, passing out medication, identifies each of them by name as she distributes the small paper cups that contain their pills.

SISTER GRACE: Madge. Gloria. Tiny. Janet.

[Janet's attention is fixed on a patient seated in a rocker against the wall.

[The camera closes on the woman. Her face is a mask of sorrow but still beautiful.]

JANET *[as if to herself]*: I noticed last night that she seemed to be rocking slower. I thought I must be mistaken because she's always rocked the same speed, never varies, but now—

MADGE *[darkly]*: Yais, she's rocking slower.

JANET: I guess she's finally slowing down from exhaustion. Rocking that fast all the time is—strenuous—exercise so she's slowed down a little. . . . And her hands have loosened a little on the arms of the rocker and her face looks—peaceful . . .

MADGE: Blank. Retired from life. Your deal, Janet. Janet, I said your DEAL!

JANET: Oh. Sorry.

MADGE *[crossly]*: Don't be sorry, just deal, it's almost lights out time.

[Gloria suddenly utters a wild, despairing cry.]

JANET: Oh, my God, they've put the sign on her door for EST in the morning!

GLORIA [*rising frantically*]: No, no, no, I can't take it, I'm seventy-two years old, they're starting me on another series of shock. I begged son to keep me off it, he promised he'd keep me off it!

MADGE: There goes the bridge game.

[*Devastated, Gloria is led from the table by Sister Grace, speaking soothingly to her.*

[*The camera picks up a small cluster of patients seated before the TV set as a commercial comes on and a patient sings along with it, loudly.*]

COMMERCIAL AND PATIENT: "Youuuu've got a lot to live/And Pepsi's got a lot to give."

MADGE: We'll play three-handed. Janet! *Deal!*

JANET: We mustn't pay any attention or they'll notice, they'll start to monitor her.

MADGE: When that rocker stops, she'll be transferred to Floor Nine, the "vegetable garden."

[*The commercial continues. A disciplinarian, Sister Grim, calls out warningly.*]

SISTER GRIM: Lights out, ladies!

[*She turns off the TV set and the scene dims out.*]

15] FADE IN: INTERIOR. THE OFFICE OF A STAFF DOCTOR AT THE ASYLUM. DAY.
The room is just a shade off the realistic, as are all the sets in the work. The desk is too particularly a desk, all precision

308

and neatness and foursquare: on it, the usual glossily conspicuous tooled-leather-framed and tinted photographs of the wife and child, the child a pre-pubescent girl whose "smile at Daddy" exposes large teeth with formidable braces. To balance this bit of decor is an autographed photo of, say, Dr. Karen Horney, inscribed to Dr. J. P. Cash with a flourish of haste and healthy assertiveness (and probably I should not have mentioned the name Karen Horney)—the sentiment is "cordially."

To the left of the desk is a photograph of Father O'Donnell wearing an entirely appropriate expression of sorrow as his photographic image looks down upon the room. On the opposite wall is one of the familiar (unsigned) photographs of Sigmund Freud. The window of the office is enmeshed with wire screen but is open almost halfway.

The staff doctor, Dr. Cash, is notable chiefly for the intense glitter of his eyeglasses, yes, despite the fact that he is portlier, especially at the paunch and hips than, say, the late President Taft and at least as important in his demeanor: his shoulders are extremely narrow, if that detail doesn't impose a casting problem.

All of this is seen through the office door, which has been opened just a second before the scene is exposed.

Dr. J. Planter Cash—the name is announced by a rather oversize desk plaque directly facing the camera through the open door—looks up for a reluctant instant from an open file before him. He looks quickly down with a tight little smile somehow less cheering than a frown or scowl. Then he looks up again at whomever has opened his door, at the same time removing his rimless glasses to rub them as if they were not already too piercingly clear.

16] CUT TO: CLOSE ONE-SHOT: JANET, FROM THE
DOCTOR'S POV.
She is obviously unnerved; she quickly crosses herself.

DOCTOR: Miss—?

JANET: No, I'm—Mrs. . . .

DOCTOR: Just Mrs.? [*He smiles a tight little professional smile.*]

JANET: My name is there on my files. You're looking at my
files.

DOCTOR: Before interviewing a patient, I always pull the file
on that patient's history at St. Carmine's. —Will you please sit
down, Mrs. Svenson?

JANET: —Wh-where?

DOCTOR [*he laughs professionally, dryly*]: There are two
chairs in the office. I'm sitting in one. Obviously you would sit
in the other. Unless you prefer the floor.

JANET: —FATHER O'DONNELL NEVER—MADE—
FUN—OF US!

DOCTOR: Father O'Donnell was not a therapist, Mrs. Svenson,
although he did occupy this office as Chief of Staff before his—
[*He regards her more sharply as she crosses herself.*] —Do you
always cross yourself at the mention of Father O'Donnell?

JANET: You mentioned his death.

DOCTOR: I didn't quite mention his death. —Do you regard
death as unmentionable, Mrs. Svenson?

310

JANET: Yes! —He was a saint.

DOCTOR: You have your own canon of saints. [*He is jocular now.*] You beat the Church to it. You confer sainthood on the deceased before their miracles and their visions have been established. [*He makes a note in her files.*]

JANET: I—meant in my—heart, in my—memory of a man who—would never make fun of—affliction.

DOCTOR: —I find that a little humor is usually—useful here.

JANET: What did you write on my files, please?

DOCTOR: I wrote the word "agitated"—followed by a long dash.

JANET: The long dash doesn't mean escape, that's not a dash for escape! [*She tries to laugh.*]

DOCTOR: —That was a rather witty remark you just made. [*He makes another quick note.*]

JANET: Please stop making notes on me, please, please. Olaf, my husband, Olaf, brought a pot of flowers to St. Carmine's on Easter but he didn't come in to see me, just delivered the card, I found the flowers and card in my room but he didn't, he couldn't come in!

DOCTOR: He couldn't deliver the flowers to you personally?

[*She shakes her head, tears starting.*]

DOCTOR: How do you interpret this rather . . . impersonal way in which he presented you with these flowers?

311

JANET: Interpret it—not *anxious* for—*personal*—*contact*!

DOCTOR: Or even perhaps reluctance might be construed, but—still he did remember you with flowers . . .

[*Watching her closely, he switches a radio on. The music, a love song, makes her gasp.*]

DOCTOR: Oh, the music disturbs you, Mrs., uh—Svenson?

JANET: A radio, oh! I thought it was in my head, no, no, I—*love* the—song, but it's been so long since the Easter flowers came to me without Olaf that they've dried up, they've been thrown away, all I've got is the card. Not "Love to Janet," but—"Happy Easter, Janet" . . .

[*He scribbles another note.*]

JANET: What note did you just write on me? Dr. Cash?

DOCTOR: A therapist doesn't usually read his notes on a patient to the patient at the patient's request, but I will read you this one. "Patient very agitated by a popular love song." —Now. —It seems from your files that once you were transferred from Ward Seven to—Ward Nine.

JANET: Yes, I spent a week in the vegetable garden. Are you planting me back there?!

DOCTOR [*with a professional smile*]: How did you like it in the "vegetable garden," as you put it?

JANET: That's how it's always put, it's the vegetable garden, Floor Nine, the floor for—motionless—people. I am not motionless, Doctor. I move. Look. I am up. I sat down and now I stand and— [*She snatches up his family photograph.*] Oh, you have—

family, a very, very attractive little girl. I had to wear braces on my teeth, too, till—will—you please tell me what to expect so I can—prepare to—expect? Is it *transfer to vegetable garden?* Please, no, you see I move, I move, I— [*She thrashes from wall to wall like a caged bird.*]

DOCTOR [*switching off radio*]: —Bravo. No. —You aren't a candidate for what you refer to as the vegetable garden but for an Ozark outing with your husband, Mrs., uh—Svenson. I must tell you I have misgivings. [*He removes the family photo from her trembling hand.*] The emotionalism which could be involved in an outing of this kind with—

JANET: Olaf!

DOCTOR: —Has already disturbed you. However—we realize what it means to you and sometimes risky projects must be allowed a chance to justify themselves, regardless of—your lips are moving as if you're speaking but you're not speaking and you're not looking at me. Whom are you speaking to and what are you looking at?

JANET: —I —am thanking—Father O'Donnell—in prayer . . .

[*The scene dims out.*]

17] CUT TO: INTERIOR. THE DAY ROOM. THE DINNER HOUR.
Sister Grace is conducting Janet to a seat at her table.

SISTER GRACE: Well, now, look here, Ladies. Janet is having dinner with you again. Nice? Wonderful? Let's have a little applause for Janet's return to your table!

[*They smile up at her and applaud; she laughs breathlessly and ducks her head in an awkward little bow, not knowing how otherwise to respond.*]

[*Dim out.*]

18] FADE IN: INTERIOR. THE DAY ROOM.
A medium shot draws in closer and clearer to its Gothic "subject." It is a two-shot when it reaches its close view. A sister, known as Sister Grim—a disciplinarian with hard, pinched features but a dutifully committed (dedicated) air— is attempting to force-feed, or "spoon-feed" an uncooperative, resistant old woman in a shapeless gray dress, much repaired.

19] THE SAME.
Sister Grace enters the frame. She has a true "vocation."

SISTER GRACE [*with apparent dislike of Sister Grim*]: How's it going this evening?

SISTER GRIM [*impatiently*]: Drooling out every spoonful I can force in her jaws. Can't you see it running down her dress?

SISTER GRACE: Let me try it a while.

SISTER GRIM: Oh, you've thought of a superior method?

SISTER GRACE: I think I can use—persuasion.

SISTER GRIM: Here! Use persuasion! [*She thrusts the tray and spoon at Sister Grace.*] You'll see it's useless. Tomorrow she'll be transferred to Floor Nine, the vegetable garden, and go on glucose; the tube. [*She stalks out of view.*]

[*Sister Grace kneels before the desicated, toothless old woman and tries "persuasion."*]

314

SISTER GRACE: Now, Emily, this won't do. You have to eat. Open. Emily, open your jaws, dear. [*There is no reaction to* "*persuasion.*"] Emily, can you hear me? Can you hear Sister Grace? It's five days you've not eaten and tomorrow you might be transferred to Floor Nine. Understand? TRANSFERRED!

[*A gradual look of awful comprehension appears on the old woman's face; slowly her jaws come unlocked a little, sufficient to admit the bent spoonful of gruel. Sister Grim re-enters the mean.*]

SISTER GRIM: It won't stay in, she'll reject it.

[*Sister Grim is proven right, to her apparent satisfaction; the gruel emerges from the corners of the old woman's mouth.*]

SISTER GRIM: —There, now, successful persuasion?

SISTER GRACE: If you would just move away. You know how it happened. After Father O'Donnell, she started grieving and resisting; it is just mourning for him. An inconsolable mourning which she can't help.

SISTER GRIM: Sister Grace, your attitudes are romantic; I think you'd better confess to that, tomorrow.

SISTER GRACE: You need confession, too. Insensibility is worse than romanticism.

SISTER GRIM: Tomorrow this old woman will be transferred! To Nine!

[*All during this episode, the camera's POV has included a banner strung across the narrow day room. It is crudely lettered; it says "Welcome Olaf!"* —*The smoky light is fading on it now.*]

315

20] INTERIOR. EARLY EVENING.

The camera pans to the entrance of a bedroom cubicle; in it stands an early middle-aged woman with a saintly face: Janet. The camera closes on her to a medium one-shot and we see that she is very agitated; she seems to be prepared for an outing. She has on her dress-up dress and is clutching a shiny red purse, twisting its handle. Sister Grace approaches her.

SISTER GRACE: Janet, you missed dinner.

JANET: Oh, we'll stop for dinner in the Ozarks!

SISTER GRACE [*reluctantly*]: Janet, your husband just phoned that the Ozark vacation has to be cancelled this weekend.

JANET: NO, NO! WHY! WITH THE BANNER PUT UP AND ME STANDING HERE WAITING IN THIS DOOR TWO HOURS! OLAF! WOULDN'T, HE WOULDN'T!

SISTER GRACE: I've saved a plate for you. The food is cold but you'd better come eat it. The trip is definitely off. I took the call, dear. You'd better—

JANET: —Can I—go to bed, please?

[*The camera draws closer. Sister Grace whispers urgently to Janet.*]

SISTER GRACE: You know what happens when food is rejected on Seven. Transference to Nine!

JANET: I will go sit at the table, but I'm still sure Olaf will come after all and we will eat in the Ozarks at sunset, but I'll— go to my table . . .

[*The camera follows her lifeless approach to a table.*]

MADGE [*at the table*]: No Olaf, no Ozarks?

JANET: Later! Don't touch the banner!

[*The scene dims out.*]

21] FADE IN: INTERIOR. DAY ROOM. EARLY DUSK.
*The wide camera view includes the banner which is fading
and drooping now. An old man with a ladder starts to remove it. There is a shriek of protest.*

JANET: NO, NO, NO, NO, NO!

[*The camera picks her up as she rushes to the old man and
pushes him violently away from the ladder; he falls to the
floor.*

[*Three sisters rush at Janet; one of them is Grace.*]

SISTER GRIM: Violence!

SISTER GRACE: Provoked!

SISTER GRIM: Not to be tolerated!

SISTER GRACE: You know what the banner means to her!

SISTER GRIM: It's hung there three weeks and Olaf Svenson is
living in sin with another woman and he has no intention of
taking his wife to the Ozarks or to the planet Mars in a rocket!
You will be *reported*! —And she goes into *restraint* in Ward
Nine, at *once*!

SISTER GRACE: Never!

317

SISTER GRIM: Are you in charge of this ward?

SISTER GRACE: Yes! —I know the life in it and all you know is the death!

SISTER GRIM: We shall see how this hysterical statement sits with Dr. Cash. George! Can you get up?

GEORGE: I'm— [*He rises.*] —up.

SISTER GRIM: I will write out a report of this incident, you will sign it, I'll deliver it to Mother right away.

GEORGE: No, no, let it go, she didn't know it was me; she's always been very nice to me.

22] CUT TO: INTERIOR. LATER.
Electric bulbs go on in the day room. The banner is down. Several patients are staring at a woman rocking more and more slowly.

ONE: I think she's going to stop rocking!

TWO [*in an awed whisper*]: If she stops, she'll go to the vegetable garden.

[*The rocker continues to slow; then suddenly stops. Janet enters the frame and begins to rock the woman. Sister Grim appears.*]

SISTER GRIM: Will you stop interfering? We are monitoring this patient; go back to your chair!

[*Janet, sobbing, covers her face. Sister Grace enters the frame and leads her away, the camera following.*]

318

SISTER GRACE: Janet, come to the chapel with me; we'll speak to St. Jude.

JANET: St. Jude of Impossible Cases!

SISTER GRACE [*her eyes closing*]: Such cases exist; we know that, so what can we do but pray?

23] FADE IN: DR. CASH'S OFFICE.
From Janet's POV we see him looking up at her with an air of controlled exasperation.

DR. CASH: I'd hoped this—interview—could be avoided.

[*The camera closes in on Janet.*]

JANET: So had I—hoped so . . .

DR. CASH: —Mrs. Svenson, I have your files on my desk.

JANET: I—recognized them.

DR. CASH: You know that you are being closely monitored lately.

JANET: Yes! Close!

DR. CASH: And for almost two weeks you have been too acutely disturbed to eat at table. You remember my misgivings about the proposed Ozark outing with your former husband.

JANET: No, not former: still! I am still Mrs. Svenson!

DR. CASH: Legally, yes, but you and I are aware that your husband Olaf Svenson is—cohabiting and has been—cohabiting with a professional colleague of his.

319

JANET: Olaf doesn't live with a—gym teacher, no! With a woman that's in mathematics.

DR. CASH: I meant a teacher in the same institution. May we get to the point? Directly? This disturbance of yours came about when the proposed Ozark outing which I didn't approve of failed to—

JANET: OLAF DIDN'T SHOW! —My disturbance and no appetite were caused by that —disappointment.

DR. CASH [*thrusting her files back in the cabinet*]: Now, Mrs. Svenson, you may not know that we are filled to capacity and somewhat over capacity here and that we have a long waiting list. Our staff's overworked, wards overcrowded, erection of the new wing postponed for six months because donations have not come in as expected and scheduled. Now if you're aware of these circumstances, not just of your private world, you must know that our staff is obliged to suggest the transference of certain patients who seem to be making unsatisfactory progress or no progress at all or—sometimes regression. These circumstances have been mentioned to your husband Olaf Svenson in a letter dated June 12 to which he replied— [*He glances down at the letters.*] —in a letter dated July 2 saying he fully appreciated our situation here and is not opposed to your transfer to the state institution at Farmington where there's an opening. Now, Mrs. Svenson, if you've been listening to me, I'm sure you must have—

[*His voice continues on its dry course but turns into mere mechanical sound, no intelligible words.*

[*Fade out.*]

24] FADE IN: INTERIOR. THE APARTMENT OF OLAF AND ALICIA. EVENING.

*It is a slightly satirical example of the genre of typical "sweet"
little suburban apartments in a condominium—the TV set is
directly before the love seat and over the love seat is a greatly
enlarged color photo of Olaf and Alicia very affectionately
posed together in almost precisely the same position in which
they are now seated on the love seat, her cheek pressed to his
massive shoulder, his arm around her—the coloring quite
similar.*

Needless to say, this is a fairly close two-shot.

*The TV is going; the subject of the program a sports event.
The sound is off or very low under the following—Alicia is
continuing a monologue which is somewhat in the style of a
speech written for her, and she delivers it with a monotony
which is too pronounced and nasal to be monotonous.*

*Olaf is trying to watch a special report of the highlights of a
baseball game between the Cardinals and the Reds. Apparently, he is accustomed to Alicia's monologue, so that it
doesn't intrude much on his consciousness.*

ALICIA [*continuing—we have seen her lips moving before the
sound comes on*]: —Even in this age of permissiveness, so-
called, there are pockets of society which are immune to it and
my family, Stone Man, as you very well know, is a conventional
family and although they pretend to ignore my position, I can
assure you, Stone Man, that they are aware of it and distressed
by it. There is a self-consciousness at the holiday get-together;
I feel it the moment that we arrive together. A certain look in
their faces, a certain tone of voice, not exactly condemning us
for the pretense of a marriage which doesn't exist in the eyes
of the law except the law which is called common and which is
just that, common, common as two alley cats—

OLAF: Two alley cats in a condominium, huh?

321

[*On this line he rises to turn up the volume of the ball game. Then he turns to her with his hand raised.*]

ALICIA: Why did you turn up the volume and raise your hand?

OLAF: My hand is raised because I am a pupil in a classroom asking permission to go to the boys' room and I turned up the volume so that I could hear the ball game in the boys' room.

ALICIA: Very, very amusing.

OLAF: Thanks.

[*He stalks to the bathroom door. She rises and turns down the TV volume to a whisper. The bathroom door is ajar. He thrusts his head into view and observes—*]

OLAF: You've turned the volume down so I can't hear it.

ALICIA: Don't you realize, Stone Man, that this ball game was played about five hours ago and a full description of it, including the final score, is right there in the *St. Louis Post-Dispatch*?

[*She points to a newspaper on the coffee table.*]

OLAF: Yes, I realize that, Alicia, but do you realize that about five hours ago I was coaching the summer basketball camp? And so was unable to see Bugsy Mahler hit the home run that puts him just one run behind the all time record of the Babe? [*He comes out, zipping his fly.*] If you were attending a lecture by one of the all time greats in the field of physics— [*He turns up the volume on the TV.*] I would not turn off his mike to a whisper that you could barely hear!

ALICIA: We have to come to a compromise on the decibel level of the ball game highlights, Olaf, because I don't intend to repeat what I am saying anytime ever again.

OLAF: Thanks.

ALICIA: I am saying that secretly in their hearts my family are seething with outrage over the perpetuation of a sham, a marriage without legal sanction—

OLAF [*rising*]: HERE COMES BUGSY TO BAT!

[*Quick as a cat, she springs from the love seat to turn off the set. He lunges toward it. She blocks him powerfully.*]

OLAF: BUGSY, BUGSY'S AT BAT! [*He thrusts her violently away from the set.*]

ALICIA: VIOLENCE?

OLAF [*uttering an outraged howl—wordless as the TV picture fades in too slowly, also the sportscaster's voice*]: Gahhhh!

ALICIA: Sometimes your behavior is downright puerile.

[*They freeze, confronting each other as the sportscaster's voice resumes.*]

VOICE: And that, folks, winds it up, the crowd is screaming in triumph, for Bugsy Mahler has slammed it out of the ball park with two men on base in the ninth.

OLAF [*with controlled passion*]: An historic moment—and you turned it off!

ALICIA: That historic moment occurred five hours ago.

OLAF: I did not SEE it!

ALICIA: Yes, you are exhibiting a side of your nature which is downright puerile.

OLAF [*fiercely*]: Downright what?

ALICIA: If I have used a word not in your vocabulary, I will define it for you. The word "puerile," spelt p-u-e—

[*He speaks the "silent word" and flings himself on the love seat, his feet on the upholstery.*]

ALICIA: Will you kindly remove your clodhopper feet from the cushion of that love seat?

[*He ignores the request. She comes to him, kneels at his feet and removes his shoes.*]

ALICIA: Now, love, I am going to spray your feet with Footguard to remove that locker-room odor, then I will give you an Electro-Vibe spinal massage because my Stone Man is in a nervous condition that I know the cause of but which he refuses to face. [*She returns with a spray can and electric vibrator.*] Separate toes.

OLAF [*exhaustedly*]: You know I take at least two showers a day.

ALICIA: Turn on stomach.

[*He complies, exhaustedly. She applies the vibrator to his spine, her voice continuing over its hum.*]

ALICIA: At family get-togethers, you may not notice that after five years of cohabitation with me, you're still greeted as Mr.

324

Svenson, with a significant inflection, never, never as Olaf. How do you interpret that except as a discreet sign of disapproval?

OLAF: Never noticed and wouldn't care if I did.

ALICIA: No, probably not, but I? —Suppose that Uncle Horace, in spite of his stroke, becomes aware of our make-believe marriage, not sanctioned by church or law. That nurse-companion of his is worming her sly way into his confidence and affections, oh, I know she'll let the cat out of the bag in the most apparently innocent way. And as for mother, you know her tendency to rattle and tattle on her constant visits to Uncle Horace. You know.

OLAF: What I know is that you're living on the purely hypothetical assumption that your Uncle Horace, the family millionaire, still holds you first in his heart and his last will and testament. You hang onto that delusion regardless of the fact that the last you heard from him was that Christmas card which he didn't bother to sign.

ALICIA: A right-handed man, paralyzed on his right side, cannot be expected to sign with his right hand.

OLAF: How about his left toes? No? His nurse-companion could have signed it for him with "love and devotion always" if that was his sentiment toward you, could have sent a live poinsettia plant instead of an unsigned card with a dead wreath on it.

ALICIA: Let us please leave Uncle Horace out of this discussion, Olaf.

OLAF: No objection to that.

ALICIA: It spoke volumes to me, that token of remembrance— [*She sobs histrionically.*] From a dearly loved man approaching

325

the "last great adventure" which is—WHERE ARE YOU GO-
ING?

OLAF: On the hottest night of the hottest summer of this cen-
tury, you're—you're climbing me up the wall and onto the
ceiling. And I am going out, O-U-T, out!

[*He lunges off the love seat: the Electro-Vibe flies one way,
the Footguard the other. He rushes out onto the little concrete balcony of the condominium: it has two chairs of
chromium and vinyl; there are imitation coach lanterns on
either side of the sliding-glass doors. Alicia follows him out
and switches on the lanterns.*]

OLAF: Turn off those lights!

[*She decides upon other tactics and presses the switch: now
the balcony is lighted only by the myriad lights on other love
nests in the high-rise condominium.*]

OLAF [*drawing a long breath*]: —You want me to explain to
you once more why it is necessary for me, morally imperative
for me, to spend a weekend with Janet in the Ozarks before
the transference that will remove me from her life. I will
gratify—Janet is an *invalid*. Invalids are *vulnerable*. I want to
break this thing to her with—*all possible—humanity* . . .

ALICIA: Darling, you're not considering yourself. Oh, you're
physically strong and health incarnate, honey, but there's a soft
core to you and this woman has been playing on it remorselessly, continually for fifteen years! This soft core you call
humanity can break a stone man down just at the point when
you need your fullest capacities to undertake a marvelous new
position.

326

OLAF: Yes, I have a soft core which I call a remnant of humanity in me, Alicia. Would you like me better without it? You call me Stone Man, fine! But do you want me to be stone outside and in, all the way through, in other words, plain heartless?

ALICIA: She has preyed on you, parasitically preyed on you to the point where—tell me something? How much do you still love Janet?

OLAF: You know how much I have dreaded every Sunday I've gone there and how I dreaded the Ozark trip with her so bad that I had to—cancel! —And I have been told that she has refused to eat since.

ALICIA: Olaf, that woman is using her mental illness to keep a hold on you, and if it continues, I will have to bow out. Did you hear me? *Bow out, quit!* —I will positively, I tell you, accept no further humiliation and insult!

OLAF: What do you think she's accepted?

ALICIA: POWER. —To move us like pawns . . .

OLAF: We are moving ourselves—a considerable distance—beyond her power, I'd say. I've been in correspondence with the chief of staff at St. Carmine's—

ALICIA: —You haven't discussed this with me.

OLAF: It does not concern you.

ALICIA: That is the basic misunderstanding between us, that the hold of this woman who belongs to your past which you can't pass—does not concern me who belongs to your present and future. Beyond her power, you say? Oh, no, she stands

327

behind you, an—emotional magnet, pulling you back, back, back. [*She sounds a bit like Billy Graham exhorting.*] How can I draw you forward against this down, down, down, back current?

OLAF: If you'll permit me to interrupt your—harangue!—I will brief you on my correspondence with Dr. Cash at St. Carmine's. He feels that Janet is not responding to treatment there and should be transferred to the state asylum at Farmington and I have left this decision entirely in his hands, but first—having once loved Janet, before I met you, Alicia, and having been loved by Janet before being loved by you—I have asked him again to allow her an outing in the Ozarks, just for a weekend, in the trailer, to our camp site, where I'll break it to her, the—necessary transfer.

ALICIA: *Ohhhhh! Ahhhhh!* —Some people deliberately expose themselves to contagion, go into cholera country, visit a leprosarium, inviting—ruin, disaster! —Do it!—if you dare!—but don't count on my continued acceptance—of an impossible situation. Stay out here and admire the polluted sky, there may be a visible star—"the night has a thousand eyes and the heart but one"—not *two*!

OLAF: Familiar quotation . . .

[*Alicia turns savagely about and charges into the interior.*]

25] **CLOSE ONE-SHOT OF OLAF.**
His face tortured, his lips form the silent word.

26] **INTERIOR. THE APARTMENT BEDROOM. EVENING.**
Alicia is rapidly stripping for action. When she is out of her dress she snatches a frilly negligee or gown from a closet and rushes into the bathroom.

27] CAMERA REVERSE.

Olaf slowly entering the bedroom with a stone face. Mechanically, he strips to his shorts and sits on the foot of the double bed. The stone face begins to show emotion; the nearly white-blue eyes shut tight. Alicia opens the bathroom door behind him. She is in her combat outfit, her negligee. She regards his back with a tight smile of expected triumph.

OLAF: This weekend—I will take her—to the Ozarks—to break—the news.

[*Alicia's face reacts.*]

ALICIA: All right. Statement accepted.

[*She sweeps past him toward the camera.*]

OLAF: Alicia, where are you—?

ALICIA: I will not share this room with a stone man turned to JELLY!

[*The door slams. There is a close one-shot of Olaf as he throws himself onto the bed, face down, and pounds it with his fists. A radio is playing in the background but is turned off.*]

[*Dim out.*]

28] INTERIOR. THE DAY ROOM. LATE DUSK.

A long shot of the room shows that Janet and three other women are seated in folding chairs about a card table. As the camera approaches the table it becomes apparent that Janet is playing mechanically, to the irritation of her partner, Madge. The game is contract bridge.

329

MADGE: Do you know what you just did? Did you all see what she just did?

JANET [*fearfully*]: Me? Did?

MADGE [*rising furiously*]: YOU TRUMPED MY ACE!

OTHER PLAYER: Never mind. Janet, take back the trump, dear, throw away a card from a different suit.

THIRD PLAYER: I'm sorry but the board's a play, we've always stuck to the rule that the board's the play.

JANET: —What—what's trump?

MADGE: It's just impossible, she doesn't know what's trump again! [*She mimics Janet furiously.*] "What's trump? What's trump?" You don't belong on this floor, this isn't the idiot floor!

[*Sister Grace sweeps into the frame, holding a hand up in protest.*]

SISTER GRACE: Now, Madge. All of you ladies have had periods of disturbance, and I know it if you don't.

SECOND PLAYER: Sister Grace, we do know. Janet didn't want to play cards tonight, it was Madge that insisted and now she blames her for every little mistake that—

MADGE: LITTLE? MISTAKE? TRUMPED MY ACE OF HEARTS A LITTLE MISTAKE?!

SISTER GRACE: Janet, Dr. Cash is on the floor with a message for you.

[*The camera closes on Janet's face; she is terrified at the mention of Dr. Cash, and no wonder.*]

29] CLOSE TWO-SHOT: JANET AND SISTER GRACE.

JANET: —Is it something—*bad?*

SISTER GRACE [*clasping her hand*]: Now, dear, he wants to talk to you for a minute to decide for himself if you are well enough to have the little vacation that was postponed. That's all. Now you must talk to him very quietly and calmly—do you understand, Janet? I told him there was every indication that nothing but good could possibly come from this outing with your husband but you know how Dr. Cash is, he is a stickler for precautions to the point of no point at all. [*She laughs to lighten Janet's mounting agitation, but it's of no use.*]

JANET [*crying out*]: DOCTOR, PLEASE!

SISTER GRACE: Janet, will you *listen?* I said to talk to him *quietly.*

30] CUT TO: INTERIOR.
A square glass-walled cubicle from which the patients are "monitored." The nurse on duty is talking to Dr. Cash who is polishing his glasses. Janet enters the cubicle.

DR. CASH: How are you, Mrs. Svenson?

JANET: Oh, I—never, never felt better in my life, never in my whole life!

SISTER GRACE [*appearing behind Janet*]: Sit down with Dr. Cash a minute, Janet. This is just a routine thing. We all know how much good you will get out of a short vacation, now, this beautiful summer.

DOCTOR [*cutting in sharply*]: Sister Grace, this interview with the patient cannot proceed until you return to the floor. There seems to be a rather charged situation at the card table tonight.

SISTER GRACE: Excuse me. I was going right back to settle a little dispute there. [*Sister Grace exits from the frame.*]

DR. CASH: Will you sit down, Mrs., uh—Svenson?

JANET [*trumpeting the word*]: WHERE?

DR. CASH [*acidly*]: Chairs always seem to be invisible to you.

JANET: It's, it's just the—

DR. CASH: Excitement, you mean, the excitement.

JANET [*taking a seat in a very straight-backed chair*]: Won't you sit down, too?

DR. CASH: Thank you, no, since there is only one chair. Or did you have the impression that there was another?

[*The nurse on duty rises.*]

NURSE: Sit down in my chair, Doctor. It's time to pass out medications.

DR. CASH: Yes. Hmm.

NURSE: Janet, here's yours, you might as well have it here. Oh. Janet, did you have a bowel movement today?

JANET: —Please—don't ask me that in front of—a man!

DR. CASH: My dear Mrs. Svenson, this is a hospital and I am a physician and a question concerning a physical function is entirely suitable under those circumstances. Now are you unable to answer the question?

JANET: No. —Yes.

DR. CASH: You have a perplexing habit of giving opposite answers. The nurse asked if you'd had a bowel movement today and either the answer to that is "no" or the answer is "yes" depending upon the facts.

JANET: I'm afraid that I—simply can't remember. [*She slowly bows her head into her hands.*]

[*After a moment, a touch of humanity seems to visit the doctor. He places his hand over Janet's. She utters a little cry of amazement and looks up at him.*]

DR. CASH: Early this morning, I received a letter from your, uh,—husband, Mr.—

JANET: *Olaf.*

DR. CASH: Informing us that he is free, now, to take you on a vacation in the Ozarks. Of course it could not be decided immediately, in the light of your extreme disturbance since the cancellation of the last outing with him, and as I said before, I have mixed feelings about the advisability of it. However.

JANET: *What?*

DR. CASH: —Sometimes—

JANET: What?

DR. CASH: Sometimes a calculated risk is worth taking and so I have phoned Mr. Svenson that after a day's consideration, the idea has been approved; and so, you will be leaving with him for the Ozark trip tomorrow afternoon. And so good night and good luck. [*He rises briskly and marches out of the glass cubicle.*]

[*Janet remains—stunned—in her chair. As the scene fades, she slowly crosses herself and begins to smile.*

[*Dim out completely.*]

31] EXTERIOR. DAY.
Janet emerges between two nuns from the Administration Building of the sanitarium. The camera keeps at a medium distance as she charges along the walk, the sisters trying unsuccessfully to moderate her pace. She is approaching something of transcendent importance to her. Her face is luminous with it; she gulps the air of outdoors . . .

SISTER GRACE: Good weather for the trip, Janet.

JANET: Yes!

SISTER GRIM: It should be cool in the Ozarks.

JANET: Oh, it *will* be *cool*, I feel I'm already *there*! —OH! [*She stops short.*] OLAF!!

32] CUT TO: ONE-SHOT: OLAF.
The man, Olaf, steps out of the cab of the "trailer."

OLAF [*tonelessly*]: Maw.

JANET: Sister Grace, my husband, Sister Gr—*Mary*, my—

SISTER GRIM: We know. [*There is a brief handshaking.*] Here are the instructions, Mr. Svenson, and here is her bag. Her medications are in it.

SISTER GRACE: And prescriptions for more if necessary. We hope you have a fine trip to the Ozarks.

[*He nods and murmurs, "Thank you."*]

SISTER GRACE [*confidentially, toward the man*]: In case there is difficulty, the phone number's with the instructions.

JANET: Oh, Sister Grace, there won't be difficulty!

SISTER GRACE: We meant—overexcitement, not—difficulty.

OLAF [*grimly*]: That could be difficulty. Let's get started, Maw. You want to sit in the back?

JANET: I want to sit in front with you, if—

[*He shrugs and gets in the cab of the "trailer"; she clambers in beside him.*]

JANET: —My first escape in five years! [*She waves to the watching nuns.*]

OLAF: A trip is not an escape . . .

33] INTERIOR. THE TRAILER CAB. LATE AFTER-
    NOON.
A close two-shot superimposed on a background of heavy traffic on a suburban thruway. Janet is in a condition of ecstasy. Little breathless laughs break from her lips at each jolt of the cab, her fingers twist spasmodically about her purse handle.

335

Olaf keeps giving her anxious little smiles of reassurance and at one point he takes hold of her hand.

OLAF: Janet? Maw? Go easy on that purse handle, honey.

JANET: —It's—just the—excitement.

OLAF: Put the purse in my lap.

JANET: It won't bother you?

OLAF: No, it won't bother me, Maw.

[*There is a stifled tenderness, almost an impulse to cry in his voice. Her lips, her fingers tremble as she lifts the purse like a sacramental chalice and deposits it lingeringly on his strong thighs. He presses her fingers a moment, then gently disengages her hand from his thigh.*]

OLAF: —Not—in this heavy—traffic . . .

JANET: I've got to get out of myself. I've got to get out of— Tell me about your life?

OLAF: —Maw, we're all confined, in a way. There is a kind of confinement in my life, too.

JANET: But not with bars at windows.

OLAF: Emotional bonds are—like bars.

JANET: Tell me about that, Olaf?

OLAF: Well, there's—sexual—enslavement, that's a bond, a barred window, a—locked door. Well. Otherwise, I do like my work. The normal activity of it with young kids still not shadowed by life . . .

JANET: And her? Alicia?

OLAF [*with effort, a muscle twitching at the side of his jaw*]: Let's steer clear of—emotionally—charged—subjects. I'll tell you about my work. I begin every morning with a cold shower, Janet, and a plunge in the pool. Did I tell you I got them to put a pool in the school? Invigorating, terrific. They wanted to heat it, I don't want it heated; it stimulates you, the cold, it makes you feel free of—

JANET: Bonds? Attachments?

OLAF: Let's—let's—forget the heavy stuff right now, lighten it up, like the kids say. —I feel pride in my basketball team's successes. Try to keep a modest, objective attitude, but sometimes I feel like shouting my fool head off when a winning point's scored in the last few seconds' play. It's good to remember about the last few seconds of play, how you can win even then, it's—stimulating, you know . . .

JANET: This—takes me out of myself, this is—sharing your life!

OLAF: Janet, I'm sorry I—haven't included you in—much as I should. This traffic is too much right now. I see a phone booth near a space to park. Mind if I make a call?

JANET: Call to who?

OLAF: —Dr. Cash, to reassure him, he wasn't sure the outing was advisable for you.

[*He places her handbag back in her hands and jumps out of the cab when he's parked the trailer. He runs to the phone booth.*]

34] INTERIOR. PHONE BOOTH.
There is a close one-shot of Olaf as he dials excitedly.

35] INTERIOR. APARTMENT. EVENING.
Alicia is seated on the love seat beside the precocious student who made a pass at her after her physics class in the spring.

ALICIA: You see, Stuart, happening to be alone this evening—I can't stand eating alone—I thought of you and I said to myself, This is an ideal time for me to discuss with you the problems involved in our little—incident after class . . .

[*The phone rings.*]

ALICIA: Oh, the phone, excuse me just a moment. Light the candles on the table, please.

36] INTERIOR. THE CONDOMINIUM APARTMENT. EARLY DUSK.
There is a close one-shot of Alicia at the bedroom phone.

ALICIA: Oh. Olaf. Report the disaster to me.

37] PHONE BOOTH. EARLY DUSK. CLOSE ON OLAF.

OLAF: —It—is not—a disaster like you—predicted. She's nervous but so—touchingly—pleased.

ALICIA: Your voice sounds strained, Stone Man. I think you're selling yourself a bill of goods.

OLAF: No, I swear. I feel decent. It hurts but it's the right way.

ALICIA: Call me a little bit later. The next report is going to be different. —Sorry you're not here for my *Boeuf Stroganoff* and *Châteauneuf-du-Pape*.

OLAF: —Who—is—there?

ALICIA [*slyly*]: Just old Mrs. Mabie, giving me counsel on—domestic matters . . .

OLAF: Do me a favor. Call Dr. Cash and reassure him, the outing is a success. [*He hangs up.*]

38] CLOSE TWO-SHOT OF OLAF AND JANET IN THE TRAILER.
During his call she has twisted the strap off her purse.

JANET: —I— [*She lifts the purse with a comically stricken expression.*]

OLAF: So you were determined to tear the strap off it?

JANET: No! —It *did* come loose, but—

OLAF [*removing it from her hand*]: It's not destroyed. I'll have it repaired by—the manual arts class at school. Well. I guess you're exhibiting the nervous excitement that the sisters warned me against.

JANET: Ha! Not Sister Grace, the other, we call her Grim. She has a fine character, a very, very fine character but a little severe with the girls. She stalks about the day room inspecting their faces for signs of excitement, you know. She likes a face to be set, you know, a set face.

339

OLAF: Yes, not agitated.

JANET: A set expression on a girl's face is what Sister Grim approves of. But that's not possible always. I mean the girls think of something or they remember something and the expression changes and Sister Grim, oh, she means well, don't say I complained, don't say it, I think it's just the hours of marching about and inspecting all of those girls' faces, set or not set, it makes her—too conscious about it, she—*monitors*! With a notebook, I mean with a long sheet clipped to a board and a pencil that hangs from a chain round her neck, and she'll stop in front of a girl whose face is changing and she will say to the girl, "I am monitoring this disturbance." And the girl whose face isn't set for Grim's inspection is sometimes very upset because if she is monitored badly, oh, brother, that girl will not be called for R.T. R is for recreation and T is for therapy, it's when we line up for a break in routine downstairs. They have a piano downstairs and several other amusements.

OLAF: Of a—respectable nature?

JANET: Very! —When Father O'Donnell was living, you remember him, Olaf, he would say to her, "Sister, you are being too grim," and that's how she got her nickname among us girls, Grim.

OLAF: These are very interesting little comments on life in the day room but can't they wait till we get through rush-hour traffic.

JANET: Very! —You promise not to report that I complained, no, no, no, not complained, I didn't complain, I just mentioned!

OLAF: Yes.

[*She heaves a great sigh of relief. A smile flickers on her face and she touches his.*]

JANET: You still use Mennen's aftershave and talcum? Yes, you do, I smell it, it's like pine woods in snow. —I'm glad that you haven't switched. You are loyal to Mennen's.

OLAF: Are you—being—sarcastic?

[*He switches the radio on and we hear a sports announcer.*]

ANNOUNCER: *Lo-ong! Hi-igh! Fly!* —Fielded by—wait! No, into the bleachers!!! —People are going WILD! [*The sound of maniacal shouting is heard over the radio.*]

[*Janet covers her ears.*]

JANET: Olaf, you know I'm terrified of baseball!

OLAF: The greatest most American sport in the world, now important all over, is—*what* to you? *Terrifying?* Tell me, Maw, is anything in the world not terrifying to you?

JANET: Yes!

OLAF: What?

JANET: YOU!

[*She seizes his arm. He slams on the brakes to barely avoid crashing into the car ahead.*]

JANET: Oh, I hope we'll be in the Ozark Mountains in time for sunset! Will we be there for sunset?

OLAF: —I've—got to stop here a minute . . .

[*He brakes the trailer to a screeching halt. A car behind strikes the rear of the trailer. Janet screams.*]

OLAF: Hush!

JANET: In—spect the—damage.

OLAF: I don't care about it.

JANET: I do, I'll—inspect the—damage. [*She clambers out of the cab of the trailer.*]

[*The camera follows Janet running, stumbling, to rear of the trailer and bending, as if searching for a time bomb. She touches the bent license plate, cries out, touches an indentation in the fender, cries out again. Slowly, stoically, he joins her.*]

JANET: Did you take the hit-and-run license number?

OLAF [*exhaustedly*]: It was my fault, Maw. Maybe he took mine.

[*He places the flats of his hands on the back of the trailer and counts aloud.*]

OLAF: One. —Two. —Three.

JANET: Olaf, what are you counting?

OLAF: I count my breaths when my nerves are uptight. It helps me control—nausea.

JANET: Aw. Let me count with you.

OLAF: No. No. I've got to do it alone. Seven. —You know better than anyone— Eight. —I am not a stone man except— Nine. —Appearance.

JANET: Ten.

OLAF: Please. Alone.

JANET: It was your nerves that affected your speech which I trained you to overcome at the speech clinic, Olaf, before the world collapsed on my head in the shape of Alicia Trout. [*She makes a gagging sound in her throat.*]

OLAF: I have Dramamine tablets back in the trailer if—you've got—car-sickness.

JANET: I suffer from—poison—trout. [*She laughs hysterically.*] Alicia, Alicia Trout.

OLAF: That is—malicious.

JANET: I can't pretend she didn't destroy my digestion. —You should have— Twelve. — Heard my confessions— Thirteen. —to Father O'Donnell.

OLAF: Please don't count along with me, my respiration is faster. I'm at fifteen.

JANET: Fifteen, yeah, yeah, me, too.

OLAF: Chriii-se! —Don't remind me again of the speech clinic, the—problem— Eighteen.

JANET: Nineteen. Twenty.

OLAF: A man, a woman—have got to put lots of things back of them and— Twenty-five. —Yes, it's—painful. —I may return—from this outing—with a speech problem again and a—butterfly stomach.

JANET: We got so much still in common. But I'm no longer an instructor.

OLAF: Shall we continue?

JANET: Counting?

OLAF: No. Driving to the Ozarks.

JANET: Yes. No stopping.

OLAF: We will return to the camper and—go on . . .

[*The camera follows their silent return to the cab of the trailer. He gently helps her back in.*]

JANET: Thanks. We still—assist each other.

OLAF: Principle of—existence. Is—mutual—assistance.

[*He makes no move to start the engine. She looks at him. Her trembling hand touches a trembling muscle at the side of his jaw. He gasps softly, she echoes.*]

OLAF: Forgot to start the motor.

[*The trailer lurches forward, and she cries out. Then a silence falls between them, desperate and lonely.*]

39] DISSOLVE TO: INTERIOR. THE TRAILER. EARLY DUSK.

344

*They are seated in silence; she keeps stealing glances at his
face. His face is set.*

Several beats of this.

JANET: —Silence! Our first real chance to talk and we sit
here speechless together . . .

OLAF: Talk if you want to talk, now.

JANET: Oh, I have this feeling I—can't express, this—feeling
like a bird in my— [*She touches her chest.*]

OLAF: Is that why you keep flapping your hands like that?

JANET: My hands are never still. Other people have noticed.

OLAF: It's—noticeable.

JANET: I've been criticized for it. You know what I think it
is? My hands feel empty, so empty. At the place, you know, I
occupy my hands. I do needlework. Oh, I brought a piece of
needlework with me; you never have seen my needlework.

OLAF: You always show me pieces of needlework; every Sunday I go there.

JANET: —You haven't been there lately. Not for—many Sundays.

[*He suddenly halts the trailer again. She lurches forward with
the abruptness of it. Olaf closes his eyes tightly.*]

JANET: —I shouldn't have said that, should I?

OLAF: Is it going to go on like this?

JANET: Olaf, you said I was silent so I—started to talk.

OLAF: Babbling isn't talking.

JANET: I'd better be still for a while.

OLAF: Yes, you'd better be still till we're out of traffic and in the open country on the thruway. Otherwise I will crash into something. Jan, I've got nerves like hot wires in me!

JANET: I won't speak again until we're out of traffic on the Ozark Highway.

OLAF: I'm going in that store.

JANET: Oh, yes, let's do!

[*Both are eager to break the unbearable tension in the trailer.*]

OLAF: I'm going in I said, me, just me, not you. I won't be long.

JANET: But I want to go in the—comfort station.

OLAF: It's not a place for—

JANET: A store that big would have a comfort station.

OLAF: The term is—lavatory, if it's not—not ladies' room.

JANET: I know, I know. But my stomach!

OLAF: There's a Red Crown station in sight down the road. Please, please, wait till—

JANET: You're ashamed to be seen in a big store with me? [*With quick, frantic movements, she adjusts her hat, her hair, her string of beads.*]

OLAF: No, no, it's—not that, I— Look! You've got to puke, I've got to puke, both of us got to—excuse me—I should've said *vomit*!

[*He rushes to some bushes beside the highway: violent retching. She cries out and follows.*]

OLAF: Ch-riiiise! Can't I puke in private?

JANET: Olaf, am I public? Don't I have to vomit, too?

OLAF: Take a different bush.

[*She staggers away a little: more retching sounds.*

[*Both convene again at the side of the road from their bushes. He is wiping his mouth fastidiously with a white handkerchief.*]

JANET: I didn't know I ate that much at lunch.

[*He closes his eyes for a moment, then rushes back to the bush. He vomits again and finally returns to her side.*]

JANET: May I have the handkerchief, please?

OLAF: It's got vomit stains on it.

JANET: I don't object to—

OLAF: *I, I* object to it.

347

JANET [*turning about*]: I'll use a—I'll use a—

OLAF: No, here. I'll—

[*He wipes her mouth. There are tears on his face.*]

OLAF: I know you—object to—nothing. —Can we get back in the trailer?

JANET: Can't we go in the big store?

OLAF: For what? Now?

JANET: I—want to buy some postcards.

OLAF: It's not a place for postcards.

JANET: I see a big rack of postcards through the front window.

OLAF: I'll buy you some. Wait in the trailer, sit tight.

JANET: I want to select them myself.

[*He is out of the trailer and charging across the road; she scrambles out behind him and is nearly run down by a car.*]

OLAF: Jan! Watch it!

40] **INTERIOR. GENERAL STORE. EARLY DUSK.**

OLAF [*approaching the clerk*]: Where's a phone booth, have you got a phone booth?

CLERK: Pay phone's there on the wall.

OLAF [*wiping sweat off his forehead*]: —Aspirin. —ASPIRIN!

CLERK: Don't have to holler for it. [*He hands him a tin of aspirin.*]

OLAF: Open, open it for me, my hands are— ! [*He lifts his shaking hands.*]

[*The clerk opens the tin. Olaf gulps two tablets as he rushes to the phone booth.*]

41] CUT TO: A SHOT OF JANET.
She enters the store, equally shaken.

42] CUT TO: OLAF AT THE PHONE.

OLAF: *I want to put through a call to Mrs. Alicia Svenson at Hi-Point; the number is Forest 6-0280.*

JANET [*directly behind him*]: Mrs.! —You call her Mrs.?

43] CUT TO: INTERIOR. THE CONDOMINIUM APARTMENT. LATE DUSK OR NIGHT.
There is a medium two-shot of Alicia and the student Stuart. They are seated on the love seat; the room is intimately lighted. She is reading his palm.

ALICIA: You see where this line transects the line that's your lifeline, there is this parallel to it.

STUART [*staring at her bosom*]: Don't see it.

ALICIA: No. Because you're not looking at your palm.

[*The phone rings.*]

ALICIA: Oh. The wires are busy tonight. Excuse me again. I'll take it in the bedroom.

[*She has sprung up, beaming lubriciously. The camera follows her to the bedroom phone.*]

ALICIA: Later report as expected?

OLAF'S VOICE [*as if in the room*]: Alicia, I'm—cracking. My nerves, my nerves are—shot. It's worse than you could imagine.

ALICIA: Your voice is hardly recognizable, Olaf. It's worse than you could imagine, not I, not I!

OLAF: Tension. —Indescribable. Nearly crashed twice on highway. Her condition—frantic. I stopped. We—vomited—in bushes.

ALICIA: Do you still want me to call Dr. Cash to assure him this outing is a brilliant success?

OLAF: Hold a minute—two aspirin in mouth too dry to swallow—wait. I think she's behind me.

ALICIA: Naturally, always, and in front of you, too. Tentacles inescapable till broken by force.

44] CUT TO: INTERIOR. THE GENERAL STORE.
There is a medium two-shot of Olaf with Janet, stricken, behind him.

OLAF [*over his shoulder*]: Janet, get me water, please get me some water!

ALICIA'S VOICE [*as if beside him*]: Olaf, I warned you this thing would be total disaster. You know I have always known

350

the terrible strength of this dependent woman and recognized the nature of this strength. It's the will to destroy, not just herself but anyone she's involved with. You've been her victim too long. Now. Listen. Save yourself, turn back, right back. Soon as you're in a place accessible to cabs, put her in one, return her to the hospital. Now, obey me, don't think, just do as I tell you, like, like a plane making an instrument landing, instructed by the tower.

OLAF: —Yes . . .

[*Janet returns behind him, her trembling hand offering a paper cup of water. Together they spill it, Janet crying out.*]

JANET: I'll get another.

OLAF: Don't—don't bother, I've swallowed. Go select postcards!

[*Janet stumbles away.*]

45] DISSOLVE TO: INTERIOR. THE CONDOMINIUM BEDROOM.
There is a two-shot, medium, of Alicia at the phone and Stuart, appearing in bedroom doorway.

OLAF'S VOICE: Alicia? Are you still there?

ALICIA: —Yes. —About how far away are you?

OLAF'S VOICE: Two and a half hours' drive from the—hospital.

ALICIA: On second thought, perhaps it's better for you to deliver her to the hospital yourself to give them a report on the disaster. Now in your nervous condition, drive more slowly.

351

OLAF'S VOICE: *How will I tell her, how will I put it to her?*

ALICIA: Don't.

OLAF'S VOICE: —Alicia, I can't—turn back till—tomorrow.

ALICIA: All right, if that's your decision, but remember, you can't go on with that woman behind you and in front of you, an all-enveloping shadow, a total eclipse of the sun.

46] **INTERIOR. THE BEDROOM DOORWAY.**
Close one-shot of Stuart: he extends his hand as he did in the classroom, he has the smile of a young satyr.

47] **CUT TO: INTERIOR. THE GENERAL STORE.**
Olaf hangs up the phone and Janet is right behind him again. Pause.

OLAF [*in a faint voice*]: I thought you wanted postcards. You wanted postcards, go get them.

JANET: —I don't—have—money.

OLAF [*snatching a bill from his pocket*]: Here!

[*She stares at him, motionless.*]

OLAF: HERE! —Have you turned to a statue? —Go to the postcard rack you saw through the window.

JANET: They're very high-priced, they're jumbo postcards, a quarter apiece and mostly duplicates, too. Only three that're different.

OLAF [*wiping his forehead*]: What's—the diff'rence?

JANET: There's one of the Elks' Lodge and one of the City Hall and one of the Moolah Temple. I want Ozark scenes, not buildings but scenes of—rivers and lakes in the mountains.

OLAF: Come on, I'll find a scene for you!

[*He charges to the postcard rack and twirls it violently; he snatches a card out.*]

OLAF: Here's one of—Dead Man's Cave.

JANET: Oh, no, no, not that one, nothing with that word on it, it would depress the girls and they're already depressed!

OLAF: Take it, pay for it. And these! Ten!

[*He thrusts them into her hand; she covers her face with a cry, dropping the cards. He snatches them up and steers her to the door.*]

48] CUT TO: EXTERIOR. FADING DUSK.

OLAF: You're making a spectacle of yourself.

JANET: I didn't know you called her Mrs. now!

OLAF: Yes, I call her Mrs. For the sake of propriety. You understand? She has to pretend that we're married and Alicia is not a woman who likes to pretend but her family insists.

JANET: I—do—understand—pretending.

[*The camera has followed them across the road to the trailer. He jerks the cab door open.*]

353

OLAF: You wallow in self-pity to make me feel guilty and I don't, I won't—get in!

[*He shoves her towards the trailer; she wails.*]

OLAF: No, go in the back with your postcards and—lamentation . . .

[*He hauls her to rear door, jerks it open and shoves her in.*]

OLAF: You got to stay in there the rest of the way since you won't shut up and it interferes with the driving.

49] CUT TO: INTERIOR. THE TRAILER.
He jerks down the hinged table and chair; then throws the postcards on the table and thrusts a ball-point pen at her.

JANET: —Ten—duplicates—buildings and—Dead Man's Cave. The girls will compare them, each should have one different.

OLAF: What if they compare them? Gives them something to do. Can we drop the subject, consider it covered and closed?

JANET: You'll—get stamps tomorrow?

OLAF: Yes!

[*He flicks on the radio and charges out of the trailer.*

[*The camera closes on Janet. She shuffles the postcards to one of Dead Man's Cave. Then addresses it to Alicia "Svenson," Apt. B, Lockland Complex, Hi-Point, Mo.*

[*The camera closes on the postcard of the cave and Janet's handwriting, a message which is — "Dear Alicia. How would you like to be here? Regards. Mrs. Olaf Svenson."*

354

[*She conceals this card.*

[*The trailer sways so violently that a plastic vase containing a plastic daisy falls off the hinged table.*

[*Fade out.*]

50] FADE IN: INTERIOR. THE TRAILER.
Janet looks dazed into space. The radio serenades her with "De Camptown Races" as the trailer jerks violently, cards and pen fly off the hinged fiberglass tabletop.

RADIO: "Camptown Ladies sing dis song, Doo-dah! doo-dah!"

[*She bends awkwardly to pick up the scattered articles and replaces them on the table.*]

RADIO: "Camptown racetrack five miles long, Oh! doo-dah-day!"

[*She now has the plastic vase in one hand and the artificial daisy in the other hand and doesn't seem to know how to get them together. She laughs helplessly at the dilemma, then solves it by placing the vase and flower beneath the table, still separate. All her actions are accompanied by "De Camptown Races" and the trailer's fantastically jerky motion. She holds tightly to the table's edges, with sporadic gasps.*]

JANET [*singing along with radio*]: "Gwine to run all night! Gwine to run all day!"

[*She claps a hand over her mouth as if fearful that Olaf could hear her.*

[*Then she grips the ball-point pen and slowly, tentatively, addresses a postcard; gets through "Miss Mary Maude, Ward Seven, Saint—."*]

[*A particularly violent jerk of the trailer cuts short this effort and she barely stays seated in the straight-back chair.*]

51] INTERIOR. THE TRAILER.
The trailer has stopped. Olaf enters.

JANET: Oh, thanks be, we're stopped and you've come back here!

OLAF [*jerking off his jacket*]: Yes, right on both counts.

JANET: Roads are rough in the mountains. I had a hard time writing just one postcard.

OLAF: Oh. Hard time. Yes!

JANET: See if you can read it. [*She thrusts a postcard toward him.*]

OLAF: It's sort of illegible. [*He sits exhaustedly on the edge of the lower bunk and closes his eyes.*]

JANET: Let me wash off your face with a wet towel and rub your forehead like I used to, Olaf.

OLAF: No, I—no . . . well, you wrote your postcards?

JANET: Olaf, the gnats are at me. They seem to have a terrific appetite for me.

OLAF: There are no gnats in the trailer.

JANET: Then what's eating me up?

OLAF: Your condition, as always.

JANET: My condition doesn't bite me continually, always, there are either mosquitos or gnats in the trailer, I swear to—

OLAF: Then spray the trailer completely with this can of insecticide—

JANET: Oh! Yes! Where?

[*Olaf rises fiercely and hands her a spray can.*]

OLAF: Spray!

JANET: —How's it operate, Olaf?

[*He seizes it from her and goes about spraying vehemently. There is a sound of "Whuff, whuff, whuff," while the radio plays "Sentimental Journey."*]

JANET: Now you want to spray me?

[*He has pointed the spray can at her. He laughs harshly and casts the spray can aside.*

[*The camera closes on her tremulous face.*]

JANET: Ten postcards; and I've only thought of one message.

OLAF: I thought the subject of the postcards was finished now.

JANET: You are breathing like you've run all the way here.

357

OLAF: So are you. —I'm sorry. —It's been a hard drive. Now what is the postcard problem, let's get that over with. For good.

JANET: Well, you see, the girls will compare the postcards and if I can't think of ten different messages to write out, they'll all have the same thing on them.

OLAF: The usual message is: "Wonderful, wish you were here."

JANET: Yes, but they'll compare them. So do you know what I think?

OLAF [*with helpless cruelty*]: Do you?

JANET: I said do you?

OLAF: Do what?

JANET: Know what I think?

OLAF: Never! Now or ever!

JANET [*slowly, with emphasis on each word*]: I think I'll send just one, addressed to all ten girls.

OLAF: A wonderful solution to the problem. Congratulations. Do that. Carry out that solution.

JANET: It would be so much better if each girl received a different message. Individual. To each only.

OLAF: On each card just change the punctuation a little, Maw.

[*He snatches up a copy of* Sports Illustrated.]

JANET: I say some silly things, don't I, like I was talking just to hear myself talk.

OLAF: Now that you mention it, yeah, and I'm reading a piece.

[*Slight pause.*]

JANET: "Girls in Ward Seven, St. Carmine's Hospital," ought to do it.

OLAF: Without a thing to do with yourself since you left the place, why can't you write ten postcards since you bought ten postcards to write. How much effort is it to compose ten slightly different messages to the girls as you call those women if they're not all the same woman multiplied by ten but otherwise no different. They all look the same to me but after years with them you may have noticed differences among them in some respects that I haven't noticed among them when I visit.

JANET: Oh, I—find them each—very different, very, very individual, each.

OLAF: They all look the same sitting around the walls in the day room on Sundays when I'd visit.

JANET: Olaf, now, that's not true, each one of those girls is a highly—individual—separate—type of person. They dress alike but that's all the similarity among them and I know, I know because I—don't just—visit on Sundays. Why, take Mary Maude for instance, she's the one plays piano at Chapel and half an hour at— Oh, I'm rattling on and you're reading a piece, I guess I make you wish you—excuse me, I'll—sit outside a while.

OLAF [*throwing down the copy of* Sports Illustrated]: Are you sure you wanted to come here?

JANET: Want to! —Olaf, what a question to ask me! Oh, no, Olaf, I—really had no intention of speaking of—making a reference to—Alicia. You know, I can't even remember what she looks like? She never visits, you know, and her appearance has faded out of my mind except that her hair is almost red as this ketchup on this table and so is her mouth but of course that's not a complete description. I don't remember her eyes, the color or anything about them.

OLAF: I don't think Alicia would mind. However, to refresh your *failing* memory of her, here is a photograph of her which I turned to the wall. [*He slaps the picture face forward.*]

[*The camera closes on the photo of Alicia, smiling with complete self-satisfaction.*]

OLAF: Now you can see that her hair isn't ketchup colored nor is her mouth. —It's in her true colors.

JANET: —Why did you do that? Turn it to the wall? I know about her importance in your life and naturally her picture should be on the wall and I want you to tell her that I would love to see her in person any Sunday you come. We would all make her welcome. Why, at O.T. we'll prepare, we'll paint a sign, "Hello Dear Alicia" like we do "Happy Birthday" signs for each other, on birthdays.

OLAF: Christ.

JANET: —You weren't swearing.

OLAF [*turning sharply away from her*]: *No.*

[*Slight pause; a close two-shot: his eyes are shut tightly against tears; tendons quiver spasmodically in his stone-like arms, fists clenched.*]

360

JANET: Remember how I used to object when you said "Christ" and I would number the times you said it and I used to insist that you tell Father O'Donnell exactly how many times at confession but you would continue to say it and finally Father O'Donnell said to me that when you said "Christ" you were not swearing at all but saying the name of your Savior and I said, "Oh, but you haven't heard him!" And Father O'Donnell said, "No, but Christ has heard him seventeen times this week!"

[*She has been preparing instant coffee. The bottle drops from her trembling hand.*]

OLAF [*without turning*]: Now what did you drop?

JANET [*reading the label*]: Instant-Freeze-Dried. I never heard of that; there're so many new products since I—left, you know.

OLAF: They've got TV in the day room.

JANET: Yes, and it's on from breakfast at six till lights out at nine-thirty. The girls say that new products are advertised all the time but do you know I have never noticed a single advertisement of anything on TV?

OLAF: Then you must have a turn-off apparatus in your head. Is that what you have in your head? That would be a very handy new product worth millions in advertisement on TV and in newspapers; it would be worth the sacrifice of space on Watergate and cease-fire and fire still going on, Jan.

[*She laughs hysterically.*]

OLAF: It's not—it wasn't that funny!

JANET: Oh, yes, it was, you say the funniest things when you open your mouth, you know sometimes you say the amusingest

361

things. The girls at St. Carmine's look forward to your visits and if you skip a Sunday, why, it spoils their day, almost as much as it does mine.

[*The camera narrows to a one-shot, a close-up of her face—an abrupt admission of her despair.*]

JANET: —The compliments you have received there these five years would have burned the ears off your head if you'd heard half! They watch with me out the windows for you to appear on the walk and all scream together when you do.

OLAF: When I do *what?*

JANET: Appear! Appear on the walk—approaching the—prison!

[*Slight pause; he hurls the* Sports Illustrated *to the floor. Automatically, she picks it up.*]

JANET [*gazing at the open magazine*]: Olympic—contestants—none of them equal to you . . .

[*He suddenly turns the tinted photograph to the wall again.*]

JANET: —Why did you turn her face to the wall again, Olaf?

OLAF: She's—considerate of you. She said I'd better remove her photograph from the wall of the trailer this weekend.

JANET: That was—considerate of her. Can I go out and take a look around?

OLAF [*too eagerly*]: Yes, yes, why not!

JANET: I'll just—scout about a few minutes before we—go to bed . . . [*She speaks the last three words in a barely audible whisper, which only makes them louder.*]

52] CUT TO: EXTERIOR. TRAILER. NIGHT.
There is a medium shot of Janet clambering down the trailer steps, awkwardly. The camera observes a scene of strange desolation: few trees, a narrow and shallow-looking river.

Sound fades in—the low, complaining murmur of the river.

The camera closes on her face. Her eyes close, then open; she approaches the river and stumbles against something.

JANET [*looking down*]: Hah!

[*She bends a little; then utters a piercing cry. The camera closes on a dead, almost skeletal creature of the sparse woods. She stumbles rapidly back to the trailer.*]

JANET [*at the door*]: No, no, no not here, we have to stop somewhere else, something is *dead* out there!

OLAF: Something is dead everywhere.

JANET: I know but let's go higher into the mountains.

OLAF: The Ozarks aren't mountains, Maw.

JANET: *No, but higher, please!*

OLAF: *Here's where I'd planned to stop and I'm not going any further.*

JANET: —Would you, could you—put the dead thing away, then?

363

OLAF: —*Yes, I would and I could and I will!*

JANET: I know that I've—annoyed you again, but—

[*The camera follows him to the dead wood creature; he lifts it savagely and hurls it into the river. Her face is desperate.*]

OLAF: I put it away for you, Maw. Now would you like me to contact Father O'Donnell to hold a funeral service or a memorial service for it?

JANET: Olaf, don't you know that Father O'Donnell has— [*Her lips tremble: tears well into her eyes.*] —passed away?

[*The elegiac murmur of the river turns subtly to a strain of lyrical music: it is as if a sudden alteration, a renascence of tenderness of Olaf's heart, were expressed in this delicate music. Involuntarily, his arms extend toward Janet. He draws her to him.*]

JANET [*as if admitted to Paradise*]: Ohhhhhh . . .

OLAF: I still have problems with speech, with expressing things, Maw. The problem makes me—fierce when I—want to—be kind . . .

JANET: Thank you for explaining, I was frightened that you'd stopped—caring for me . . .

OLAF: No. No.

[*His great hand trembles as it caresses her hair, her face, brushes the tears from beneath her eyes.*]

OLAF: It's just—the problem with speech that you—corrected for me, it comes back with—emotion and—soft words, love words, I—have trouble with . . .

JANET: I knew, I knew, I KNOW! That's why the muscles at the corners of your lips twitch and tighten. Remember how I touched them, in speech correction class, and said to you, "Loosen, don't tighten these muscles?" And you did, slowly, and the fierce look disappeared from your eyes as they looked in mine and you took hold of my hand and said to me, "Miss Janet, thank you, I love you." —From that day on, the speech problem was solved! —Can you say it again, not the thanks but the love?

OLAF [*struggling*]: Is it—wise to go back?

JANET: Love is not going back.

OLAF: Maw, Janet, you're shaking.

JANET: Naturally, in your arms, after so much—!

OLAF: —Time. —Can't be—turned back.

JANET: To?

OLAF: Emotions passed away as far as—

JANET: Father O'Donnell?

OLAF: Yes, that far, and as far as the river's taken the remains of the—

JANET: Dead wood creature . . .

[*He draws back from her and adjusts his manner and clothes as if for a more formal occasion.*]

JANET: This has been an intimate talk between us.

OLAF: Probably too much so.

JANET: Maybe not enough so.

OLAF: Much, much too much so. The—ob-se-quies—of the wood creature being concluded, we can leave the tomb.

JANET: Let me just once more ask: isn't it low country here? Couldn't we go higher?

OLAF: This is where I stop. I always stop here to fish.

JANET: Are you going to fish?

OLAF: No. I don't fish at night. Let's go back to the trailer and sleep till it's day.

53] CUT TO: INTERIOR. TRAILER.
The space is cramped with two bunks, upper and lower.

OLAF: Which one do you want, upper or lower?

JANET [*unconsciously bitter*]: You are always—considerate of me, ask me what I prefer—but you won't go higher into the mountains where it's cool.

OLAF: That subject is done with.

[*He turns off the light and strips his clothes off, barely a silhouette; or perhaps just a shot of the clothes seen thrown.*]

JANET: It's so wonderful being anywhere with you. —Can I sleep in the upper?

OLAF: I offered you a choice. Is your choice the upper?

JANET: I prefer the upper if you don't mind the lower.

OLAF: See the ladder?

JANET: It's cute. —I'll take my Thorazine now and then climb up there. [*Slight pause.*]

[*The camera closes in on Janet's face.*]

JANET: I'm not sure that Thorazine is right for me with my condition, it's a powerful tablet, but—

OLAF: You'd better accept the doctor's recommendations.

JANET: Yes, there's no way not to. —At the place.

[*She has taken the tablet; the camera sees her clothes folded by her hands over the table. Then her hands open a very old valise and remove a nightgown.*]

54] INTERIOR. TRAILER.
There is a shot of Olaf lying straight out on his back in the lower bunk, his look tormented.

OLAF: We were speaking of changes that go on outside of the day room at the place, Maw.

JANET: —I wish—

OLAF: What?

JANET: That what you have to tell me you won't till on the way back.

[*The camera pauses on her face; her fist is pressed to her mouth as if to suppress a cry.*]

OLAF: Wouldn't it be better to know it now and get adjusted before then?

JANET: *NO!* Not now, tonight!

OLAF: It's best to adjust to it now. —Maw, you live in a world that's protected from any important changes. Almost a timeless world is what you live in.

JANET: Oh, no, no, it changes all the time. The changes aren't very sudden in most cases.

OLAF: What are the changes, Maw?

JANET: Like Sophie. She always rocked faster than anyone else in the room. Almost as fast as if she was racing to get somewhere in that rocker with the plaid cushion she made for it in O.T. —Then, Olaf, early this spring she began to slow down a little. Hardly noticeable at first but by the middle of April, Sally said to me, "Have you noticed how Sophie rocks?" —I didn't know until then that anybody had noticed it but me. Sally is quick to notice. I admitted that I had noticed the slow-down, too. And we both felt that it meant something, not just accidental, but—

OLAF: Significant? [*He smiles with a hint of cruelty in his lean face.*]

JANET: Yes, significant. That's the word I meant. And after Sally noticed the slowdown of the rocker, the other girls began to mention it, too.

OLAF [*cruelty plainer*]: Oh. It became a *cause célèbre*.

JANET: —What?

OLAF [*fiercely, almost*]: A celebrated subject, a subject of much discussion among the ladies.

JANET: —Yes. It did. By the end of spring she was rocking slower than anyone in the day room and Sally said: "I think she's preparing—to stop . . ."

[*She begins to cry soundlessly, the moon washing her face now and then through the monotonous trees along the empty road.*]

OLAF: —Did she? —Stop?

JANET: Stopped completely last week.

OLAF: In late July.

JANET: The day before they told me we could—I was *allowed* to, *you'd invited me out* to go on this—beautiful trip —she stopped rocking completely and Sally said to me, she's the girl who talks most, she said to me: "Sophie isn't going to sit in the room anymore." And Sally was right. The very next morning she didn't come out to the day room but stayed in bed. We took turns visiting with her till she—

OLAF: Died?

JANET: No. Removed. They removed her. To *where*—nobody is sure.

OLAF: —Wipe your face, Maw.

JANET: I didn't know I was crying. I—didn't mean to. I only meant to convince you that even at the place we know about time. And changes. —Now. I'm prepared to hear what you want to tell me. [*Pause.*] Aren't you going to tell me?

OLAF: Later. I think it will keep till morning. —Go to sleep . . .

[*Fade out.*]

55] INTERIOR. TRAILER. NIGHT.
The camera observes both, sleepless. The interior of the trailer is oppressively warm and Janet is just under its ceiling; she starts to get up, stealthily—bumps her head on the ceiling and gives a startled cry.

OLAF: *What?*

JANET: I sat up too sudden—bumped my head on the ceiling, it's—very low.

OLAF: You had your choice of bunks and you chose the upper.

JANET: I know I did.

[*She is slowly, awkwardly crawling backward to descend the ladder.*]

OLAF: Are you getting up?

JANET [*with a little laugh*]: No. Down, if I can make it.

370

[*There is a shot of Olaf, impassive as a stone figure and curiously unaged in the dim light; he had thrown the covers back.*]

JANET: Now I've just about made it.

[*He draws the covers over his massive chest.*]

JANET: I think the trailer wasn't designed for me.

OLAF: No. It wasn't designed for you, Maw. It wasn't custom made for your specifications.

JANET: I'm not fat anymore but I was never intended by nature to be graceful or—dainty.

OLAF: No. The trailer wasn't designed with you in mind.

JANET: I knew you weren't sleeping either.

OLAF: That's very perceptive of you.

JANET: Don't look a minute, my nightgown is hitching up.

[*She is gingerly climbing down the ladder and her coarse-fabriced gown—hospital issue—has been lifted half up her thighs.*]

OLAF: I'm studying the stars.

JANET: You say such strange things in a strange voice to-night.

OLAF: —"The night has a thousand eyes and the heart but one."

JANET: Eyes. Stars? —You didn't use to express yourself this way.

OLAF: In five years time every cell of the body is replaced by others. —Physically you're a totally new person and you have to accept it; it can't be refused as a fact of human existence.

JANET: Your feelings—too?

OLAF: Oh, they change faster than the cells of the body, Maw.

[*She is now down and standing beside the bunks as if she didn't know why she'd climbed down from hers, for what purpose or reason.*]

[*The faint elegiac murmur of the river is heard from a distance.*]

JANET: Mine, mine—don't at all.

OLAF: They could without your knowledge.

JANET: Olaf, why did we stop here in the foothills?

OLAF: You wanted to go higher?

JANET: Yes, higher and cooler. Further up in the mountains.

OLAF: The Ozarks are called mountains but the title is just honorary.

JANET: When did you start talking this new way, when all the old cells changed to the new ones, Olaf?

OLAF: I haven't sat still rocking five years in a day room.

JANET: I know you don't mean to make me feel what I—feel.

OLAF: What did you get up for? I mean come down for?

JANET: To ask you to drive further, into the mountains.

OLAF: Now?

JANET: Since neither of us could sleep, why not go higher? I know the Ozarks aren't mountains but they're not all of 'em this low.

OLAF: You want to go into the Alps or the Himalayas? Where there's snow? Perpetual?

JANET: Not snow but not gnats and mosquitos.

OLAF: This is where we always go on weekends.

JANET: You and—

OLAF: Yes.

JANET: She doesn't want to go higher?

OLAF: A weekend doesn't allow much of an excursion for us.

JANET: But this is more than a weekend, this is your summer vacation from the school.

OLAF: I thought you knew that I don't work in a high school but am the head of the Athletic Department at Springfield Community College.

JANET: Do you talk to the athletes like this, Olaf?

OLAF: No, I don't, but you are not an athlete.

JANET: And she is still in the Mathematics Department?

OLAF: She is Alicia, Maw, and she's in physics.

JANET: Is physics—physical, too?

OLAF: No. It's been described as the poetry of mathematics.

JANET: I see, I see, it's very clear to me, now!

OLAF: Something's clear to you now?

JANET: What you want to tell me tonight for me to adjust to is very clear to me now. We are not going any higher and cooler, we're stopping here because I just have a weekend.

OLAF: Take another tablet of Thorazine, Maw.

JANET: No. No.

OLAF: You are getting hysterics.

JANET: No, no.

[*He springs up and seizes her arm and takes her into the kitchenette end of the trailer; still holding her tightly by the arm, he unscrews the bottle of tablets with his teeth and presses the bottle top to her clenched teeth.*]

OLAF: OPEN!

JANET: MMM!

OLAF: Open like I told you or we drive back tonight.

374

[*She submits.*]

JANET: How many did you put in my mouth?

OLAF: Here. Swallow. Wash down.

JANET: I'm used to doing what I'm told to do now. But the doctor's prescription for me is one at night only.

OLAF: Nights—change.

[*Pause. She turns slowly to open the trailer door. The river's elegy is louder.*]

JANET: Yes, they do, they're not the same everywhere.

OLAF: In a minute or two your condition will be relaxed enough for me to tell you what I have to tell you.

JANET: Why didn't you just write on your typewriter: "Dear Maw. All the cells of the body are replaced by new cells in"—how many years? Five? The length of our separation which is the length of my time in the day room.

OLAF: You go sit on a campstool out there till the tablets work on you, don't come back in here till you're ready to sleep and then I will tell what I have to tell you and you will have to accept it, it's not subject to change, so go out and sit on a campstool till you're prepared to accept it as absolutely decided.

JANET: Oh, that's now. You're—

OLAF: I'm transferred.

JANET: Oh. Transferred . . .

375

[*The implication of the word, which is total and final separation from Olaf, is registered in a close-up of her face.*]

JANET: To *where?* Somewhere near or—far?

OLAF [*swallowing with difficulty, not facing her*]: To Colorado State Teachers.

JANET: —Colorado is—in high country, in mountains, not the foothills of Ozarks, the *honorary* mountains . . . [*Something breaks in her mind: she half rises to crouch before him like a frenzied cheerleader.*] Colo-rah-rah-rado! Colo-*RAH-RAH—RAHDO! Yea. Team!* Over and up to the snow line—goalpost! Alicia is transferred with you?

OLAF: Alicia has been offered—

JANET: *Chief? Staff?*

OLAF: Head of the Physics Department, but she refuses to go until this thing is settled, once and for all.

JANET: Oh, is something not settled, what is it that's not settled now, Olaf?

OLAF: My RELEASE!

JANET: *From?*

OLAF: *You!*

JANET: —Tell her that was settled—five years ago! —To her—satisfied face, and heart and—*body!*

[*She reaches for the door; he seizes her wrist and holds her in the trailer.*]

OLAF: Maw! What is *this*?

[*He snatches a jumbo postcard up and holds it toward her panicky eyes. She screams.*]

OLAF: WHAT! [*He twists her arm.*] IS! THIS!

JANET: The jumbo! Postcard picture of! Dead Man's—Cave! You selected it for me from the rack!

OLAF: And you addressed it to Alicia, telling her to go there, signing it "Mrs. Svenson"?

JANET [*leaning exhausted against the door*]: It isn't—stamped, I—I wouldn't have mailed it to her.

OLAF: —The important thing is the message, confessing the hate, stamped, mailed, or not, the hate confessed in the message.

JANET: Yes! —If I said Christ, he would know that I wasn't swearing. —I send no message of hate. I wrote it but didn't stamp it and mail it. Felt it, oh, deep, deep felt as love for you, Olaf. —No more Sunday visits, now, ever, not longer between but never, never ever—those—long words, never ever—not even the potted Easter flowers by Western Union, delivered to wither before you—return. . . . What else is there not settled, what question? Has Alicia a question to ask me which is not yet settled?

OLAF [*overlapping*]: —You—*pity* yourself . . .

JANET [*overlapping*]: Which—came first—the chicken or the—egg, is that a question not settled?

OLAF: And try to use pity to—revive a thing dead as the animal by the river which I—removed!

377

JANET [*with pride*]: I do *not* pity myself, I have *contempt* for myself because I surrendered to *her*, poetess of—mathematics!

[*The excessive tablets have crazed her and made her stagger as she crosses to the trailer door.*]

JANET: Now can I go out, now, and sit on the campstool by the river till the tablets—more than prescribed!—work on me? Already working on me like—hammer on head of—Swift, Armour—product, penned for slaughter? Isn't that your suggestion? *I—follow—suggestions . . .*

[*She stumbles to her knees before the door. He flings it violently open. She rises with effort and stumbles, half falls, out of the trailer.*]

JANET: Hah!

56] EXTERIOR. NIGHT.
Everything is now seen from Janet's POV as she hallucinates. Then the camera draws back but retains the hallucinated (visionary) view. It follows Janet out to the pair of canvas campstools by the river. One of them is occupied by an apparitional figure.

JANET [*with great wonder*]: —Father—O'Donnell!

[*An elderly priest, in vestments, rises from the campstool.*]

JANET: *Please! Hear my confession!*

[*The apparition speaks in a voice that blends with the troubled, elegiac murmur of the river.*]

PRIEST: Child, I've always heard it.

JANET: —Give me *penance*, Father.

PRIEST: I give you—absolution.

JANET: Father, I have to do penance before—absolution.

PRIEST: Child, absolution is given without penance.

[*She stares at him a moment; then starts to the river.*]

JANET: Excuse me. I can't stop moving.

[*Janet looks back over her shoulder. The priest is dissolving in the river mist. She stumbles desperately on. The margin between the shore and the river is indistinct until she enters the water and still stumbles desperately on.*]

JANET: Can't—stop—rocking!

[*Her white gown rises in the current to her knees. Moonlight breaks through the mist and irradicates it and is full on Janet's face in which fear and anguish are passing into a kind of ecstasy.*]

[*The bang of the trailer door is heard.*]

57] EXTERIOR. NIGHT.

A startlingly clear shot of Olaf in the door clutching Sports Illustrated, *the vivid cover to the camera, his face inscrutable as stone.*

Sounds are heard: thrashing in the water and involuntary, strangulated outcries.

The camera remains on Olaf's stone face.

379

58] EXTERIOR. NIGHT.
*The "hallucinated" POV: Janet is in the river, her gown now
swept about her breasts. She lifts her arms as if surrendering
to the river—and then disappears beneath the rolling surface.*

59] EXTERIOR. THE RIVER. NIGHT.
*The rolling surface breaks upon Janet; she is washed against
a tangle of rocks and rotting timbers. She appears lifeless for
several beats; then, mindlessly, she begins to crawl along the
obstruction to the weedy shore.*

JANET: Fa-father!

[*It is Olaf who has entered the river to save her, his con-
flicting impulses resolved, but his figure is merged in her
hallucinated sight with that of the apparitional priest.*]

OLAF: I am not your father. Move! Move, I said, move!

[*Slowly, with the look of a somnambulist she allows him to
lead her toward the trailer.*]

60] THE ENTRANCE TO THE TRAILER.
He supports her.

OLAF: Why, why, *WHY*?

JANET: —I wanted—transfer—away. There was nothing to
stay for . . .

61] INTERIOR. TRAILER. NIGHT.
*She looks about her wondering, without recognition. She is
like a fountain figure, her wet gown clinging to her, hair
twisted wet about her face and throat. She stands quite still
as if listening to something vocal in the river's murmur.*

JANET: —So far from Colorado.

62] CLOSE TWO-SHOT. NIGHT.

OLAF: Here, towel, dry off!

[*He thrusts it into her hands; she stares at it vaguely a moment, then drops it.*]

OLAF: Okay, be a child, I'll dry you.

[*He turns her this way and that, rubbing her roughly with the towel.*]

OLAF: Now dress, coat, hat! [*He has to put them on her.*] We have to go right back.

JANET: Such a long wait for such a—short vacation . . .

OLAF: Imagine the consequences for me and—

JANET: Her.

OLAF: If you'd, if I'd not—prevented.

JANET: Why did you want to? Prevent?

OLAF: Maw, Janet, think of something besides self now.

JANET: I thought of you, Olaf. Giving you release from past to future—advantage.

OLAF: You have your fantasy world, better than the real one ever could be.

JANET: Yes, I'll transfer there, be planted on Floor Nine.

381

63] CLOSE ONE-SHOT OF OLAF.
He hurls the torn, wet nightgown out of the trailer.

OLAF: Now. No evidence.

[*He notices and snatches up* Sports Illustrated. *She staggers from the trailer.*]

OLAF: Yes, get in the cab with me, you can't be trusted alone.

JANET [*with a violent but silent laugh*]: Not alone? For the rest of my life?

OLAF [*moving her gently now*]: No, not alone, with fantasies, apparitions, perfect companions for you. Creatures you invent make no demands on you. You'll dream your own world, Maw, with complete possession of it. A prospect better than mine. For me: contention, effort, demands relentless, no stopping. Reality gives no rest, it gives no peace. For you: stopping, resting.

JANET [*turning her face slowly to his through the cab into which he's thrust her*]: Planted? Among plants?

OLAF [*with eyes shut tight*]: *Pax vobiscum.*

[*He slams the door: runs around to the driver's side.*]

64] NIGHT.
The camera comes in for a close two-shot of Janet and Olaf in the trailer. It is passing through spectral country. Janet herself is entering a similar country in her dimming consciousness. From time to time he glances at her face as it records the nature of this change which is voluntary, submissive.

OLAF: Janet? Jan? Maw?

[*Janet responds with an unintelligible murmur.*]

OLAF: Speak so I can hear you.

[*Janet again murmurs unintelligibly.*

[*Olaf mouths the "silent word."*

[*Janet takes a loud breath as the set look locks itself as unbreakably on her face as the "maximum security" gate of a prison.*

[*Olaf halts the trailer, turns the pocket flashlight on Janet's face and observes its final lack of expression. The return is resumed through a country of bleak landscapes and lightless buildings. He speaks to her, more to reassure himself.*]

OLAF: So. No more anxiety, now. —Know where we're going? We are going above the honorary mountains into the higher country, near the silence. Near the silence and snow.

65] DISSOLVE TO: EXTERIOR. THE STREET CURB BEFORE THE ASYLUM. DAY.
Evidently Olaf has phoned ahead to alert them of the early return. Sister Grace and Sister Grim move into the shot, behind them an orderly with a wheelchair. Then Dr. Cash in a gray topcoat and hat, polishing his glasses impassively.

SISTER GRIM: When did this happen?

OLAF: I will write an exact account for your records.

SISTER GRIM: I would like a spoken account of what happened before the written account, Mr. Svenson. Spontaneity is important sometimes.

OLAF [*uncertainly*]: It seems—unnecessary—to speak to me in this way.

[*Abruptly he covers his face with his hands as Sister Grace and the orderly draw Janet out of the trailer.*]

SISTER GRACE: Janet?

SISTER GRIM: Can't move. [*She speaks to the orderly.*] Into the chair, quick.

[*Janet is supported on either side by the sisters. Dr. Cash peers at her closely through his brilliant glasses.*]

DR. CASH: Total withdrawal.

[*The wheelchair is rushed to the curb. Janet is unnecessarily strapped into it.*]

SISTER GRACE: Floor Seven.

DR. CASH: No, Floor Nine, till Mr. Svenson and I have made arrangements for her transference.

66] EXTERIOR. DAY.
There is a close-up of Janet's face, utterly peaceful and "resigned from life."

Briskly the chair is turned about and wheeled up the walk between regimental ranks of zinnias.

Fade out.

THE END

New Directions Paperbooks—A Partial Listing

Walter Abish, *In the Future Perfect.* NDP440.
How German Is It. NDP508.
Ilango Adigal, *Shilapa-dikaram.* NDP162.
Alain, *The Gods.* NDP382.
Wayne Andrews. *Voltaire.* NDP519.
David Antin, *Talking at the Boundaries.* NDP388.
Tuning. NDP570.
G. Apollinaire, *Selected Writings.*† NDP310.
C. J. Bangs, *The Bones of the Earth.* NDP563.
Djuna Barnes, *Nightwood.* NDP98.
Charles Baudelaire, *Flowers of Evil.*† NDP71,
Paris Spleen. NDP294.
R. P. Blackmur, *Studies in Henry James,* NDP552.
Wolfgang Borchert, *The Man Outside.* NDP319.
Johan Borgen. *Lillelord.* NDP531.
Jorge Luis Borges, *Labyrinths.* NDP186.
E. Brock, *Here. Now. Always.* NDP429.
The River and the Train. NDP478.
Buddha, *The Dhammapada.* NDP188.
Frederick Busch, *Domestic Particulars.* NDP413.
Manual Labor. NDP376.
Ernesto Cardenal, *In Cuba* NDP377.
Hayden Carruth, *For You.* NDP298.
From Snow and Rock, from Chaos. NDP349.
Louis-Ferdinand Céline,
Death on the Installment Plan NDP330.
Journey to the End of the Night. NDP84.
Jean Cocteau, *The Holy Terrors.* NDP212.
Robert Coles, *Irony in the Mind's Life.* NDP459.
Cid Corman, *Livingdying.* NDP289.
Sun Rock Man. NDP318.
Gregory Corso, *Elegiac Feelings.* NDP299.
Herald of the Autochthonic Spirit. NDP522.
Long Live Man. NDP127.
Robert Creeley, *Hello.* NDP451.
Later. NDP488.
Mirrors, NDP559.
Edward Dahlberg, *Reader.* NDP246.
Because I Was Flesh. NDP227.
René Daumal. *Rasa.* NDP530.
Osamu Dazai, *The Setting Sun.* NDP258.
No Longer Human. NDP357.
Coleman Dowell, *Mrs. October . . .* NDP368.
Robert Duncan, *Bending the Bow.* NDP255.
Ground Work. NDP571, The Opening of the
Field. NDP356, *Roots and Branches.* NDP275.
Selected Poems. NDP198.
E. F. Edinger, *Melville's Moby-Dick.* NDP460.
Wm. Empson, *7 Types of Ambiguity.* NDP204.
Some Versions of Pastoral. NDP92.
Wm. Everson, *The Residual Years.* NDP263.
Lawrence Ferlinghetti, *Her.* NDP88.
A Coney Island of the Mind. NDP74.
Endless Life. NDP516.
The Mexican Night. NDP300.
The Secret Meaning of Things. NDP268.
Starting from San Francisco. NDP220.
Ronald Firbank. *Five Novels.* NDP518.
F. Scott Fitzgerald, *The Crack-up.* NDP54.
Robert Fitzgerald, *Spring Shade.* NDP311.
Gustave Flaubert, *Dictionary.* NDP230.
C. Froula, *Guide to Ezra Pound's Selected Poems.*
NDP548.
Gandhi, *Gandhi on Non-Violence.* NDP197.
Goethe, *Faust,* Part I. NDP70.
Henry Green. *Back.* NDP517.
Allen Grossman, *The Woman on the Bridge
Over the Chicago River.* NDP473.
Of The Great House. NDP535.
Lars Gustafsson, *The Death of a Beekeeper.*
NDP523.
The Tennis Players. NDP551.
John Hawkes, *The Beetle Leg.* NDP239.
The Blood Oranges. NDP338.
The Cannibal. NDP123.
Death Sleep & The Traveler. NDP391.
Second Skin. NDP146.
Travesty. NDP430.

Samuel Hazo. *To Paris.* NDP512.
Thank a Bored Angel. NDP555.
H. D., *End to Torment.* NDP476.
The Gift. NDP546.
Hermetic Definition. NDP343.
HERmione. NDP526.
Tribute to Freud. NDP572.
Trilogy. NDP362.
Robert E. Helbling, *Heinrich von Kleist,* NDP390
William Herrick. *Love and Terror.* NDP538.
Kill Memory. NDP558.
Hermann Hesse, *Siddhartha.* NDP65.
Vicente Huidobro. *Selected Poetry.* NDP520.
C. Isherwood, *All the Conspirators.* NDP480.
The Berlin Stories. NDP134.
Ledo Ivo, *Snake's Nest.* NDP521.
Alfred Jarry, *Ubu Roi.* NDP105.
Robinson Jeffers, *Cawdor and Media.* NDP293.
James Joyce, *Stephen Hero.* NDP133.
James Joyce/Finnegans Wake. NDP331.
Franz Kafka, *Amerika.* NDP117
Bob Kaufman,
The Ancient Rain. NDP514.
Solitudes Crowded with Loneliness. NDP199.
Kenyon Critics, *G. M. Hopkins.* NDP355.
H. von Kleist, *Prince Friedrich.* NDP462.
Elaine Kraf, *The Princess of 72nd St.* NDP494.
Shimpei Kusano, *Asking Myself, Answering Myself.*
NDP566.
P. Lal, *Great Sanskrit Plays.* NDP142.
Davide Lajolo, *An Absurd Vice.* NDP545.
Lautréamont, *Maldoror.* NDP207.
Irving Layton, *Selected Poems.* NDP431.
Christine Lehner. *Expecting.* NDP544.
Denise Levertov, *Candles in Babylon.* NDP533.
Collected Earlier. NDP475.
Footprints. NDP344.
The Freeing of the Dust. NDP401.
Light Up The Cave. NDP525.
Life in the Forest. NDP461.
Poems 1960-1967. NDP549.
The Poet in the World. NDP363.
Relearning the Alphabet. NDP290.
To Stay Alive. NDP325.
Harry Levin, *James Joyce.* NDP87.
Memories of The Moderns. NDP539.
Li Ch'ing-chao, *Complete Poems.* NDP492.
Enrique Lihn, *The Dark Room.*† NDP452.
García Lorca, *Deep Song.* NDP503.
Five Plays. NDP232.
The Public & Play Without a Title. NDP561.
Selected Letters. NDP557.
Selected Poems.† NDP114.
Three Tragedies. NDP52.
Michael McClure, *Antechamber.* NDP455.
Fragments of Perseus. NDP554.
Jaguar Skies. NDP400.
Josephine: The Mouse Singer. NDP496.
Carson McCullers, *The Member of the
Wedding.* (Playscript) NDP153.
Stephen Mallarmé.† *Selected Poetry and
Prose.* NDP529.
Thomas Merton, *Asian Journal.* NDP394.
Collected Poems. NDP504.
Gandhi on Non-Violence. NDP197.
News Seeds of Contemplation. NDP337.
Selected Poems. NDP85.
The Way of Chuang Tzu. NDP276.
The Wisdom of the Desert. NDP295.
Zen and the Birds of Appetite. NDP261.
Henry Miller, *The Air-Conditioned Nightmare.*
NDP302.
Big Sur & The Oranges. NDP161.
The Books in My Life. NDP280.
The Colossus of Maroussi. NDP75.
The Cosmological Eye. NDP109.
From Your Capricorn Friend. NDP568.
The Smile at the Foot of the Ladder. NDP386.
Stand Still Like the Hummingbird. NDP236.

The Time of the Assassins. NDP115.
Y. Mishima, *Confessions of a Mask.* NDP253.
  Death in Midsummer. NDP215.
Eugenio Montale, *It Depends.*† NDP507.
  New Poems. NDP410.
  Selected Poems.† NDP193.
Paul Morand, *Fancy Goods/Open All Night.*
  NDP567.
Vladimir Nabokov, *Nikolai Gogol.* NDP78.
  Laughter in the Dark. NDP470.
  The Real Life of Sebastian Knight. NDP432.
P. Neruda, *The Captain's Verses.*† NDP345.
  Residence on Earth.† NDP340.
New Directions in Prose & Poetry (Anthology).
  Available from #17 forward. #48, Fall 1984.
Robert Nichols, *Arrival.* NDP437.
  Exile. NDP485. *Garh City.* NDP450.
  Harditts in Sawna. NDP470.
Charles Olson, *Selected Writings.* NDP231.
Toby Olson, *The Life of Jesus.* NDP417.
  Seaview. NDP532.
George Oppen, *Collected Poems.* NDP418.
István Örkeny. *The Flower Show/*
  The Toth Family. NDP536.
Wilfred Owen, *Collected Poems.* NDP210.
Nicanor Parra, *Poems and Antipoems.*† NDP242.
Boris Pasternak, *Safe Conduct.* NDP77.
Kenneth Patchen, *Aflame and Afun.* NDP292.
  Because It Is. NDP83.
  But Even So. NDP265.
  Collected Poems. NDP284.
  Hallelujah Anyway. NDP219.
  In Quest of Candlelighters. NDP334.
  Selected Poems. NDP160.
Octavio Paz, *Configurations.*† NDP303.
  A Draft of Shadows.† NDP489.
  Eagle or Sun?† NDP422.
  Selected Poems. NDP574.
St. John Perse.† *Selected Poems.* NDP545.
Plays for a New Theater. (Anth.) NDP216.
J. A. Porter, *Eelgrass.* NDP438.
Ezra Pound, *ABC of Reading.* NDP89.
  Collected Early Poems. NDP540.
  Confucius. NDP285.
  Confucius to Cummings. (Anth.) NDP126.
  Gaudier Brzeska. NDP372.
  Guide to Kulchur, NDP257.
  Literary Essays. NDP250.
  Selected Cantos. NDP304.
  Selected Letters 1907-1941. NDP317.
  Selected Poems. NDP66.
  The Spirit of Romance. NDP266.
  Translations.† (Enlarged Edition) NDP145.
Raymond Queneau, *The Bark Tree.* NDP314.
  Exercises in Style. NDP513.
  The Sunday of Life. NDP433.
  We Always Treat Women Too Well. NDP515.
Mary de Rachewiltz, *Ezra Pound.* NDP405.
John Crowe Ransom, *Beating the Bushes.*
  NDP324.
Raja Rao, *Kanthapura.* NDP224.
Herbert Read, *The Green Child.* NDP208.
P. Reverdy, *Selected Poems.*† NDP346.
Kenneth Rexroth, *Collected Longer Poems.*
  NDP309. *Collected Shorter.* NDP243.
  The Morning Star. NDP490.
  New Poems. NDP383.
  100 More Poems from the Chinese. NDP308.
  100 More Poems from the Japanese. NDP420.
  100 Poems from the Chinese. NDP192.
  100 Poems from the Japanese.† NDP147.
  Women Poets of China. NDP528.
  Women Poets of Japan. NDP527.
Rainer Maria Rilke, *Poems from*
  The Book of Hours. NDP408.
  Possibility of Being. (Poems). NDP436.
  Where Silence Reigns. (Prose). NDP464.
Arthur Rimbaud, *Illuminations.*† NDP56.
  Season in Hell & Drunken Boat.† NDP97.

Edouard Roditi, *Delights of Turkey.* NDP445.
Jerome Rothenberg, *That Dada Strain.* NDP550.
  Poland/1931. NDP379.
  Vienna Blood. NDP498.
Saigyo,† *Mirror for the Moon.* NDP465.
Saikaku Ihara. *The Life of an Amorous*
  Woman. NDP270.
St. John of the Cross, *Poems.*† NDP341.
Jean-Paul Sartre, *Nausea.* NDP82.
  The Wall (Intimacy). NDP272.
Delmore Schwartz, *Selected Poems.* NDP241.
  In Dreams Begin Responsibilities. NDP454.
K. Shiraishi, *Seasons of Sacred Lust.* NDP453.
Stevie Smith, *Collected Poems.* NDP562.
  Selected Poems, NDP159.
Gary Snyder, *The Back Country.* NDP249.
  Earth House Hold. NDP267.
  The Real Work. NDP499.
  Regarding Wave. NDP306.
  Turtle Island. NDP381.
Gustaf Sobin, *The Earth as Air.* NDP569.
Enid Starkie, *Rimbaud.* NDP254.
Robert Steiner, *Bathers.* NDP495
Stendhal, *The Telegraph.* NDP108.
Jules Supervielle, *Selected Writings.*† NDP209.
Nathaniel Tarn, *Lyrics . . . Bride of God.* NDP391.
Dylan Thomas, *Adventures in the Skin Trade.*
  NDP183.
  A Child's Christmas in Wales. NDP181.
  Collected Poems 1934-1952. NDP316.
  Portrait of the Artist as a Young Dog.
  NDP51.
  Quite Early One Morning. NDP90.
  Rebecca's Daughters. NDP543.
  Under Milk Wood. NDP73.
Lionel Trilling, *E. M. Forster.* NDP189.
Martin Turnell. *Baudelaire.* NDP336.
  Rise of the French Novel. NDP474.
Paul Valéry, *Selected Writings.*† NDP184.
Elio Vittorini, *Women of Messina.* NDP365.
Vernon Watkins, *Selected Poems.* NDP221.
Nathanael West, *Miss Lonelyhearts &*
  Day of the Locust. NDP125.
J. Wheelwright, *Collected Poems.* NDP544.
J. Williams, *An Ear in Bartram's Tree.* NDP335.
Tennessee Williams, *Camino Real,* NDP301.
  Cat on a Hot Tin Roof. NDP398.
  Clothes for a Summer Hotel. NDP556.
  Dragon Country. NDP287.
  The Glass Menagerie. NDP218.
  Hard Candy. NDP225.
  In the Winter of Cities. NDP154.
  A Lovely Sunday for Creve Coeur. NDP497.
  One Arm & Other Stories. NDP237.
  Stopped Rocking. NDP575.
  A Streetcar Named Desire. NDP501.
  Sweet Bird of Youth. NDP409.
  Twenty-Seven Wagons Full of Cotton. NDP217.
  Vieux Carré. NDP482.
William Carlos Williams.
  The Autobiography. NDP223.
  The Buildup. NDP259.
  The Farmers' Daughters. NDP106.
  I Wanted to Write a Poem. NDP469.
  Imaginations. NDP329.
  In the American Grain. NDP53.
  In the Money. NDP240.
  Paterson. Complete. NDP152.
  Pictures form Brueghel. NDP118.
  Selected Poems. NDP131.
  White Mule. NDP226.
  Yes, Mrs. Williams. NDP534.
Yvor Winters, *E. A. Robinson.* NDP326.
Wisdom Books: *Ancient Egyptians,* NDP467.
  Early Buddhists, NDP444; *English Mystics,*
  NDP466; *Forest* (Hindu), NDP414; *Spanish*
  Mystics, NDP442; *St. Francis,* NDP477;
  Sufi, NDP424; *Taoists,* NDP509; *Wisdom of*
  the Desert, NDP295; *Zen Masters,* NDP415.

For complete listing request complete catalog from
New Directions, 80 Eighth Avenue, New York 10011   † Bilingual